Using Methods in the Field

A Practical Introduction and Casebook

Using Methods in the Field

A Practical Introduction and Casebook

■

Victor C. de Munck
Elisa J. Sobo

Editors

A Division of
ROWMAN & LITTLEFIELD PUBLISHERS, INC.
Walnut Creek • Lanham • New York • Oxford

ALTAMIRA PRESS
A Division of Rowman & Littlefield Publishers, Inc.
1630 North Main Street, #367
Walnut Creek, CA 94596
www.altamirapress.com

Rowman & Littlefield Publishers, Inc.
A Member of the Rowman & Littlefield Publishing Group
4501 Forbes Boulevard, Suite 200
Lanham, MD 20706

PO Box 317, Oxford, OX2 9RU, UK

Copyright © 1998 by AltaMira Press
Production Services by Carole M. Bernard, ECS

British Library Cataloguing in Publication Information Available

Library of Congress Cataloging-in-Publication Data

Using methods in the field: a practical introduction and casebook / edited by
Victor C. de Munck, Elisa J. Sobo.
   p. cm
   Includes bibliographical references and index.
   ISBN 0-7619-8912-9 (cloth)
   ISBN 0-7619-8913-7 (pbk).
   1. Ethnology—Methodology. 2. Social sciences—Methodology.
I. Munck, Victor C. de. II. Sobo, Elisa Janine, 1963–
GN345 .I38 1998
305.8'001—ddc21   98–9073

Printed in the United States of America

♾™ The paper used in this publication meets the minimum requirements of American
National Standard for Information Sciences—Permanence of Paper for Printed Library
Materials, ANSI/NISO Z39.48–1992.

Contents

Section III: More Advanced Means to Model Culture

Foreword

In 1985, Bert Pelto and I received a grant from the National Science Foundation to hold a conference on the then-current state of research methods in cultural anthropology. We held the conference at NSF in April of that year. Beside Bert and me, the conference members were: John W. Adams, James Boster, Ronald Cohen, Roy D'Andrade, Patricia Draper, William Dressler, Carol R. Ember, Joel Gittlesohn, Daniel Gross, Allen Johnson, Brian Johnstone. Alice Kasakoff, Christopher McCarty, John Roberts, A. Kimball Romney, and Lee Sailer. One of our main conclusions was that "more methodological training is needed, not only for graduate students but for experienced field anthropologists as well" (Bernard et al. 1986:392). Pelto and I applied to NSF for funding for a three-week summer institute. We got support for three years and held the first NSF Summer Institute on Research Methods in Cultural Anthropology at the University of Florida in 1987.

The Institute (which quickly became known as "methods camp" because its official name was such a mouthful) continued for nine summers. Most of the 12–14 participants each year held teaching positions at colleges and universities in the United States. (A few were applied anthropologists who worked outside the academy and a few were from abroad.) Contents included instructions on how to collect data using freelists, pile sorts, triad tests, ratings, rankings, and paired comparisons and on how to analyze data using methods like multidimensional scaling, cluster analysis, consensus analysis, and Guttman and Likert scaling. At various times, network analysis, decision-tree modeling, and text analysis rounded out the curriculum.

Except for 1987, the instructors at methods camp were Bert Pelto, Stephen Borgatti, and me (Lee Sailer taught with Pelto and me in 1987). Borgatti was director of the institute in the seventh, eighth, and ninth years (1993–1995). His suite of computer programs, ANTHROPAC, became the centerpiece of instruction.

The importance of ANTHROPAC will be quite apparent as you read these chapters. In 1988, Susan Weller and A. Kimball Romney produced a readable, detailed manual about how to collect data using systematic ethnographic methods (freelisting, pile sorts, triad tests, paired comparisons, etc.). The problem was, analyzing these data required methods like multidimensional scaling, cluster analysis, quadratic assignment. . . . With ANTHROPAC, Borgatti almost single-handedly made all these methods accessible to thousands of researchers. (ANTHROPAC has the data collection routines *and* the data analysis routines all in one place.)

The chapters in this book, then, are mostly (but not entirely) case studies of anthropologists actually using the various methods that Pelto, Borgatti, and I taught at methods camp. Each chapter focuses on one or more methods of data collection and analysis. Elisa Sobo and Victor de Munck introduce the book with a panoramic view of field methods in Chapter 1, and in Chapter 2 de Munck gives an overview of the strategic method of participant observation. Systematic ethnographic methods, after all, are used in the context of ethnographic research—that is, research based on participant observation fieldwork.

Chapters 3, 4, and 5 are about lists. In Chapter 3, Gery Ryan and Thomas Weisner tell us about turning the words in interview texts into lists and how to analyze those lists. Mark Fleisher relates in Chapter 4 how he, with the assistance of Jennifer Harrington, used freelisting as the main tool of data collection in his study of a federal prison. In Chapter 5, Juliana Flinn shows how she used freelists to get at the criteria for selecting courses at her university and how she used those lists to produce a rating scale for those courses.

Chapter 6 focuses on pile sorts. Gun Roos used several methods to produce a list of 40 foods. She used pile sorts to test whether preadolescent boys and girls in the U.S. understand the domain of foods differently. They do.

In Chapter 7, Allen Johnson walks us through his Guttman scale analysis of Matsigenka men's skills. Johnson takes us through every step as he decides what to do with outliers and how best to cut down the data so as to reduce scaling errors.

Robert Harman asked Karen people in Thailand four freelist questions: What do old people get pleasure from? What do old people worry about? What do old people suffer from? What kinds of work do elders do? In Chapter 8, Harman shows us how he used these lists to select items for a triad test and how he used triad tests to examine possible differences among Karen subgroups.

In Chapter 9, Carole Hill uses three cases studies to illustrate decision-tree modeling. One of those studies is her recent work on a decision model for the treatment of mental disorders.

Chapters 10, 11, and 12 illustrate the use of consensus analysis. In Chapter 10, Penn Handwerker shows how consensus analysis can be used to select knowledgeable informants. In Chapter 11, Douglas Caulkins uses consensus analysis to test—and ultimately disconfirm—his hypothesis that different kinds of Scottish business advisers would have different models of success. And in Chapter 12, Javier García de Alba García and his colleagues use consensus analysis to test whether people of different ages in Mexico have different ideas about the causes of high blood pressure.

In Chapter 13, Jeffrey Johnson and David Griffith lay out some of the many possibilities for using visual stimuli to collect data.

Finally, in Chapter 14, Lauren Clark and her colleagues use QAP to compare an empirical model of children's pain (built from children's responses to questions about pain) to the model that the children's parents have.

Congratulations to the editors of this volume, Victor de Munck and Elisa Sobo, for bringing together these excellent papers on systematic ethnographic methods. Colleagues from across the social sciences can use this book in their courses on methods of field research. I know I will.

Foundations

ELISA J. SOBO ■
VICTOR C. DE MUNCK

One

The Forest of Methods

Clearing the Path

Imagine yourself lost in a dense pine forest. The air is brisk and misty; night is about to fall. You feel cold and miserable. Your morale, like the sun, is sinking fast—and it takes a decided plunge when you realize that you have been walking in a circle. You need to find a way out. What to do?

You collect your thoughts and begin to observe and think carefully about your present location. You ask yourself, "What is it about this place that I recognize? How do I know that I have been here before? What do I know that might help me find a way home if I can't recall the way I came to be here?"

You systematically retrace your steps. You remember coming down a slight slope at the crest of a hill on which grew two particularly old and tremendous Jefferson pines. You go back up the slope to the twin pines. There, you recall once hearing that a fire road to the east side of the Twin Pines Crest connects with the main highway. You know that the sun sets in the west so you head away from the quickly setting sun and, sure enough, there's the fire road. After walking 15 minutes, you see the highway and in just under an hour, you are home safely.

It was thinking methodically—carefully, logically, systematically—that saved you. The central goal of this volume is to promote methodical thinking in relation to research pursuits. The book may not possess much in the way of woodsy natural beauty, but the lessons it contains can make finding your way in and around the theoretical and methodological forests of the world of social science an easier task.

The Research Process

As the twin pines story implies, methods are generated in keeping with the perceived needs, questions, and capabilities of the researcher to assess the socio-cultural terrain. The classical view of methods holds that they are part of a linear research design process that begins with theory and ends with an outcome that either validates or invalidates the theory. However, a number of researchers have argued that the very notion of "design" implies a comprehensive blueprint and thus falsely represents research as a programmatic process.

Howard Becker (1986), a leading qualitative researcher in education, suggests that research is a shared and ongoing process undertaken between the researcher and his or her subjects. Regarding their now-classic research on medical students, Becker et al. (1961) wrote that:

> In one sense our study had no design. That is we had no well-worked out set of hypotheses to be tested, no data-gathering instruments purposely designed to secure information relevant to these hypotheses, no set of analytic procedures specified in advance. Insofar as the term design implies these features of elaborate prior planning, our study had none. If we take the idea of design in a larger and looser sense, using it to identify those elements of order, system, and consistency our procedures did exhibit, our study had a design. We can say what this was by describing our original view of the problem, our theoretical and methodolgcial commitments, and the way these affected our research and were affected by it as we proceeded. (p. 17)

Martin (1982) holds a similar view of research. He refers to his model as a "garbage can" model, making the point that methods, theory, resources, and solutions are in a continuous feedback relationship, being modified by and modifying each other during a research project. The garbage-can metaphor suggests that research is actually a messy, ad hoc affair only tidied up when put on display. But in reacting against the immaculate structure of the classical linear model, the garbage-can model may have swung too far to the antistructural extreme.

Maxwell (1996:3) notes that both models—garbage can and classical linear —provide equally distorted views of what actually goes on. His compromise solution is to propose an "interactive" butterfly-like model of research (see Figure 1.1) in which methods and validity form the empirical wing of the model, while what he calls "purposes" and "conceptual context" form the ideational wing. Research questions form the head and thorax, connecting and integrating the two wings. Maxwell's model allows for interactive feedback between the different parts of a research design while still retaining a research structure.

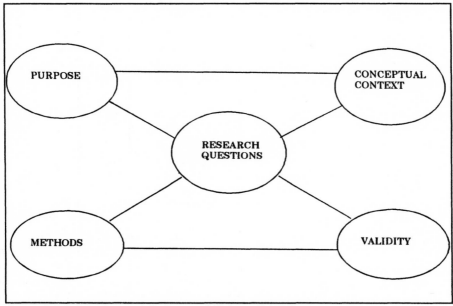

Figure 1.1. Interactive model of research (Maxwell 1996).

Linear, garbage-can, and interactive models of research design all have in common the idea that methods are connected to other components of a research design. In a linear model, methods follow from theory. In a garbage-can model, methods and other components all "swirl about," with none taking priority over the other (Grady and Wallston 1988:12). In an interactive model, there is a definite division of labor and temporal organization, but there is also recognition that research is an ongoing process in which methods, purposes, conceptual context, research questions, and issues of validity all influence and are influenced by one another. We agree with Maxwell that the choice and use of methods are embedded in and interact with other major components of a research design. Our focus here is to introduce readers to what scientific methods are and to describe them against the backdrop of actual research activity.

Goals and Overview

The goal of this volume is to show how researchers use methods in the context of *doing* research (for the history of methodology in anthropology, see the Appendix). Most methods volumes consist either of a string of unrelated articles that describe as many different types of methods as possible or articles that are variations on the same methodological theme. This volume presents studies that use ethnographic methods to examine the relationship between cognition (that is, what people think) and social practice (what people do). Thus, its methodological focus is broader than volumes that focus on one particular method alone but narrower than volumes that attempt to cover everything. The chapters assembled here form a coherent whole, even while they represent a wide variety of methods.

In each chapter, the author describes a particular research problem and tackles it with an appropriate set of methods. In the process, the author explains, step by step, why each particular methods-related choice was made and how these choices contribute to and affect the project as a whole. The collection thus serves as a methodological source book, teaching by example or demonstration.

All of the authors in this volume conducted **ethnographic** (versus laboratory) research. We therefore begin by presenting our position concerning the importance of ethnography. After explaining that the choice of methods must be adapted to the ethnographic setting rather than selecting the methods and then the research context, we discuss the fact that the selection of particular methods by a researcher stems from an attempt to juggle and coordinate a number of interrelated but often very different types of issues. These issues are: (1) the human connection between researcher and participants; (2) research ethics; (3) theory; (4) research questions; (5) the costs and benefits of each method; and (6) validity. It is unlikely that appropriate methods can be selected without considering these issues. A discussion of these issues follows the overview below, and we conclude with a description of the organization of this volume.

What Can Ethnography Tell Us?

Just the Facts

The purpose of ethnographic research is to pin down the facts about people. We test our impressions against these facts by formulating a wide range of **hypotheses** or propositions about what is happening and then figuring out ways to test those hypotheses. For example, an ethnographer studying U.S. political party affiliation may surmise that "Republicans tend to prefer cats to dogs, while Democrats tend to prefer dogs to cats." But a certain amount of work needs to be done to claim with any degree of certainty that this is true or even interesting (as it might be, for example, if linked to the notion that cats don't need as much care as dogs).

Many social scientists would disagree with our position. **Postmodernists** would argue that there are no facts per se to pin down, even if we indirectly acknowledge the ambiguity of facts by encasing the term in quotation marks. On the other hand, **modernists** who believe that ethnographers can pin down the facts would argue that ethnographic methods provide factual information about lifeways in a particular locality or society. At the same time, they would warn that this information cannot be used to test causal models, particularly those generalizable to a larger population than the one sampled (to **generalize** is to assume that what applies in one case applies in another). For example, Golden (1976) writes that ethnographic "field studies use real groups in natural settings; they focus on a particular context, are strong on naturalness, weak on control and representativeness, and are most likely to be used in exploratory or descriptive research" (p. 16).

Strauss and Corbin (1990) summarize three goals of qualitative (read: ethnographic) research: (1) "Let the informants speak for themselves"; (2) Provide accurate descriptions of the contextualized stream of social life; and (3) Build theory inductively from the data (that is, after collecting it) (pp. 21–22). Bogdan and Bilken (1992:29–32) list five characteristics of qualitative research: (1) Behaviors are studied in their natural settings; (2) It is descriptive; (3) The emphasis is on understanding processes rather than outcomes; (4) It is inductive, so that theory is grounded in data; (5) The goal is to accurately describe the meaning systems and the use of symbols of the people being studied.

Although we agree with these summaries, we think they're too limited in scope and perpetuate a taken-for-granted divide between qualitative and quantitative methods. We think ethnographic research and methods can have practical applications and can be used to develop and test causal models.

Spradley (1979) accepts the postmodern axiom that all knowledge systems, including science, are culture bound, and that ethnographic research "alone seeks to document the existence of alternative realities and to describe these realities in their own terms" (p. 11). He suggests that ethnographic methods serve to help discover or describe and delineate "folk" categories and realities (the **emic** perspective) rather than test or clarify a priori and supposedly universally applicable models into which those categories and realities are meant to fit (the **etic** perspective). For Spradley, the ultimate goal of ethnographic research is to "serve humankind" by eliciting "informant-expressed needs" that can be "synchronized with scientific methods" to reduce human suffering (pp. 14–15).

The Qualitative-Quantitative Divide

In arguing that science and ethnography should be synchronized, Spradley retains a distinction between quantitative and qualitative. Generally, researchers use the term "**quantitative**" when speaking of numerical data and use "**qualitative**" to refer to data of the nonnumerical kind (narrative data or descriptions of beliefs, which ethnographers traditionally gather). Because of cultural associations that we make between numbers and science, some researchers have come to interpret quantitative as if it means scientific but, for various reasons—some of which we explain here and some of which we explain a little later—this isn't so.

Qualitative and quantitative data types and distinctions between scientific and nonscientific investigations on the basis of data type begin to blur when we consider that categorizing any item involves making qualitative distinctions. For example, the researcher determines criteria for categorizing research participants as being rich, of average income, or poor and also draws the line used in determining whether a participant is in middle or old age for a given piece of research. Our cultural assumptions about when these categories begin and end are just that—cultural assumptions, and thus value linked and amenable to qualitative description. Even age, often thought of as a number, is derived from qualitative assumptions about when to begin counting and at what time interval one's assigned number changes.

Not only do qualitative judgments determine many quantitative category boundaries, they also determine the meaning of quantitative findings once we have calculated them. That is, quantitative findings must be interpreted to have any meaning, and meaningful interpretations are based on an understanding of the qualitative data that relate to such findings. We can find that 28% of Americans like dogs better than cats and 21% like cats better than dogs (Crispell 1994:59), but only qualitative data can help us understand the meaning of this, or why it might be so.[1] Further, to interpret the output of either qualitative or quantitative data analysis techniques, we need to know something about the ethnographic context in which the data were elicited and we need to know how the participants described each item of data that they provided or named .

The relationship between qualitative and quantitative data demonstrates that research isn't just a matter of input and output. Rather, a great deal of creativity is needed to plan and carry out good research. From the beginning steps of hypotheses generation and determination of one's data needs to the final steps of interpretation of the output of a given computer operation, research demands the ability to synthesize and think creatively.

In part due to the interpenetration of qualitative and quantitative approaches, a growing number of researchers have suggested that the so-called qualitative/ quantitative divide is unnecessarily divisive (Rossi and Berk 1991:226; Robson 1993:42; Miles and Huberman 1994:144–148; Maxwell 1996:20). Miles and Huberman (1984) write that:

> In fact, it is getting harder to find any methodologists solidly encamped in one epistemology or the other. More and more 'quantitative' methodologists, operating from a logical positivist stance, are using naturalistic and phenomenological approaches to complement tests, surveys and structured interviews. On the other side, an increasing number of ethnographers and qualitative researchers are using predesigned conceptual frameworks. (p. 20)

Werner and Schoepfle (1987) emphasize that "No qualitative study can afford to leave implicit its qualitative aspects" and go on to argue that "ethnography can be systematic and its methods explicit and replicable" (p. 44).

Field or Lab? Case or Variable?

New methodologies have been developed that purposively use qualitative and quantitative data in tandem, each complementing the other. The remaining divide between quantitative and qualitative research is now predominantly a result of where data are gathered: in the field or in the lab.

Ethnographic methods are necessarily different in kind from **experimental** methods because the researcher has to physically go to where the participants of his or her research live and study them in situ. Everyday life is a mixture of the routine and the unusual, the predictable and the exceptional. Chance events happen that we cannot control. Experimental methods, on the other hand, bring the subjects to the researcher, taking them out of their natural, rather uncontrollable settings.

The goal of experimental methods is to test hypotheses about the relationship(s) between two or more **variables** (discrete influences or states). To ensure that other variables aren't influencing a hypothesized causal relationship, the researcher needs to control the situation by eliminating extraneous variables. Experimental methods involve creating artificial conditions or posing hypothetical situations that are designed to eliminate extraneous variables and allow the researcher to focus only on the study variables (Golden 1976:16). This clarity notwithstanding, experimental studies are said to be high on internal validity but low on external validity. That is, the parts fit together with impeccable internal logic, but it is questionable whether they actually mirror what goes on outside the lab (we'll come back to validity later).

In comparison with the experimenter, the ethnographer has little to no control over variables. However, she or he can still build valid and reliable local causal models of cognitive and event processes. Miles and Huberman (1984) write that fieldwork involves talking with people about *their* explanations of why things happen. They argue that ethnographers should elicit the "mental maps" of informants, from which network diagrams of "local causality" can be constructed (pp. 131–132). Weiss (1994) writes that demonstrating causation through interview methods "rests heavily on the description of a visualizable sequence of events, each event flowing into the next" (p. 179, cited in Maxwell 1996:21). In other words, although demonstrating causation is done differently when research is done in the field and not in the lab, it can still be done.

Qualitative methods, no less than quantitative methods, can produce causal models that explain the relationship between variables. The difference that we want to highlight here is that qualitative methods tend to focus on case-oriented causal processes, whereas quantitative methods focus on variable-oriented causality (Maxwell 1996:20). That is, qualitative studies focus on the linkages between events or activities at a particular site—in a particular case—rather than linkages between trait variables across sites.

Be Explicit and Systematic

It is feasible to test whether qualitatively generated models of local causality are generalizable through cross-cultural or cross-site comparisons (see Miles and Huberman [1984, 1994] for descriptions of cross-site analysis). But for a study to have practical application or theoretical validity, and for it to be useful in making comparisons, it's essential that its methods be systematic and explicit. When the researcher explains which methods were selected and how they were used, then the latter requirement of explicitness is satisfied. Furthermore, systematic and explicit methodologies (or studies of methods, or explanations for methods choices) are a means to communicate to readers and to other researchers what you did, why you did it, and why your analyses and ethnographic descriptions should be believed and accepted over someone else's. Your descriptions and conclusions should never appear like those of the sorcerer—as if magically spun out of thin air.

In addition to **systematic data collection**, good research requires that a method be applied systematically. When the researcher uses the same data collection and analytic procedures with all research participants (or across all events or contexts), we can say that the methods are systematically applied. For example, if one is trying to identify problems first-year students experience at college, then the same questions, preferably in the same order, should be asked of a number of first-year students. By using systematic methods, grounded theory can be induced, problems identified, and solutions proposed, because descriptive and explanatory (or causal) statements will be grounded in empirical data obtained through explicit and democratic (that is, publicly open, accessible, and replicable) methods. Such standardization of methods means that the research can be repeated or replicated at other sites to determine whether localized, case- or site-specific theories are generalizable.

We believe explicit and systematic methods also make for ethical research. Fieldwork is time consuming and labor intensive. Researchers depend on the goodwill and sympathetic spirit of the members of the community or group that they are working with and often living among. Although other ethical considerations come into play, here we stress that researchers must accurately report and describe the lives and thoughts of the people with whom they work. Fiction writers and unscrupulous journalists needn't be constrained by what people actually think or do, they can select or invent behaviors and thoughts to prove their point. Social science is different. Social scientists use methods like those described here to cull fact from fiction and to construct models and descriptions that are as accurate as possible.

The Human Connection

Pelto and Pelto (1978:25–26) argue that, before the emergence of postmodernism, reliance on anecdotal evidence and vagueness in arguments and definitions were pervasive problems in anthropological research. Another problem concerns the ethnographer's motivations. Some say that people who feel alienated from their own society and culture are often drawn to anthropology to find a culture more suitable to their personality. This anti-Western impulse (for ethnography, as we know it, is a Western construct and endeavor) has led to the "romantic antimodernist" spirit prevalent in contemporary ethnographic writings (di Leonardo 1997:36).

Ethnography that is motivated by a romantic antimodernist spirit and that relies on anecdotes to depict native thoughts and traditions as noble and (inevitably) corrupted through contact with the West not only simplifies and does a disservice to the study group, but moves anthropology to the margins of social science. Clifford (1986) writes that ethnography is really pastoral allegory in which the researcher is motivated to inscribe traditional non-Western "primitive" cultures that are quickly becoming extinct. The researcher positions him- or herself as hero and archiver, recording, preserving, and sometimes fighting for the cultures he or she is writing about (Richardson 1975). We agree that much of the time this is so.

Although not substitutes for data derived by systematic and explicit methods, a romantic antimodern disposition is not "bad," nor is anecdotal evidence necessarily worthless. But the debates that surround their use attest to the fact that doing ethnography can be an epistemological minefield. **Epistemology** is the study of how we know what we know. Postmodernists argue that all knowledge is subjective and therefore ethnographers can't portray other people's knowledge independent of both their own biases and the informants' or participants' reactions to the researcher.

Heider (1988) used the phrase "the Rashomon Effect" to describe the subjective nature of perceived reality. Taken from a Japanese Samurai movie directed by Kurosawa, the Rashomon Effect is a well-known dramaturgical term that refers specifically to the multiple versions of a murder presented by witnesses in the film. Each version is said to contain another angle or perspective on the truth about the murder, with none presenting the whole truth. Heider espouses a multicultural position, in which truth is distributed and relative to the personal and cultural experiences of the researcher and where the more positions presented (providing what is called "multivocality"), the richer (and truer) will be the reader's understanding of a culture. On the other hand, when murder does occur, it's important to find out who did it and how.

Postmodernism teaches us that the phenotypical, psychological, and cultural attributes of the researcher and of the participants do matter. Certainly Sobo's (1995) research experiences with inner-city African American women who shared information about their sexual practices would have been very different had she been male, darker skinned, or substantially older.

We could make similar arguments about all ethnographers who have done fieldwork. We would do so to highlight the concepts of bias, reactivity, and reflexivity, all recently popularized terms that highlight the fact that field research is carried out by humans interacting with other humans. **Bias** refers to the cultural "filters" or "lenses" that anthropologists use to select what data they consider important and how these data are gathered and interpreted. Postmodernists would consider the idea of culling a piece of data from the stream of human activities as a scientific bias applied by the researcher.

In responding to arguments about subjectivity, Peshkin (1991) writes that "The subjectivity that originally I had taken as an affliction . . . could . . . be taken as 'virtuous.' My subjectivity is the basis for the story that I am able to tell. It is a strength on which I build. It makes me who I am as a person and as a researcher" (p. 104). Peshkin argues, as do many other anthropologists (for example, Rabinow 1977; Obeyesekere 1981), that we should attempt to write explicitly about both our own biases and the way that participants in our research react to our very presence (called reactivity, more on this later). The act of the observer attempting to measure something influences the position of the thing measured.

Maxwell (1996) writes that "Explaining your possible biases and how you will deal with these is a key task of your research proposal" (p. 91). This inclusion of the researcher as a research variable is called "**reflexivity**." Reflexivity refers both to the researcher's own internal biases and to the effects of the researcher on the subjects under study. Ethnographic methods are particularly susceptible to problems of personal bias and reactivity. The ethnographer is not a fly on the wall or a purely objective observer, therefore the ethnographer's perspective should be recognized as influencing the choice of questions and methods.

For example, in the introduction to his book *Medusa's Hair*, a study of Sri Lankan men and women with thick, matted locks who became possessed by Hindu-Buddhist folk deities, Gananath Obeyesekere (1981) notes that he was initially repelled by a woman informant. He asks "Was it the anthropologist's own castration anxiety that provoked this reaction? Or was it the ordinary disgust of a fastidious scholar for something dirty and anomalous sticking out of her head?" (p. 7). Through introspection, Obeyesekere developed a psychodynamic theory of how public symbols become internalized as private symbols. He then used this theory to explain how popular religious beliefs and practices provided a symbol system for resolving the personal psychic conflicts of his informants. In other words, the researcher's own emotional responses were used methodically to formulate a theoretical model.

The postmodernist position has enhanced our understanding of and sensitivity toward the inherent subjectivity of field and laboratory research. Kuhn (1970) argued that the criteria by which "good science" is judged is based on what fits the scientific paradigm of that time period, not on any timeless, universal criteria. What constitutes good science and truth in one era may be judged bad science and false in another era. Scientific truths, in other words, are grounded in human (that is, subjective) consensus (that is, culture) about what is true and what is false rather than in some objective truth outside the human purview.

Justification for Methodical Practices

In claiming Kuhn as a forefather, postmodernists ignore his recognition that scientific paradigms shift when enough evidence mounts that can't be explained by or that contradicts the old paradigm (the normal way of thinking and doing science). So there *is* a march of science, and it is precisely because reflexivity, bias, and reactivity influence our research and the way it is received by our readers that we should try to adhere to systematic and explicit methodologies whenever possible. The anthropological lens described by Peacock (1978) differs from the journalistic or the artistic lens. The latter aim to project biases onto the lives portrayed in order to enhance and magnify their features into a unique and creative vision. In contrast, the anthropologist's creativity is derived from using methodological tools to construct depictions and propositions about how culture works that are as accurate and verifiable as possible.

Research Ethics

All researchers, whether students or professionals, are ethically bound to use methods correctly. In addition to avoiding mistakes, such as those that sloppy methodology can engender, they must not knowingly misrepresent their findings. They must not twist findings to suggest unsound conclusions, and they must not falsify findings to this end. Researchers mostly work on an honor system, according to which falsification of data, or messaging the data to fit a certain model, is absolutely unacceptable. Fiddling the facts is not only unethical and reprehensible, it also is damaging to one's career. Falsifying or knowingly misrepresenting facts can lead to forfeiture of professional credentials, loss of professional status, and employment termination.

In addition to professional integrity and scrupulousness, researchers are also expected to ensure that participants' rights and interests are always protected. In many institutions, before research is even begun, approval must be secured from a human subjects board or committee. The committee, often called an internal review board (IRB), evaluates the research proposal in relation to the risk it holds for participants rather than on its intellectual or academic merit (that is necessary but not sufficient for IRB certification). Many committees ask researchers to have participants sign a written consent form on which the possible costs and benefits of the research to them are clearly spelled out. Alternately, they specify that participants must give explicit verbal consent after the researcher explains all this in jargon-free conversation. Any coercion is frowned on, as when potential participants are made to feel that by opting out they may be endangering themselves in some way.

Rightly or wrongly, until recently much ethnographic research has preceded without undergoing the human subjects approval process. Nonetheless, it's essential that the principles of ethical research on human subjects be adhered to—all the more so in anthropological undertakings in which participants might be easily exploited due to language or cultural differences. To this end, the American Anthropological Association has maintained a code of ethics, the last version of which was published in 1996 (*Anthropology Newsletter:*7–8).

Basically, the code gives anthropologists "guidelines for making ethical choices in the conduct of their anthropological work" (p. 7). The code states that research proposals must make clear the purpose and potential impacts of a project along with the funding source. They must state who will be provided with information gleaned from the project; after research has been conducted "researchers must intend and expect to disseminate results" (p. 7) and they should make their data and field research materials available in response to all reasonable requests. Accordingly, anthropologists should also seek to preserve these materials wherever possible.

The code goes on to state that anthropologists are ethically obligated first and foremost to the people they study, and must "do everything in their power to ensure that their research does not harm the safety, dignity or privacy of the people with whom they work [or] conduct research" (p. 7). This means making sure that anonymity is protected when it is requested or promised, and that confidentiality is never breached. It also means making sure that participants are not exploited, and to this end informed consent procedures are advocated in the ethics code. Further, anthropologists should "continually monitor the effects of their work" (p. 8), taking all steps possible to ensure that people's lives are not adversely affected by participation in the research.

Theory

We are not professional methodologists: We are anthropologists who want our research results and claims about social problems and cultural issues to be supported by solid evidence. The best way to ensure that our claims will be heard and considered is to use appropriate methods of data collection and analysis. The proper use of methods adds to the market value of a project's findings: It ensures that they will not be discarded as ungrounded.

It's impossible to imagine an academic or scientific discipline that doesn't rely on a core set of agreed-on procedures for procuring, organizing, reading, and interpreting information. While methods are the means by which we do these things, theories stipulate the goals we hope to achieve through the application of methods by shaping the research questions we ask in the first place: Method follows theory.

Theories can be cosmological and grand (higher order); or local, specific, and narrow (lower order); or somewhere in between (midrange). Generally, lower-order theories are themselves based on higher-order theories about human nature or the order of the universe. Whether low, midrange, or high order, all theories follow a certain syntactic or structural pattern in which one or more complex of things is connected to another or more other complexes through an act or process.

All theories are derived from core propositional statements about how X and Y are related and all are claims or conjectures about the nature of reality. For example, the proposition that "There is no such thing as reality" is a statement about the nature of reality that posits the absence of a connection or relationship between reality and the world (the place where we assume reality, if it existed, would be located). Theories may be said to be higher-level propositions. For example, the statement "John loves Mary" is a proposition stating a relationship at one level; at another level—say, for example, when connected to the lower-level (more concrete) statement "John brought Mary flowers"—it's an explanatory theory.

Theories are sometimes used like spotlights to illuminate particular aspects of the human condition. We all use them daily to make sense of what we and others do. Those developed during the research process are called "**grounded theories**" and are common, if not the norm, in qualitative research (Glaser and Strauss 1967). For example, in Sobo's (1995) condom-use research, carried out among impoverished inner-city women, she first thought that women with less money forgo condoms because by doing so they seek to gain financially from their condom-averse partners. Sobo thought that if this were the case, noncondom-using women would start each month poorer than condom-using ones and that they would report that their male partners gave them more financial assistance than condom-using women would report. Actually, the reverse was the case: Condom users reported receiving more money from men than did nonusers (income is relative; both categories of women were equally poor). Because Sobo looked at her data as they came in, she realized her hypothesis was wrong. While conducting her research, she revised it in light of what she was learning. Grounded theory refers to this kind of interactive way of revising theory while applying methods to collect information relevant to the theory.

Sobo used the financial data she collected (along with a mix of other forms of data on how women perceived their relationships) to propose and investigate a new theory that concern over status and self-esteem and other motivations linked to love, not money, drove the women to have unsafe sex. Many of her findings could be accounted for by this new theory. The more data that fit with or can be accounted for by a theory, the stronger or more robust the theory is. A nontrivial theory is one that explains more than one particular kind of phenomenon.

Research Questions

Formulating Hypotheses

Theory spurs research questions. While theories may often remain implicit, research goals or questions must be explicitly stated. Before choosing methods, researchers must be able to state succinctly and unambiguously what their area of interest is and what questions about that area of interest they want to examine and answer. To do so, they must formulate a hypothesis. **Hypotheses** are propositions derived from theories and phrased as verifiable or falsifiable statements. The hypothesis about political affiliation and pet preference was itself derived from a certain theoretical stance about the personality types attracted to certain political platforms. That theory, in turn, derived from a higher-order theory about personality (for example, altruism and egoism are the two main dimensions or types of personality).

The hypothesis provides guidance as to how to test the validity of the theories in a given context. Falsification of a hypothesis doesn't necessarily mean that a theory is wrong, but it does mean that it might be wrong and that, in any case, the hypothesis stemming from it needs to be rethought. "Americans will do anything for a lousy buck" is a hypothesis, loosely speaking: It is based on the theory or unquestioned understanding that Americans are greedy. The loose hypothesis is a more scientific kind of statement than the theoretical statement because it suggests ways to test whether it is true or false. But to turn it into a *scientific* hypothesis, we would need to refine it so that the means for testing it are specific.

Independent and Dependent Variables

There are two kinds of variables: independent variables and dependent or outcome variables. **Independent variables** are those considered important in determining a specific kind of outcome. **Outcome variables** are often called dependent variables because they depend on the independent ones: A certain alignment of independent variables produces a dependent variable as an outcome (providing that a hypothesis is correct).

For example, if we hypothesize that eating hamburgers leads to heart attacks, then "eating hamburgers" is an independent variable and "heart attacks" is a dependent or outcome variable. If we hypothesize that eating fatty foods leads to ill health, then we would have a number of independent variables (for example, ice cream, hamburgers, cheese, etc.) and a number of dependent variables (for example, heart attacks, diabetes, cancer, etc.). Although it's simpler to have only one of each type of variable, social scientific research rarely allows for this. Generally, a whole constellation of complexly interrelated variables are implicated.

To test our hypothesis about fatty foods and health we need to **operationalize** both the dependent and independent variables. Operationalizing variables involves determining how to measure them and making the measures explicit. For example, in relation to the simpler hypothesis, will we measure hamburger consumption by the pound or by the burger? Will a slice or other unit of meatloaf count as one unit of burger? Will we rely on self-reports or will we observe people eating first-hand? How long will the period of observation last? Operationalizing even one variable can be quite time consuming; operationalizing many is hard work indeed. But this step is imperative if the goal of conducting scientific research is to be achieved.

Methods

Dual Demons: Jargon and Math

One barrier to gaining methods skills and knowledge—one of the demons that has made what is really a beautiful forest seem dark and forbidding—is the vocabulary or jargon that inevitably accompanies any specialized field. We have attempted to limit the introduction of jargon in this collection to what is absolutely necessary. The jargon we do include is what Bernard calls "the good kind" (1994:viii); that is, it's here because it's necessary and because it's helpful. To make life easier, we have also included a glossary (pp. 227–233).

Another barrier to gaining methods skills and knowledge has been a lack of mathematical background and computer skills. Methods such as multidimensional scaling, pile sorting, freelisting, and Likert and Guttman scales have been used by researchers for over 30 years, but in the past researchers needed special knowledge to collect, collate, and analyze the data these methods use. This is no longer true. There are price- and user-friendly menu-driven software applications that don't require knowledge of sophisticated math or program languages.

ANTHROPAC is one multimethods program that features a wide variety of applications for collecting, manipulating, and analyzing data. We recommend it because it's easy to use and very versatile. While ANTHROPAC and other such programs are helpful, you don't need to use or know ANTHROPAC or any other methods program to acquire the skills needed to use many of the methods described here. Nor do you need one to interpret articles and reports in which computer-assisted methods and related findings are discussed.

Methods Strategies Will Reflect Research Types

Research areas of interest can be (1) exploratory; (2) classificatory; (3) associational or relational; and (4) causal (Golden 1976:10). Ethnographic research is generally type 1, 2, or 3; it's rarely causal (although, as shown above, it can be). Exploratory (type 1) ethnographic research or "old-fashioned" ethnography uses a method called **participant observation** (see de Munck, this volume) and seeks to familiarize the audience with a group, the setting, and a general research problem.

Hypotheses are usually the products of, rather than the motivation for, such research. Exploratory research is typically open and flexible and concerned with discovery rather than the resolution of a problem.

Classificatory studies, such as ethnobotanical studies of native flora (for example, Conklin 1954; Brown 1984), depend on methodological strategies for eliciting names of categories, the criterial features of the things in the categories (for example, trees have trunks and branches), taxonomic relations of inclusion (for example, a tree is a kind of flora; a red oak is a kind of a tree), and levels of contrast (a red oak tree has acorns and broad leaves; birch trees have no acorns and narrow, serrated leaves; grasses have no trunks or leaves). Researchers must find out what the names of the categories are and discuss whether they use native (emic) or universalist (etic) criteria for specifying the relevant characteristics of the category items.

In associational or relational studies, researchers investigate the relationship between variables and try to determine the relationship's direction. Direction refers to whether variables move in the same direction (in a positive relationship, both go up or down together) or in opposite directions (in a negative or inverse relationship, as one goes up the other goes down). Causal studies try to learn if the relationship depends on or is caused by one (or more) independent variables.

Cause or Correlation?

A perennial problem in research is that we have a tendency to confuse a **correlation** or the simple co-occurrence of two variables with a **causal relationship**, in which one causes the other. Arguments for causal links are extremely difficult to support because co-occurrence can be by chance rather than by design. Even if a correlation exists by design—if it's not due to chance (and there are statistical tests to measure the probability of this happening)—it's not necessarily there because of the reasons we think. Researchers should be extremely cautious when tempted to speak of relationships between variables as causal.

For example, until recently it was thought that being a person of color necessarily entailed having an IQ ("intelligence quotient") that was lower than the norm for people with white skin. It was true that low IQ and dark skin correlated positively, or co-occurred. But this had more to do with racism and poverty than with a genetic link between so-called race and intelligence. Correlation and cause were confused in a manner that fit neatly with a racist agenda. Clearly, correlations not due merely to chance or environmental conditions (such as the co-occurrence of cars and sunshine in San Diego) should alert researchers to the possible existence of complex relationships between variables rather than assure them that their culturally shaped assumptions are correct.

Other Common Errors

A number of types of low-level errors can, like high-level ones, poison research results. With foresight, errors can be avoided. Measurement error involves the erroneous measurement of a variable. It occurs, for example, when a research assistant misreads—or hasn't been trained to properly read—a thermometer or scale. Recording error occurs when a measurement is inaccurately recorded in data record forms, generally due to carelessness or sloppy note taking (for example, miscopying "sow" as "cow" or miskeying 23 as 32). Data entry error is similar, and happens when data recorded on paper or tape are misentered when computer files are created. One way to avoid these types of errors is to measure, record, and enter all data twice and to compare entries. Some researchers skip the recording stage and enter data directly into the computer when possible (for example, when a portable computer is available for field use or when data are collected in a laboratory). However, it's best to be as careful as possible to begin with. (Another kind of error is sampling error; we'll come back to that later when we discuss sampling.)

What Makes a Method Scientific?

We have mentioned the possibility (and, indeed, the unavoidable reality) of blending qualitative and quantitative approaches. We also mentioned several differences between the two: the nature of data (narrative or numerical); the location and nature of research (in situ, the lab, or another controlled environment); and the type of focus (case specific or on a narrow range of specified variables). Some might call those on the narrative, in situ, case-specific side of the fence "humanists" and those on the numerical, lab-experimental, independent-dependent and operational variable side, "scientists." Scientists tend to be generalizers, concerned with random sampling and statistical significance as means to examine how specified factors vary across cases; humanists tend to be **particularists** who focus on holistic, richly detailed accounts of social life (Wellman and Sim 1990:1–2).

Validity

Validity refers to the extent that one's conclusions about the world are correct (Kirk and Miller 1986:19). Using explicit and systematic methods increases the probability that your study is valid, but it doesn't guarantee validity. Early positivist approaches assumed that scientific knowledge was discovered through development of logically coherent and impeccable arguments (that is, theories) validated by empirical (sense) data gathered by systematic methods. But, for example, even if we systematically measure fat intake in terms of the number of hamburgers subjects eat, we miss other sources of fat. We therefore have to ask ourselves if our measure has validity; that is, does it measure actual fat intake?

There are two problems of validity that must always be considered with regard to variables: (1) Are our variables (for example, hamburger intake) accurate reflections or indicators of the stream of life we are trying to describe, measure, or explain?; and (2) Are our methods for measuring variance or change in relation to our chosen variables useful or effective? For example, does counting the number of hamburgers informants eat tell us more than other variables? Is counting the number of hamburgers eaten a more useful measure than, say, weight? The researcher must be able to defend his or her position both in terms of defining variables and in the manner in which they've been operationalized.

Other problems of validity involve the more philosophical issue of whether it's possible for humans to be scientific or objective. This issue, touched on earlier, is usually divided into two components: reactivity and research bias.

Reactivity

Reactivity refers to the effect the researcher has on participants and the context in which work is carried out, as mentioned above. In fieldwork, the problem of reactivity diminishes over time; after a year of living in an area, the researcher's effect on surrounding people's behavior has—or should have—*effectively* disappeared (see de Munck, this volume, and Maxwell 1996:91). In general, the subject's or informant's behavior will be affected in proportion to the intrusiveness of the research. Bogdan and Bilken (1992) put it well: "If you treat people as 'research subjects,' they will act as research subjects, which is different from how they usually act" (p. 47). Because reactivity can never be eliminated in the use of intrusive, formal methods, generalizations to the real world are suspect if they are made from the results of such analyses.

Research Bias

Research bias refers to the theoretical preconceptions researchers bring to bear on choice and use of methods. For example, an anthropologist who assumes that all behavior is rule governed may infer the presence of a particular rule for explaining a behavior when no such rule is actually present. Most researchers recognize that "*all data* are theory-, method-, and measurement-dependent (Ratcliffe 1983:148, cited in Phillips 1990:25; emphasis in original).

Quantitative methods attempt to minimize research bias by emphasizing the use of instruments for data collection and measurement, thus eliminating the researcher's bias in both the data collection and analysis processes. However, as Kirk and Miller (1986) point out, researchers often select methods that have a high probability of substantiating their predictions or theories. Even so, researchers can minimize these "threats to validity" in a number of ways. We will discuss four of them: reliability or replicability, verifiability, triangulation, and sampling.

Reliability

Like validity, **reliability** depends to a large degree on the construction of a given question or measurement technique. A faulty thermometer may lead to invalid (wrong) or unreliable (inconstant) readings, just as a poorly worded question may generate invalid and unreliable answers. For instance, if we wanted to know how many children a woman had, we might ask, "How many children do you have?," leaving her to self-report the answer. But without specifying that we mean living or surviving children (or whatever it is that we mean), we might find a mother reporting one number when asked in one context and another number in the next. Her answers won't be reliable or consistent because we haven't given her a firm enough idea of what we want; our tools aren't good enough to ensure reliability. Although each of her answers may be valid in relation to her situational reading of the question, some or all may not be valid in relation to our conception of the actual question asked (number of living children, in this case). And, of course, she may be lying (see Wolcott 1990), which will correlate positively with the sensitive nature of the topic under question. If she lies consistently, her answers will be reliable. But they still won't be valid.

It's better to revise the question during a pilot study or an exploratory research phase so that participant and researcher agree about what each question means. Otherwise, because of its very vagueness (Does the researcher mean only living children, or living and dead children, and, if the latter, would miscarriages and abortions count as dead children, or only stillbirths?), the question may elicit a different response each time it's asked, even if it's asked of the same participant. For this reason, a pretest is necessary.

In part because of explicitness and attention to reliability, another hallmark of scientific research is its **replicability**. That means that an experiment or project carried out by one person can be carried out again by another person, which may be the case if the second person wishes to verify the findings. While one ethnographer might have better rapport with the participants in his or her study than the next ethnographer would, in general the replicability of a project helps show that the findings were sound. That is, if I find x, and another ethnographer finds x, we are all the more sure that x is the answer to our research question. If the methods of a study are not replicable or reliable, then the conclusions can never be verified by an independent study. We are then left with either accepting or rejecting the results of a study based on the authoritarian claims of the research team rather than on the findings themselves.

Verifiability

Scientific studies also are verifiable. For a study to be verifiable, the definitions of concepts and methods must not only be explicit and replicable, they must also correspond to empirical referents or phenomena. Another key feature of science—that it is based on observation—is paramount here. Introspection or thought experiments such as those undertaken by philosophers are not scientific endeavors; they cannot be replicated or verified. **Verifiability** depends on the means by which we measure concepts and demands that the methods of measurement and the values of measurement are standardized.

Studies are verifiable if they state the method of measure and the value of measure so that comparisons can be made and similar findings ascertained. For example, we may measure height either by feet or meters, or by assessments of short, average, and tall. But while feet and meters can be converted into one another, unless the value of tall is provided by the original researcher, there is no way to convert it to feet. Similarly, socioeconomic studies that rely on class measures of lower, middle, and upper aren't verifiable by studies that rely on numerical measures of class unless the former studies specified the income and other quantitative indicators that they used to determine their class classifications.

Triangulation

One of the techniques that helps us verify conclusions and limits our desire to replicate others' work (although not the need to build on it) is called **triangulation**, after navigational techniques by which three points are used to steer a straight line or go toward a particular destination. In triangulation, data collected with one specific method are compared with data collected with other methods. This is one way to try to correct for the biases inherent in specific methods of data collection.

Recall our question about number of (living) children. While the low reliability of answers tipped us off to problems with the operationalization of that variable, triangulation might have done the same. Let's say that when a woman is asked, "How many children do you have?," she reports that she has three. When we double check her answer through triangulation (for example, by asking her sister, by asking her partner, or by observation), we may learn she actually has two living children. This doesn't mean she was lying; she may have been answering her conception of our question. She may have had three children at one time and may have taken our question to be in relation to this total. Nonetheless, her answer would be invalid in relation to our (poorly operationalized) conception of what the question asked.

Triangulation also gives a richer and more complete picture of the study material. For example, we can legitimately obtain data on eating habits by using the following types of methods: (1) participant observation; (2) self-reports of food intake over the past 24 hours; (3) freelists of most commonly eaten foods; (4) Likert-scaled (never to always) questions relating to frequency of intake of these foods; (5) clinical assays of blood and urine chemistry; and (6) interviews concerning cooking techniques. Combining two or more of these techniques will lead to a fuller understanding of people's eating practices and beliefs than data obtained from only one of these techniques.

Sampling

A sampling method is usually necessary if you want to generalize findings from a small sample population to a larger population. However, it's not always necessary. For example, the existence of plow horticulture in a society is evident from seeing one plow from a train window. Similarly, answering the question of whether polyandry is practiced in a society is also confirmed by one case. Basic or self-evident generalizations can be asserted without using sampling procedures. For more complex sorts of generalizations, such as the percentage of polyandrous marriages or determining the conditions that enhance or reduce the probability for a polyandrous marriage, one must use methodical sampling procedures. Researchers rely on samples because it's usually unfeasible to collect data from the entire population. Thus, the **sample** is intended to be a microcosm of the larger population in terms of the relevant characteristics the researcher is interested in.

Unsound generalizations occur when the sample population isn't representative of the larger population. Randomizing selection procedures for including informants into a sample is one way of increasing the probability that a sample is representative of the larger population. For example, in a given study area, houses or people can be chosen according to a random number table. Random number tables are found in the back of most statistics and many methods books. For a review of how to use random number tables, see Bernard (1994:71–101).

Sampling is important when you want to know about causal relations and population variance. When variance is close to zero in a population, there is no reason to use sampling procedures. Ethnographers seldom use sampling methods because they frequently work with a small population (for example, a classroom, village, or small group) where there is either little variation in a given variable (that is, all are adolescents or Muslims) or, when there is variation, researchers have access to the entire population. Second, ethnography, by definition, involves a concern with thick description, so breadth is sacrificed for depth. Because the ethnographer has lived with a population and studied them for an extended period of time, there's some assurance that she or he knows the population well enough so that causal explanations and descriptions of what is typical of it can be trusted.

The myth of ethnography's inherent reliability was exploded by Derek Freeman's (1983) critique, some say demolition, of Margaret Mead's work on

Samoan adolescents. Briefly, Mead's (1928) work, *Coming of Age in Samoa*, had become an anthropological classic. Many anthropologists used it in their under-graduate classes as an example of good ethnography. Mead had argued that Samoan adolescents didn't suffer the same kinds of rebellious and self-conscious growing-up pains that American adolescents did. She argued that this was primarily because there were no sanctions against premarital sex (and everyone was doing it) and because emotional ties were diffused among the kindred rather than concentrated on one love object. Mead depicted a relatively sexually carefree Polynesia, devoid of sexual guilt and angst, which appealed both to anthropologists and their students.

Freeman noted that most of Mead's generalizations were based on interviews with two women. Mead, as Orans (1996) mentions, wrote to her mentor, Franz Boas, worried about the difficulties in obtaining a representative sample. But, in fact, most ethnographers rely on key informants and convenience (ethnographic) sampling, based on interviewing those who are willing and able to be interviewed.

Most anthropologists today try to combine thick, particularist description and simple statistics in an attempt to provide ethnographic detail and embed community data into wider fields of relevance. In collecting their data, they generally rely on ethnographic samples—small numbers of participants knowledgeable about the topic under question but not necessarily representative or typical in terms of their demographic traits (for example, age, occupation, etc.)—rather than relying on probability samples, in which every member of a population has an equal probability of being selected.

An **ethnographic sample** establishes the range of cultural phenomena, but not the frequency distribution of those phenomena. Only a probability sample can do that (Werner and Bernard 1994). In other words, ethnographic samples cannot tell us the percentage of people in a population who are Republicans or Democrats, but they can tell us the range of political parties that people belong to and why people are Republican, Democrat, or anything else.

An ethnographic sample can tell us what is in the phenomenal or experiential, lived, perceived world of the people we are studying and how they think about those things (Dreyfus 1987). Boster (1985), Romney and Weller (1988), and D'Andrade (1995) tell us that comparatively small ethnographic samples (less than 20 people) are sufficient to obtain confidence that members of a culture agree on the array of items or symbols that constitute a cultural domain or category (for example, types of birds, grasses, vegetables) or agree on the core attributes used to identify similarities among those items (for example, wing and beak shapes) and to contrast them with other cultural domains (Kronenfeld 1996).

In discussing Kluckhohn's *Navajo Witchcraft* (1944), Werner and Bernard (1994) conclude that "to do ethnographic sampling well . . . the ethnographer must learn another culture systematically and not casually" (p. 9). Thus, ethnographic sampling, like probability sampling, requires controls. We can only have confidence in findings from ethnographic samples if the ethnographer has taken these steps: (1a) demonstrated familiarity with that culture through knowledge of previous publications and duration of stay (over a year) or (1b) focused on a particular cultural domain and has, through freelisting, established the range of elements that constitute a domain; and (2) understood that the material presented represents a model of culture as represented by the informants and is not a model of the culture itself.

Developing a Systematic Methodological Approach

When entering the field, it's not always possible to know what data you might deem necessary at the end of the research period. One of the strengths of ethnographic research in general has been the freedom to examine concerns that emerge as important during the fieldwork experience and to discard questions developed before entering the field if they aren't relevant to the participants. However, it's increasingly recognized that all data collected must be collected in a systematic way so that they are useful at the end of the day. If you encounter a new issue while in the field, it's well worth taking the time to develop a systematic methodological approach so that any information collected will actually be of use. Flexibility is important. Whyte (1984) boldly argues that "When the field situation reveals opportunities to do a more valuable study by changing the research design, seize the opportunity" (p. 37). However, it's almost always better to have developed systematic methods before you enter the field.

One dimension of research that affects data's usefulness is the mode of analysis planned. If you plan to determine frequencies related to dishwashing, for example, then you need to collect frequency data in the field. On the other hand, if you're interested primarily in the meaning of dishwashing practices, you probably intend to use narrative or content analyses on interview transcripts; therefore, you need to elicit verbal data amenable to such techniques.

Finally, methods for data collection are only useful if researchers plan to use the data collected. This point may seem simple minded, but every year we encounter students with arrays of data that they have no idea how to use. Goals for analysis should be a primary consideration when planning research methods. Careful planning involves thinking about the hypotheses to be tested, specific analysis goals, and the methods by which to collect the kind of data needed to accomplish this.

Specific Methods for Data Collection

The methods chosen for a particular research project reflect, as we have noted, the questions asked and the types of answers desired. However, one also needs to know what methods exist in order to choose between them. While we cannot introduce every possible method in this volume, we have assembled a wide variety of chapters spanning the range of key methods. Most chapters deal with the more basic methods and are arranged so that more difficult or derivative methods come later, giving readers a chance to build their competence and confidence before encountering them. Competence building is enhanced by the inclusion of study or discussion questions for each chapter.

The methods covered include participant observation, freelisting, pile sorts, ratings and rankings, Guttman and Likert scale questions, hierarchical clustering, multidimensional scaling, network analysis, consensus analysis, correspondence analysis, timed observations, and decision modeling. As you will see, the application of some methods depends on data obtained through the application of previous methods. So, terms from a particular domain (for example, favorite children's foods) elicited through freelisting can then be used to generate a list of terms for pile sorting. This doesn't have to be the case, as favorite children's foods can be obtained through survey data, focus groups, or by other means. In turn, pile sort data are frequently submitted to multidimensional scaling or hierarchical clustering for analysis. There are many ways in which methods can be productively combined, whether by chaining them to achieve one kind of finding or by using them simultaneously for triangulation.

Methods' Temptations

With the development of new, systematic data collection techniques that don't entail years of fieldwork, it is tempting to engage in what has become known as rapid ethnographic assessment. This involves using only one or a few methods; the researcher foregoes participant observation and long-term study. This may be convenient and even necessary and excusable when there are time-sensitive problems, as in the field of development or the context of a health crisis. However, this technique is only truly appropriate when researchers have already done extensive fieldwork or already know a lot about the population involved and have taken the time, in developing their study and in writing up the findings, to take existing knowledge into account. Otherwise, they might be misled as they attempt to interpret their findings, and they might mislead others with their (unsound) conclusions.

Parting Words

No matter what topic you are interested in, or what group of people you work with, if you take the time to think carefully, logically, and systematically about your data collection and analysis needs you can develop and implement a sound methods plan.

It is critical to do so, for without good methods, it is impossible to produce valid and reliable results. Findings will be unsupportable, spurious, or nonsensical. Frustration will run high. You will be lost in the forest again.

NOTE

1. Crispell's study addressed "popularity" rather than "preference" of pet; we took the liberty of translating popularity as a measure of preference.

VICTOR C. DE MUNCK ■

Two

Participant Observation: A Thick Explanation of Conflict in a Sri Lankan Village

Participant observation is the only method I know that enables the researcher to get close to the realities of social life. Its deficiency in producing quantitative data are more than made up for by its ability to minimize the distance between the researcher and his subject of study.   (Herbert Gans, 1976, p. 59).

I had been living in the Sri Lankan Muslim village of Kutali for 22 months when, at about 1:00 A.M. on December 14, 1981, there was a knock on my door and a man named Rafi called out in an urgent whisper, "_Grama sevaka, ende ikemente!_" ("Officer, come quick!"). The _grama sevaka_, the sole government official involved in the day-to-day runnning of the village, had been sleeping at my house. He and my 18-year-old assistant, Lafir, woke up, shook the cobwebs from their heads, and the three of us followed Rafi up the dirt road. Barefoot, with my flashlight sweeping the dirt road for cobras and vipers, we made our way to the Kutali junction. There we found three Sinhalese Buddhist men on a bullock cart filled with recently cut timber. The cart was surrounded by five angry Muslim villagers, demanding the immediate arrest of the Sinhalese men for illegally harvesting and transporting timber.

It soon became apparent that the situation at the junction was not as it appeared. The Sinhalese men had been hired by Mohideen, a Muslim and one of the richest, most powerful, and feared men in the village. In confronting the angry villagers, the *grama sevaka* ultimately had to confront Mohideen. Ethnicity now became an important factor, complicating what had first appeared to be a straightforward situation. Sri Lanka has a population of 16 million, of which 64% are Sinhalese Buddhists, 20% Tamil Hindus, 7% Muslims, and 7% Christians, predominantly of Sinhalese and Tamil ethnicity. For the villagers, the Sinhalese *grama sevaka* symbolized and represented a government and nation dominated by the Sinhalese and favoring Sinhalese interests.

In chronicling this conflict, I was concerned with answering three questions: What were the resources that the *grama sevaka* and Mohideen had at their disposal? What do these resources signify? How does ethnicity influence access to these resources? The types of resources these antagonists used against each other illuminated and affirmed, to the villagers and myself, who had power, what constituted power, and how the protagonists used power. Power is most clearly represented in situations of conflict or contests where the opponents have to use whatever symbolic and material resources are available in order to defeat their opponents.

The method I used for obtaining data is **participant observation**. This is the primary method used by anthropologists who do fieldwork, and it's what distinguishes anthropology from the other social sciences. The rest of this chapter is organized as follows: (1) a discussion of the advantages and limitations of participant observation; (2) a description of the procedures for coding conflict events; (3) a description of the conflict; (4) and an interpretation of this conflict case.

Participant Observation: Advantages and Limitations

Is Participant Observation a Method?

As an undergraduate, I didn't consider participant observation a "true" method. Participant observation was, I thought, just academic jargon for "hanging out." In fact, Bernard (1994) has a subsection of his book on anthropological methods called "Hanging Out." He says that hanging out is a skill and it's what anthropologists should do a lot of to gain trust and rapport. In "Street Corner Society," Doc, Whyte's key informant, admonishes him to "Go easy on that 'who,' 'what,' 'why,' 'when,' and 'where' stuff, Bill. You ask those questions, and people will clam up on you. If people accept you, you can just hang around, and you'll learn the answer in the long run without even having to ask questions" (1984:303).

Raybeck (1992) uses the apt metaphor of swimming and "getting below the surface" to describe participant observation. Participant observation, Raybeck suggests, humanizes the relationship between the anthropologist and villagers by making the anthropologist "vulnerable." Spradley (1979, 1980) describes it as an unfolding process, proceeding from mutual apprehension and ignorance to cooperation, trust, and, eventually, participation.

Hanging Out

Hanging out is the single best way to gain entry into the **backstage** life of a society or group that you are interested in studying. Only through systematic hanging out do you build up friendly and informal relationships with members of the community. Conversely, only through hanging out do a majority of villagers get an opportunity to watch, meet, and get to know you outside your "professional" role.

You hang out to observe and meet people, to have pleasant conversations, and to socialize. When you hang out, you shouldn't carry the obtrusive badges of your profession (for example, a camera, tape recorder, and, nowadays, a notebook computer). A pocket notebook and pen are fine—they don't need to be used and they are not "foreign" or "prestige" items. You must remember that you are not going out *only* to collect data. You can't develop intimate relations with people if you always interact with them as a data gatherer. You need to show and convince them that you have an interest in them as friends and acquaintances. This means going to public places and being prepared to stay out a relatively long time.

In peasant communities like Kutali, the cycle of work is based on the seasons and is periodic, with weeks of intense activity followed by weeks of relative idleness (see A. Johnson 1975). Except during periods of intense activity—at the beginning and end of cultivation cycles—adult male villagers hang out much of the time, while women are daily busy collecting foodstuffs, washing clothes, cleaning, collecting firewood, making mats, bathing and caring for children, and preparing meals. Men in Kutali hang out at a number of places: at one of the five major shops in the village; at the junction where the bus arrives three times daily; at the mosque; at the river or public wells where they bathe daily; or on the verandahs of houses. I made it a point to distribute my periods of hanging out at each of these primary hang out spots. Kutali is a nucleated village with an elliptical configuration, and it takes no longer than 20 minutes to walk from one end to the other, thus it was easy to visit each spot daily, if one were so inclined.

The Stages of Hanging Out

There are three distinct stages to hanging out. Ideally, one moves from a formal, intrusive, and incompetent beginning stage to an intimate, welcomed, and competent end stage (the idea of these stages comes from Dreyfus [1984], by way of Holland [1992]).

The first, "stranger" stage, is characterized by a process of learning the rules and language for social interaction and becoming familiar with the community (or group) and they with you. During this stage, villagers tried to teach me their language with the associated gestures and intonation patterns. I learned informal social etiquette, names, faces, and personalities. I became aware of the patter and pattern of social interactions, who hangs out with whom, and the themes of everyday conversations. In other words, I learned what one needs to know in order to act and think as a relatively competent member of that community.

In the second stage, having learned basic social skills, the community and I had become familiar and relatively comfortable with each other. I could now go out in public without having a noticeable effect on ongoing interactions. This is the "acquaintance" stage, where the researcher and villagers begin to recognize each other as individuals, with particular quirks and characteristics. During this stage, the researcher is accepted (though not necessarily liked) as part of the audience at the various public arenas in the community. The researcher begins to learn how to act competently "as a local" in the various social settings. However, the researcher's behavior and speech are very limited, and he or she is incapable of speaking and behaving fluidly and unself-consciously.

In the final stage, the reseacher is a full-fledged participant observer, acting and responding automatically—without first having to consciously construct his or her behavior and speech—to the actions of those nearby. This is the "intimate" stage of hanging out, where villagers and ethnographers have accumulated a mutual history and repertoire of experiences so that they think of each other as individuals rather than as social identities.

Hanging out is not all there is to participant observation. Raybeck notes how he volunteered for guard duty in the Malaysian village where he worked in order to become more integrated into the community. Many anthropologists participate in the same work, religious, and leisure activities as do the members of the community. For example, I offered free English lessons, cleaned and bandaged wounds, and, in emergencies, took villagers to the hospital on my 1956 Java motorcycle.

Participant observation also requires taking discrete notes of observations and interpretations. I always carried one notebook with me and often a second memo-diary notebook. The first notebook was the official one in which I had a list of questions that I wanted to answer. Usually, these were a series of formal survey questions on a particular subject (for example, How do you find a spouse? How do you acquire more land?). When there was a major event—a wedding, exorcism, or during the harvest period—my time was spent observing and asking questions about that event.

My second, more personal, notebook contained whatever I felt like writing, from short comments, addresses of informants, queries that I wanted to follow up on, to poems and cathartic passages. I usually took my second notebook with me only when I "meant business." For example, if I attended a wedding or was interviewing villagers about a particular topic, I kept the primary data in the first notebook and wrote down questions, odd observations, and things that "didn't fit" in the second notebook. This kept the first official notebook clean and relatively uncluttered with extraneous material.

The Advantages of Participant Observation

Participant observation has three distinct advantages over other methods: (1) It allows access to backstage culture; (2) It allows for a thick description of a society or group; and (3) It provides opportunities and a means to report on unscheduled sorts of behaviors and events. Each of these advantages is discussed below.

The term "**backstage**" is taken from the theater and is meant to suggest that what happens backstage makes what happens on the **frontstage** possible. Goffman (1959) was perhaps the first to adopt these terms to study how people alter their behaviors as they move between various backstage and frontstage arenas of social life. Frontstage behavior is what is normative, expected, and conventional behavior meant for public viewing. Backstage behavior is meant to be hidden from the public eye, it occurs behind the scenes, and only intimates participate in or can witness it. The key advantage of participant observation is that it provides access to the backstage arenas of social life.

A goal for most sociocultural anthropologists is to write an ethnography of the community or group they studied. An ethnography consists of a "**thick description**" of life as lived and interpreted by members of the study group (Geertz 1973). Thick description is not code for correlating the validity of an ethnography with the amount of descriptive material provided; rather, it invokes the ethnographer's goal of describing behaviors, intentions, situations, and events as understood by one's informants. The anthropologist works as a cultural translator, using participant observation to learn the meanings of another culture and translating these meanings into "standard Western culture." To learn how people of another culture assign meanings to their lives and their world, you have to live and interact in that world. Participant observation gives anthropologists the means to observe and describe how individuals use and make meanings in everyday social interactions.

Certain sociocultural events can only be studied through participant observation. These are unforeseen or unscheduled events (Frake 1964). The night Rafi knocked on my door was one such event. No other methodological approach would have given me an opportunity to provide a thick description of this conflict process.

The Disadvantages of Participant Observation

To obtain the trust and sympathy of a community so that they will be sympathetic to your work and accepting of your presence take time and commitment, and, for most of us, it cannot be faked. To be able to decipher and translate both backstage (informal, hidden, and intimate) and frontstage (public) information requires a high degree of competency in the meaning systems of a given culture. To acquire both cultural competency and mutual trust take more time and skill than most anthropologists have. Many important social and cultural events, such as political contests and funerals, are public and frequently available through the media, so developing intimate relationships in order to gain access isn't necessary.

Often, anthropologists aren't interested in what happens backstage, or they believe backstage information is unimportant. (When attending the theater, do you care about what goes on behind the scenes?) When conditions of poverty are associated with high rates of malnutrition, crime, and illness, survey types of data are more efficient and may be better than participant observation for developing models of cause and effect and social policy. This is because participant observation, by definition, lacks a systematic sampling procedure.

Another potential problem is that participant observation frequently relies on information provided by one or two **key informants**. Intimate relations are, by definition, formed only with people you become friends with. Had the *grama sevaka* and I not been friends, my access and understanding of this conflict case would have been significantly different. There are many cases of ethnographers drawing very different conclusions and characterizations of the same people because of their reliance on different key informants (see the discussion in the Introduction on sampling and the Mead-Freeman controversy). One reason this happens is that anthropologists often choose key informants who are most like themselves and/or who are atypical members of their own society either because they are leaders or because they are marginal. To minimize this type of bias, Boster (1985) and Bernard (1994:165) recommend selecting key informants who are either pretested as or known to be culturally competent in the subject matter you are collecting data on. For example, if you want to know about folk theories of illness, you should rely on local healers as your key informants.

A competent informant is someone who knows what other members of the community know and are astute observers of their own culture. My guess is that, over time, the anthropologist makes friends with the members of the community most like him- or herself, people who are intellectually interested in thinking and asking questions about what human beings do and why they do it. My key informants were all, I thought, culturally competent, articulate, and thoughtful.

Ethnographers don't just choose key informants as if all the villagers are lined up shouting "Choose me!" The ethnographer is also "chosen" by someone who likes and will help you. In that sense, obtaining a culturally competent key informant is often a matter of luck. You can't make a person your key informant if he or she is unwilling to play that role.

Key informants are a necessity for a thick description and for writing about culture, but they are not suitable for hypothesis testing or asserting a causal model as social fact. Spradley (1979:30–31) writes that ethnographies are about description and laying the groundwork for building theory and hypothesis testing. Similarly, Golden (1976:16) classifies "field studies" as "exploratory" studies on which one can formulate theories and hypotheses. Confirmation of theories and hypotheses grounded in the statements of key informants can only come through methods based on sampling procedures. This doesn't imply that you can't develop good causal models through participant observation. Indeed, participant observation may be the best way to develop good, verifiable, causal models. However, such models are always exploratory until they are verified with empirical data gathered through a representative sample of the study population.

Writing Up Field Notes

As mentioned earlier, I used two notebooks simultaneously, numbering them by date and sequence (for example, Books No. 1 and 1a, March 4–10, 1990). Book 1 was my official field book, containing all my field jottings, maps, diagrams, interviews, and observations. Book 1a was a memo book and contained my "unofficial" mullings, questions, comments, quirky notes, and diary type entries (see Figures 2.1a and 2.1b).

I also used index cards to index and cross-reference materials from both books (see Figure 2.1c). Indexes are arranged in terms of headings such as conflicts, gender, jokes, religion, marriage, kinship, men's activities, women's activities, and so on. Each day's notes are indexed by book, page number, and a brief descriptive phrase. Thus, if I am interested in conflict between Muslims and Sinhalese over land I would look for the Conflict index cards and search under the interethnic and/or land dispute subsections.

Coding Procedures

Participant observation involves writing down what people say and do in a given context at the time of the event (or just after it). Because it is easy to be overwhelmed by too much data, it is important to develop a coding procedure for targeting, selecting, and organizing information.

Werner (1989a, 1989b) describes a contact tree method for keeping track of interviewees in the field. The contact tree is a simple diagram in which you first list your initial contacts and branch out from there as they introduce you to other informants or contacts. This method can also be used to graph any other relevant parameters. For example, I used a numbering and naming system to identify conflict cases. This particular one was conflict case #36, and the field note jottings in Figures 2.1a and 2.1b was my fourth record of this case. This allowed me to keep track of the aggregate number of conflict cases and the sequence of events, or at least my records on these events, for each case.

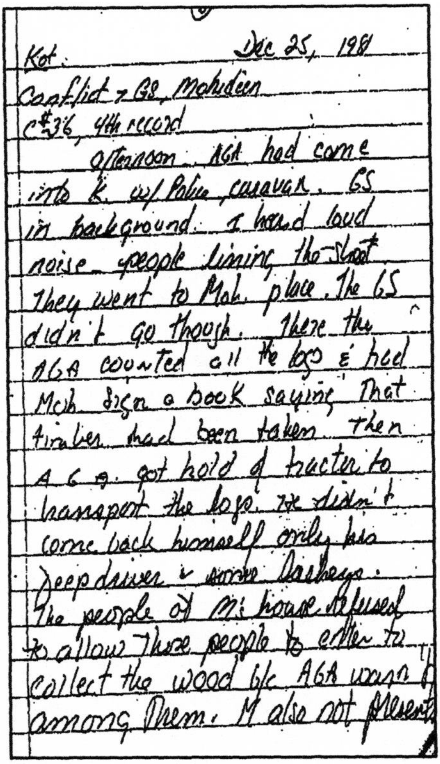

Kot. Dec 25, 1981
Conflict = GS, Mohideen
C#36, 4th record
afternoon. AGA had come into K w/ Police caravan. GS in background. I heard loud noise people lining the street They went to Moh. place. The GS didn't go though. There the AGA counted all the logs & had Moh. sign a book saying that timber had been taken. Then AGA got hold of tractor to transport the logs. He didn't come back himself only his jeep driver & some lackeys. The people of M's house refused to allow those people to enter to collect the wood b/c AGA wasn't among them. M also not present

Figure 2.1a. Field notes.

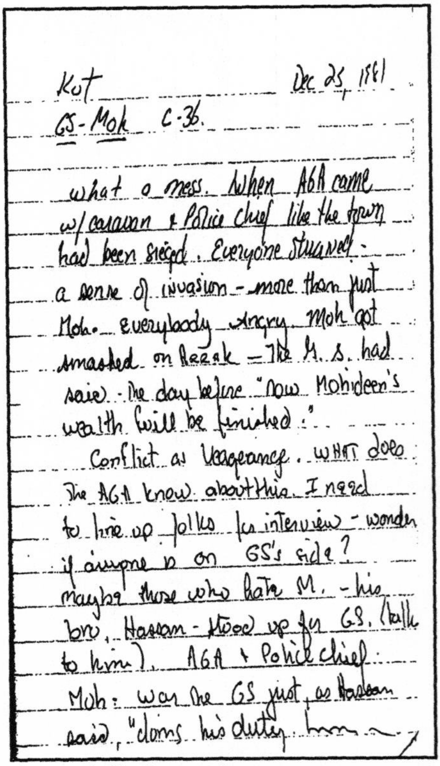

Kot Dec 25, 1981
GS-Mok C-36.
what a mess. When AGA came w/ caravan & Police chief like the town had been sieged. Everyone stunned - a sense of invasion - more than just Moh. Everybody angry. Moh got smashed on Razak - The G.S. had said the day before "now Mohideen's wealth will be finished."
Conflict as vengeance. WHAT does the AGA know about this. I need to line up folks for interview - wonder if anyone is on GS's side? maybe those who hate M. - his bro, Hassan - stood up for GS. (talk to him). AGA & Police chief Moh: was the GS just, as Hassan said, "doing his duty. hmm ~

Figure 2.1b. Personal notes.

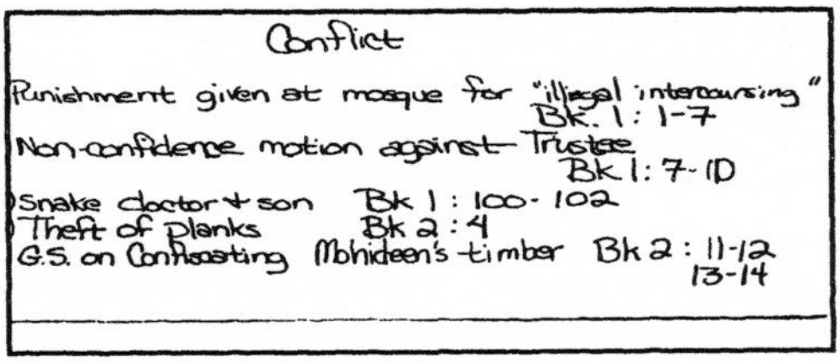

Conflict
Punishment given at mosque for "illegal intercoursing" Bk. 1: 1-7
Non-confidence motion against Trustee Bk 1: 7-10
Snake doctor + son Bk 1: 100-102
Theft of planks Bk 2: 4
G.S. on Confiscating Mohideen's timber Bk 2: 11-12 13-14

Figure 2.1c. Index cards.

I divided conflict cases into beginning, middle, and end stages. The beginning stage describes the triggering event and its immediate ramification. For example, if X sets fire to Y's house and Y goes out to search for X and the two have a huge fight, this is recorded as the beginning stage. The middle stage consists of marshaling resources, recruiting allies, and making strategic moves. The end stage marks the end of the conflict case, either through recognition of a winner or loser, a negotiated settlement or simply that it runs out of steam.

Beginning, middle, and end stages are often imprecisely marked. Stage codes are important for apprehending patterns in the flow of events that comprise a conflict process. For example, escalation of a conflict may be preceded by a period of intensive and successful recruitment of allies. Events are recognizable in terms of the "moves" that actors make. A move is any recognizable action taken by a protagonist or ally to move the protagonist nearer to his or her goal. Moves involve using resources to overcome obstacles or to place obstacles in the way of one's opponent(s).

In conflict situations, opponents usually make many moves, but a few are critical moves intended not just to marshal resources or counter the opponent but to gain victory. One should be alert to such moves; they are not always obvious. Moves toward conflict resolution may be preceded by a disinclination of opponents to maintain relations with allies. The escalation and resolution processes involve different patterns of events and may be seen as separate stages in a conflict process.

Conflicts usually involve the recruitment of allies and the use of resources. When possible, a resource is marked as a little "r" or a big "R" to note its degree of importance. The assessment of importance is determined by the researcher. Since allies are a type of resource, they are connected to an "r/R" by a hyphen so that one can have R-AGA (meaning that the resource is the assistant government agent and that this is an important ally). Resources are marked within the stage of the conflict process in which they are used or recruited.

In conflicts, protagonists face obstacles and attempt to overcome them. The obstacles are usually the lack or loss of a resource or a resource controlled and used by one's opponent. When obstacles were apparent, they were included in the above string at the appropriate stage. Big obstacles were signaled with an upper-case "O" and minor ones with a lower-case "o."

These codes were selected because of my adherence to the **transactional** game theory of conflict that became prominent in the 1960s as a result of the pioneering works of Beals and Siegel (1966) and Bailey (1969). From this perspective, conflicts are processes motivated by the ambitions of actors to obtain culturally defined prizes (for example, a political office or prestigious job). The emphasis is on individuals as motivated agents, moving and manipulating personal, social, and cultural resources to gain their objectives. Protagonists recruit allies, gather resources, and develop strategies to overcome obstacles, defeat their opponents, and gain the "prize." A game theoretic approach views conflict as a process of tactical interactions between protagonists until one wins or the conflict fizzles out, at least overtly.

The analyst's job is to understand the reasons for the actions of the main actors involved in the conflict process. Thus, though my coding system was intended to help me describe conflict processes, it was consciously embedded in a theoretical perspective. As Pelto and Pelto (1978) note, description is never "mere description," it's always motivated by a theory.

Coding procedures are used to evaluate and select the information you think is important enough to record. A coding procedure allows you to create a mental guideline targeting the type of data you need to attend to. Without one, your focus is likely to waver and your field notebooks will be the written analogue of zapping between TV shows. This doesn't mean you cannot code switch or zap, but that you need to always have a methodological "home" to return to. Coding procedures are also, to paraphrase Lévi-Strauss, good to think with. Like grammar, codes are rules for organizing symbols into larger and more meaningful strings of symbols. It is important, no, imperative, to construct a coding system not because the coding system represents the "true" structure of the process you are studying, but because it offers a framework for organizing and thinking about the data.

Describing the Conflict Case

Historical Prelude

In 1963, the Sri Lankan government replaced the traditional village headman post *(arraci mahatmeya)* with government-appointed civil servants called *grama sevakas* (often simply called "*GS*" by the villagers). The *arraci mahatmeya* was an inherited position because the local-level political structure of a Sri Lankan village was based on kinship relations. The *grama sevaka* post is an achieved post, determined by nationally prescribed criteria. Applicants must possess the equivalent of a high school diploma, pass a special exam, and undergo a training program. *Grama sevakas* are rotated every three years and seldom serve in their own community. The intent of these changes was to bureaucratize the local-level political structure and to mediate local-level disputes impartially. The changes also minimized the exchange of favors between politicians and the few powerful villagers.

The Kutali *grama sevaka* and I had become friends quickly. He found a house for me, spoke English, was seriously interested in my work, and was a highly intelligent man who spent hours explaining village customs, social relations, intrigues, and so forth. He came to the village on his bicycle about three times a week and frequently ate and slept at my house.

The Beginning Stage

The morning after the *grama sevaka* had spoken with the Sinhalese men who were transporting the timber, he met with Mohideen, the villager who had hired the Sinhalese to cut and transport the timber. Lafir, my cook and assistant, went with him. The following description was told to me by Lafir and its gist was confirmed by the *grama sevaka* and Mohideen.

Mohideen had opened a bottle of *arrack* (coconut rum) and offered the *grama sevaka* a drink. The *grama sevaka* had turned to Lafir and said, "Mohideen is trying to get the job done [that is, bribe him] with only a bottle of *arrack*." It was openly acknowledged by the *grama sevaka* and others that small "gifts" [*tagge*] kept relations between the *grama sevaka* and villagers cordial. The *grama sevaka* refused Mohideen's offer of a drink. and asked to see the permit for cutting the timber. Mohideen replied that he did not have it but could get it the next day. I'm not sure why the *grama sevaka* refused Mohideen's offer. Had he accepted the drink, it would possibly have implied that the conflict was resolved and Mohideen could keep his timber; certainly it would have compromised the *grama sevaka*'s authority. His rejection of the drink was a move that signified that he was on official business.

The Middle Stage

Nothing much happened for 10 days. On the afternoon of the 11th day, three jeeps came down the main dirt road of the village. It was the only time in my two years and ten months in Kutali that more than one government vehicle entered the village. The regional police chief and the assistant government agent (AGA) were in the front jeep, while the *grama sevaka* was in the last jeep with some police officers. (The AGA administrates state policies, disburses funds for development projects, and oversees the activities of the 12 or so *grama sevakas* in his district.) The jeeps stopped in front of Mohideen's house. The AGA inspected and counted the timber, and Mohideen signed a document confirming the amount of timber that was to be impounded. After the AGA and police chief left, a tractor came and hauled the timber to the police station. This was the *grama sevaka*'s critical move.

The villagers were furious at the *grama sevaka* and said that he was a "snake in the grass," so tricky that he could "light a fire under water." Most thought that the *grama sevaka* was motivated by revenge because Mohideen hadn't offered a large enough bribe. But the *grama sevaka* never implied that to me, and I believed him. Mohideen first dismissed the *grama sevaka*'s actions, saying "After all, what is the most I can lose, five thousand rupees? Other people lose . . . more than that. So with Allah's help I can get that back. But the *grama sevaka* I can't understand, I have been doing so many things for him. He eats over at my house, now he also shits at my house." Later, Mohideen began to drink and became progressively more enraged. Villagers watched passively as Mohideen, bottle in hand, hurled curses into the night: "It is written on my forehead that I will drink and do bad things for the rest of my life . . . this doesn't matter, I am somehow or other going to cut the *grama sevaka*'s Achilles tendon . . . somehow or other I will gain my revenge!"

The following night, the *grama sevaka* met secretly with two mosque officials *(marikars)* at my house. They asked him why he had started all this trouble, and he replied, "If I don't confiscate, or at least inquire, about the timber then my presence here is useless. If Mohideen had said, 'It's true I have some timber but I am poor, so please help me,' then I would have dropped the whole affair. Most villagers regard me as a puppet. I have a job to do, and if I don't do it, then I am nothing. I am also a God-fearing man; each morning and night I worship god Kataragama. If I ignore these illegal activities that are taking place under my own nose then God will also become angry with me and turn His back on me."

The villagers thought that the *grama sevaka* was guilty of breaching an implicit social contract between himself and the villagers. The *grama sevaka* was the only government agent who regularly entered the village. A previous one had been beaten to near death by villagers, and the culprits were never identified. It was important for both the villagers and the *grama sevaka* to establish and maintain hospitable relations. Hence, they struck up an implicit social contract: The *grama sevaka* would use his authority lightly and with discretion and, in turn, villagers would feed him and provide him with small gifts. By recruiting the AGA and police chief, the *grama sevaka* had broken this contract, which the villagers conceived of as both moral and pragmatic. From that day on, the *grama sevaka* rarely came to the village, and to my knowledge, when he did, he always came at night.

Mohideen wasn't completely powerless. He and another villager, Pitchai, were the village representatives of the United National Party (UNP), the political party in power then. They were also the leaders of the local Rural Development Committee (RDC). As the UNP representatives and respective RDC presidents, Pitchai and Mohideen received funds to carry out local development projects. Mohideen had received funds to build a rice storage building and an addition to the Kutali school.

Three days after the timber had been impounded, Mohideen and Pitchai went to Colombo, the capital of Sri Lanka, to meet with the local member of parliament (MP). Members of parliament are elected and are said to have nearly autocratic control over their electoral region. They returned with a letter from the MP stating that no further action should be taken until he had personally investigated the matter. This was Mohideen's critical countermove.

The End Stage

In February, the MP returned to the Kutali region. He told me that, although Mohideen's timber permit wasn't quite right, it was good enough for him and he would order the timber returned. A few days later, Mohideen went by oxcart to the police station and hauled the timber back to his house. The *grama sevaka* was transferred, and a new one was appointed soon afterward. This marked the end of this conflict case.

Charting the Conflict Process

I will go over the conflict case again below, in abbreviated form, by focusing on the previously described coding procedure. This allows me to rewrite and reduce the thick description to its critical details in order to induce grounded theory or explanatory models from the organizational structure of the empirical data. Codes are in italics within parentheses.

> *Beginning Stage*: The *grama sevaka* detains (official *move*) the bullocks cart at the request of Muslim villagers who thought the Sinhalese men were transporting illegally obtained timber (*triggering event*). In his official capacity (*Resource*), the *grama sevaka* asks to see Mohideen's timber permit (official *move*). Mohideen tries to bribe the *grama sevaka* with a bottle of *arrack* (*resource/backstage move*). The *grama sevaka* rejects the bribe (critical *move*).
>
> *Middle Stage*: Both opponents are concentrated on marshaling their resources. The *grama sevaka* had many resources at his disposal: the responsibility of his job, political power, and religious influence. The *grama sevaka* makes his *critical move* when he uses his position to recruit government and police representatives (*Resource-allies: police chief and AGA*) to enter the community and impound the timber. Mohideen responds by marshaling anger and revenge (emotional *resources*). Mohideen recruits Pitchai (*resource-ally/move*); they go to Colombo to explain their case to the member of parliament (R*esource-ally/critical move*). The MP was a more powerful political ally resource than the *grama sevaka*'s midlevel civil servant allies. Villagers collectively turned against the *grama sevaka* (*obstacle*) and are unified in their support of Mohideen, even though most did not particularly like him (*Resource-ally: village support*).
>
> *End Stage*: The MP supports Mohideen's claim (official and critical *move*); the *grama sevaka* is transferred to another district (official *move*); and Mohideen hauls his timber back from the police station (concluding *event*).

Interpreting the Conflict Case and Developing Grounded Theory

This conflict case was triggered by the villagers wanting to test the *grama sevaka*'s willingness to exercise his authority as a civil servant against his own kind (that is, Sinhalese). By the time the *grama sevaka* went to talk with Mohideen, the situation had become public knowledge. Bribes, as a means to persuade government officials to ignore illegal activities, should occur backstage, unknown to the public. The conflict escalation was, I believe, a consequence of the impossibility of moving the negotiations over the timber backstage. The *grama sevaka* said as much when he said that he would be viewed as "a puppet" and that "God would turn his back on him." In this case, God may also symbolize the public world watching him. There was no way that he could accept a bribe, however large, without his authority in the village being compromised. Worse, perhaps, was the real possibility that if the AGA heard what had happened, he would take action against, and possibly discharge, the *grama sevaka*. Thus, because the situation could not be moved to the backstage, the *grama sevaka* was forced to affirm and exercise his role as a government agent.

In the second stage, the *grama sevaka* recruited higher-level civil servants to substantiate and exercise his authority in the village and over Mohideen. The cost of this move to the *grama sevaka* was the end of his cordial relations with villagers. Mohideen countered the *grama sevaka*'s official move by recruiting Pitchai and the MP. It was important for Mohideen to recruit Pitchai, because now both UNP representatives were allied against the *grama sevaka*, an active supporter of the Sri Lanka Freedom Party (SLFP), the major opposition party. By symbolically politicizing the conflict, Mohideen muted the conflict's ethnic underpinnings (Sinhalese versus Muslim interests) and gave the MP a political incentive to support Mohideen's cause.

Mohideen told me that he had a legitimate timber permit and the MP supported him because he was in the right. No villager I knew seriously believed that Mohideen had a valid timber permit. Most thought that the MP supported Mohideen for political reasons and because they were "drinking buddies." The *grama sevaka* explained to me that the MP needed Mohideen's political support to obtain the Kutali vote. He said:

> Mohideen gets contracts to build roads, irrigation channels, and the new paddy storehouse. Villagers depend on Mohideen for jobs on these projects in return for their political support. When a new politician gets elected, Mohideen will visit him and promise to get him timber, clothes, and labor to renovate his house. In this way, Mohideen establishes links with the new MP.

Mohideen's alliance with the MP shifted the conflict in his favor and illustrated the complementary relationship of interests between local-level patrons who control village voting banks and politicians who control state resources.

Through their connections to outside funds of power and capital, Mohideen and Pitchai were the two most prominent village patrons. In the social network literature, Pitchai and Mohideen hold the position of **gatekeepers** because through them, outsiders—in this case politicians—gain access to village resources (votes) and, through them, villagers gain access to outside political-economic resources. By building a loyal vote bank—a valued political resource—Mohideen (and Pitchai) gained access to and influence over the MP and development funds.

This triadic exchange relationship—involving villagers, Mohideen, and the MP—sustains itself only as long as villagers have limited access to outside (state) economic resources and as long as the elective branch of government can overrule policy decisions under the jurisdiction of the bureaucracy. The nonelective, bureaucratic branch of government is intended to dispense national resources (for example, drivers' licenses, timber permits) and mete out justice impartially. The interference and apparent dominance of elected politicians over bureaucrats has a two-pronged effect on local-level politics: (1) It encourages bribery because bureaucratic authority can be overruled through partisan politics; and (2) It promotes and establishes the gatekeeper role through which local and national resources are funneled for personal gain.

The elective, political branch of government is, by definition, partisan and partial. If there were a clear separation of powers between the bureaucracy and the elective branch of government, the MP could not contravene in the decision of the AGA to impound Mohideen's timber and the *grama sevaka*'s ruling to impound the timber would have been upheld. It is not in the interest of politicians to eliminate gatekeepers, as that would deny them easy access to vote banks. Nor is it in the interest of the villagers to withhold giving their votes to a village gatekeeper, as that would deny the villagers access to political and economic goods. Hence, we can say that this triadic relationship can be maintained from the "top down, the bottom up, and from the middle out."

Conclusion

The above narrative is a chronological description of the events of a conflict case from beginning to apparent resolution. Participant observation spotlights insiders' perspectives and consequently allows the researcher to develop case-based explanatory models of social processes. All such explanatory models are tentative and hypothetical until they have been subject to more extensive research endeavors that: (1) Explicitly test the explanatory connections suggested by the case-based model; and (2) Use representative sampling to establish the validity of these models for that population.

I believe Golden (1976) is right when she refers to participant observation as an "exploratory method," with reference to hypothesis testing. I can only conjecture, but not claim, that this conflict case is representative of the distribution of interests and power between villagers, gatekeepers, the bureaucracy, and politicians in Sri Lanka. To test this relationship, I would have to look at and analyze similar types of conflict cases across a representative sample of villages. Participant observation, done right, offers an accurate, thick description of sociocultural processes. The next step is to discover if the descriptions and explanation obtained through participant observation are generalizable to similar cases in the same or other places.

QUESTIONS

1. What is the primary method that distinguishes anthropology from the other social sciences?
2. What are the *stages* of hanging out?
3. What does the author mean by the "backstage" of culture?
4. Can you test hypotheses through participant observation? Explain your answer.
5. What is a "gatekeeper"?

Generating and Analyzing Lists

GERY RYAN ■
THOMAS WEISNER

Three

Content Analysis of Words in Brief Descriptions: How Fathers and Mothers Describe Their Children

Introduction

Our objective in this study is to understand parental perceptions and attitudes of Americans toward their adolescent children. From our background readings in anthropology, we know that parental impressions of adolescents and children vary across cultures. When Super and Harkness (1986) asked Kipsigi parents in western Kenya to describe boys, descriptions included the terms "warrior" and "fierce." When Raghavan (1993) asked South Asian parents living in the United States about their daughters, descriptions included "hospitable" and "responsible." Such phrases or words would strike most American parents as unusual or odd. American parents are more likely to use such terms as "athletic," "independent," "argumentative," and "well-rounded"—terms that would seem odd to most Kipsigis or South Asians.

The data for this article come from a follow-up survey in the Family Lifestyles Project—a 20-year longitudinal study of conventional and nonconventional families in the United States.[1] As part of the survey, we asked parents: "What is your teenager like now? Does she or he have any special qualities or abilities?" This was a relatively easy, comfortable task for most people we interviewed. Parents wrote their answers in short descriptive phrases. We focus now on these data.

We could have asked many questions about these descriptions. For our research purposes, however, two were particularly important: "How did parents describe their children?" and "Did mothers and fathers describe their children differently?"

In 82 of the 200 families interviewed, a male and female parent independently described their child. Nearly all the descriptions came from the biological parents. In three cases, the male parent was a step-father, and in one case the female parent

57

was a step-mother. Because we are interested in how parents raise their children, we treat biological and step-parents as equal in our analysis. We thus have two descriptions for each of 82 children, one from the mother and the other from the father, for a total of 164 descriptions.

Each of the 82 children are different (some are more artistic, social, academic, or temperamental than others), but we can make comparisons across children because: (1) We were systematic in how we asked parents to describe their experiences (we always asked the exact same question each time); (2) Each pair of parents described the same child; and (3) We have the same number of descriptions (82) from mothers and from fathers. Of course, the child is not "the same" to each parent. Children respond and identify differently to each parent and parents to each child. So, when parents are asked to describe their child, they are not reacting to exactly the same stimuli, but to a comparable family situation that has different meanings to each family member.

Selecting an Analysis Strategy

Here is a classic example of anthropologists collecting good, rich, ethnographic data from their informants, and deciding how to analyze it afterward. Usually, you want to know how you are going to analyze your data before you collect it. Choosing an analysis strategy is analogous to planning a road trip. You need to know first where you are starting from (what kind of data you have) and then you need to know where you want to go (what research goals you have). We had textual data that came from **open-ended questions**. This meant that respondents were not confined to a fixed set of predetermined answers. They simply told us what they thought in their own words. As analysts, we had two goals. We wanted to *describe* the kinds of answers that parents gave and we wanted to *compare* fathers' and mothers' answers.

The analysis strategy that best links open-ended textual data with the research goals requiring a systematic description and comparison is loosely referred to as *content analysis*. There are several flavors of content analysis (see Bernard and Ryan [1998] for a broad overview). Classic content analysis is based on judgments the researcher makes. In this case, the researcher identifies a fixed set of themes or categories, then reads each text and marks down how often the text refers to each theme. Sometimes, they mark down whether the theme is mentioned anywhere in the text; at other times, they count the number of words or paragraphs that pertain to a theme. During World War II, when the approach was first developed to analyze German propaganda, coders actually measured the number of column inches in newspapers dedicated to particular themes.

Because of the increased use of computers due to their improvements and lower costs, a new type of content analysis has appeared. In this approach, the researcher doesn't pick a fixed set of themes or categories, but analyzes the words used by the informants. How much can we learn from a simple word analysis of qualitative data? Jehn and Doucet (1996, 1997) used word lists derived from informants' descriptions of recent confrontations to learn to better understand inter- and intracultural conflicts. Schnegg and Bernard (1996) relied on computer-generated word counts to identify central themes that graduate students in anthropology used when describing their own fields of study. Jang and Barnett (1994) were able to distinguish between American and Japanese companies based on the words used in each company's published annual reports. (For additional examples of content analysis, see Krippendorff [1980], Weber [1990], and Roberts [1997].)

We rely on standard word-processing programs and other readily available software. No special formatting or coding is needed. The methods we describe are useful for discovering patterns in any body of text, whether field notes or responses to open-ended questions, and are particularly helpful when used along with ethnographic data and other sources of information. Word analysis can tell us about a word's salience. By "salience" we mean the importance of a word as measured by the number times it is used informants. We can also use word analysis to examine word patterning, where "patterning" refers to how often pairs of words are found close together (for example, within the same sentence, paragraph, or interview). Word analysis, however, cannot produce a holistic interpretation of cultural data because it takes the words out of their original context.

In our data, we asked two questions: (1) What do the words parents use in their descriptions tell us about the goals they have for their children?; and (2) What do differences and similarities in word use tell us about the differences and similarities in parents' perceptions of their children?

Organizing the Data

We transcribed the parents' verbatim answers into a word processor text file (in this case, WordPerfect 6.0). For each answer, we typed in the family identification number, the type of family, the sex of the child being described, the sex of the parent who gave the description, and the complete description. Each description was followed by a single hard return. Figure 3.1 shows the first three descriptions in our master file (MASTER.WP).

To facilitate analysis, we separated each unique phrase/descriptor by a period and a space. The period/space combination has two advantages: (1) A period indicates the end of a sentence, and we can then use the word processor or style checker to count the number of sentences in a document (Harris 1996); (2) We can use the period as a delimiter for importing the text data into a spreadsheet or a database (like Excel or Quattro Pro).

ID009. F1030. Boy. Fthr. Loving. Obedient. Maintains own identity. Likes being home. Independent. Anxious to go to California to school.
ID016. F1130. Boy. Fthr. Smart. Energetic. Arrogant. Dependent. Slick. Passive. Lack of imagination. Attraction to inner-city lifestyle.
ID124. F1130. Girl. Mthr. Great kid. Willing to communicate with parents. Listens. Motivated in school. Helpful around the house. Healthy. Active. Lots of friends. Tends to play it safe.

Figure 3.1. Examples of master file of parents' descriptions of their children.

Once we had our master file of descriptions, we sorted the descriptions by parent's sex. Since we consistently made parent's sex the fourth word of the paragraph, we can do this with our word processor. Select all your text and tell the word processor to use the fourth word to sort the highlighted paragraphs.[2] (Before sorting, back-up your file!)

We then copied mothers' and fathers' responses to separate files (MOTHER.WP & FATHER.WP). At this point, we were only interested in the descriptors, so we stripped out the extraneous information in each file. This is easily semiautomated with a **macro** that goes to the beginning of each paragraph and deletes the first four words (ID, family type, child's and parent's sex). Our two stripped files contained only the verbatim descriptions provided by mothers and fathers.

Simple Tricks with a Word Processor

We used WordPerfect's document information function to calculate some general statistics.[3] Document information is located under File on the top menu. Among other things, it calculates the number of characters, words, and sentences, plus the average word length, the average number of words per sentence, and the maximum words per sentence. Table 3.1 compares these statistics for mothers' and fathers' responses.

These statistics tell us that:

1. Mothers use more words to describe their children than do fathers. Of all the words used to describe the 82 children, 56% come from mothers and 44% come from fathers.
2. On average, mothers used 28% more sentences than did men. (Mothers used $528/82 = 6.4$ phrases to describe their children, while men used $411/82 = 5.0$ phrases. Mothers and fathers use the same number of words per phrases, but mothers said more things about their children.)
3. Mothers and fathers use roughly the same size words, about 5.7 characters each.

TABLE 3.1
Text Statistics Generated from WordPerfect 6.0

	Mothers	Fathers	Total
Characters	9,748	7,625	17,373
Word Count	1,692	1,346	3,038
Sentence Count	528	411	939
Average Word Length	5.76	5.66	5.72
Average Words per Sentence	3.20	3.27	3.24
Maximum Words per Sentence	14	17	17

Fathers and mothers are more similar in this sample than they are different. Mothers use more words, but not very much more, and on other measures, fathers and mothers are about equal. Clearly, parents used the same "standard social science questionnaire schema" to answer our questions—writing a series of terse phrases and words for a minute or so.

Learning from Unique Word Lists

We next examine whether mothers and fathers use *different* words to describe their children. WORDS 2.0 (E. Johnson 1995) is a useful program that counts the number of running words in a text, identifies the number of **unique words forms**, and lists the number of occurrences of each unique form.[4] (See Bernard [1995] for a review of WORDS 2.0.) Other programs, such as CATPAC, and the latest version of ANTHROPAC (Borgatti 1992) also count the frequency of unique words. (See Doerfel and Barnett [1996] for a review of CATPAC.)

To get the files ready for WORDS 2.0, we first saved our WordPerfect files (MOTHER.WP and FATHER.WP) in ASCII format (calling them MOTHER.ASC and FATHER.ASC so as not to overwrite the original files). When we analyzed each file, we used WORDS 2.0's **"common word list"** to exclude 125 of the most-used English terms. Figure 3.2 shows a portion of the two outputs. Each output tells us how many words each file contained originally,[5] how many unique words were found (including unique common words), and how many words were removed when we eliminated the common ones. WORDS 2.0 outputs the list of unique words with their respective frequency of occurrence. We indicate the rank order of each word under the # sign. (You can do this in your word processor by turning on the line numbering option.)[6]

Figure 3.2 shows that the MOTHER file contained a total of 1,721 words in 734 unique word forms. It contained 542 instances of the 125 common words that were eliminated from further consideration. In the end, there were 666 unique words in the file, and mothers mentioned the words "good," "friends," "loving,"

Mothers' Descriptions

File MOTHER.ASC:
Total number of running words in file: 1,721
Number of unique word forms in file: 734
The following counts exclude 542
occurrences of 125 common word forms.

Fathers' Descriptions

File FATHER.ASC:
Total number of running words in file: 1,355
Number of unique word forms in file: 607
The following counts exclude 419
occurrences of 125 common word forms.

Rank	Frequency	Word	Rank	Frequency	Word
1	22	good	1	23	good
2	12	friends	2	16	school
3	11	loving	3	11	hard
4	11	out	4	9	intelligent
5	11	people	5	8	bright
6	10	doesn't	6	8	independent
7	10	hard	7	8	out
8	10	school	8	8	well
9	9	responsible	9	7	doesn't
10	9	sense	10	7	lack
11	8	caring	11	7	loving
12	8	intelligent	12	7	people
13	8	lacks	13	7	sensitive
14	8	sensitive	14	7	sports
15	7	bright	15	7	student
16	7	honest	16	6	caring
17	7	others	17	6	does
18	7	self	18	6	life
19	7	time	19	6	others
20	7	well	20	6	work
21	7	work	21	5	ability
22	6	creative	22	5	enjoys
23	6	does	23	5	great
24	6	great	24	5	lacks
25	6	mature	25	5	likes
26	6	sports	26	5	mature
27	5	academically	27	5	own
28	5	artistic	28	5	sense
29	5	cares	29	5	social
30	5	concerned	30	5	wants
31	5	goals	...	...	...
32	5	going	548	1	zero
33	5	humor			
34	5	independent			
35	5	other			
36	5	social			
37	5	times			
...	...	...			
666	1	zest			

Figure 3.2. Counts of words used more than five times by mothers and fathers.

"out," and "people" at least 11 times. The last word on the mothers' list, "zest," was mentioned only once.

We can think of unique word lists as *concentrated* data or, as Tesch (1990: 138–139) called them, distillations. **Concentration rates** are also called **type-token rates**. Concentration rates refer to the average rate at which words in a text are used multiple times. The rates are calculated with the formula: 1– (total unique words/total words). We can produce three different measures of concentration and can compare any of these measures across the MOTHER and FATHER files.

The first concentration rate uses *all* the unique words (regardless if they are common words or not) in the calculation. With 734 unique words in a corpus of 1,721 words, mothers have a concentration rate of 57% (1–734/1,721). Fathers have a concentration rate of 55% (1–607/1,355). The second concentration rate doesn't include the common words in its calculation. For mothers, we calculate the new concentration rate based on the 666 unique substantive words (eliminating all occurrences of words in the common-word file). Thus, the rate for mothers is 1–666/1,721 = 61%. For fathers the rate is 1–548/1,355 = 60%. We also can calculate a third concentration rate based on words that occur more than once. In the MOTHER file, just 207 of the 666 substantive words occur more than once. This produces a concentration rate of 1–207/1,721 =88 %, identical to the rate (1–159/1,355 = 88%) for fathers.

We lose a lot of information when we examine unique words. We don't know the context in which the words occurred, nor whether informants used words negatively or positively. Nor do we know how the words related to each other. But distillations like these introduce very little **investigator bias** (we *do* have to choose what words to leave out of the analysis), and they can help us identify constructs used by parents to describe their children.

The word lists suggest things about parents' values and goals for their children, and the lists can be compared across fathers and mothers. For example, from Table 3.1 we don't know if fathers have less to say about their children or they just have less to say about all topics. From Figure 3.2, however, we see that men's vocabulary for describing children is as rich as women's vocabulary. [The ratio of unique words to total words is roughly equivalent for men (607/1,355 = .45) and for women (734/1,721 = .43).]

Figure 3.2 lets us make crude comparisons between men's and women's use of different words. (The measures are crude because they represent **rank order data** and don't take into consideration the total number of words used by each group.) Both mothers and fathers use the word "good" a lot more than any other word. Women, for example use that word almost twice as much as "friends," their second most popular word. Antonyms of good aren't prevalent among the word list, indicating that people might have a tendency to be optimistic in describing their children, have a response bias on questionnaires to use positive words, and are accessing a cultural model for describing one's child that emphasizes positive, growing cultural careers.

Figure 3.2 also suggests that men and women focus on different characteristics of their children. A comparison of the most frequently used words shows that "friends," "loving," "people," and "responsible" are ranked higher for women than they are for men. In contrast, "school," "hard," "intelligent," "bright," and "independent" are ranked higher for men than for women. This suggests that mothers, on first mention, express concern over interpersonal issues, while men appear to give priority to achievement-oriented and individualistic issues.

Figure 3.2 is very informative but is somewhat deceptive. For both men and women, the most frequently mentioned word was "good." Women mentioned it 22 times, and men mentioned it 23 times. This similarity in frequencies at first *seems* to suggest that men and women and women are equally likely to use that word to describe their children. But here lies the deception. Word frequencies don't consider the total number of words mentioned by men and women. (Remember, women used more words than did men!) To eliminate this deception, we can **standardize** the word frequencies according to what we expect to find if men and women used the same number of words. Standardize means to make two measures equivalent so they can be compared. Here we want to compare the use-rates of words across genders. Table 3.2 shows the results of such a process.

To create this table, we put mothers' and fathers' responses in a single ASCII file and counted the words again. We then selected the 131 words that informants mentioned at least four times. We picked four because it gave us a reasonable number of words to work with. (If we had selected three as our cut-off point, we would have had to work with over 200 words—something that seemed too daunting.) We put the these 131 words in the first column of a spreadsheet and their frequency counts in the second column. In the third and fourth columns, we put the number of times each word was mentioned by women and by men respectively. Next we calculated the *expected* word frequencies for men if men used the same number of words as women. Since women on average used 1.27 (1721/1,355) times more words as did men, we multiply the observed mens' frequency by 1.27. We put the result in the fifth column.

To compare mothers' and fathers' word use, we subtracted the expected mens' frequencies in column five from the observed women's frequencies in column three. We put the results in column six. This gave us a more accurate difference in word use between the files. Negative numbers in column six mean that the word was more likely to be used by fathers than used by mothers. Positive numbers mean that the word was more likely to be used by mothers. Numbers close to zero mean that there wasn't that much difference between the men's and women's descriptions. Finally, we sorted the rows in the spreadsheet by the values in column six. In Table 3.2, we show some selected results of this comparison: Words whose frequencies varied a lot between men and women as well as some examples of words whose frequencies varied little.

TABLE 3.2
Word Frequencies Sorted by Standardized Frequency Difference in Gender

TERM	Both	Mother	Father	Expected Father	Standardized Differences
school	26	10	16	20.3	−10.3
good	45	22	23	29.2	−7.2
lack	9	2	7	8.9	−6.9
student	9	2	7	8.9	−6.9
enjoys	6	1	5	6.4	−5.4
independent	13	5	8	10.2	−5.2
extremely	4	0	4	5.1	−5.1
like	4	0	4	5.1	−5.1
ability	7	2	5	6.4	−4.4
own	7	2	5	6.4	−4.4
wants	7	2	5	6.4	−4.4
high	5	1	4	5.1	−4.1
interested	5	1	4	5.1	−4.1
great	11	6	5	6.4	−0.4
mature	11	6	5	6.4	−0.4
humor	9	5	4	5.1	−0.1
times	9	5	4	5.1	−0.1
attitude	7	4	3	3.8	0.2
caring	14	8	6	7.6	0.4
adult	4	4	0	0.0	4.0
average	4	4	0	0.0	4.0
difficulty	4	4	0	0.0	4.0
goes	4	4	0	0.0	4.0
kid	4	4	0	0.0	4.0
lots	4	4	0	0.0	4.0
respect	4	4	0	0.0	4.0
talented	4	4	0	0.0	4.0
uses	4	4	0	0.0	4.0
honest	9	7	2	2.5	4.5
time	9	7	2	2.5	4.5
creative	6	6	0	0.0	6.0
friends	16	12	4	5.1	6.9

Now look at the word "good" in Table 3.2 (the second line). The table shows that if men and women used the same number of words in their descriptions, we would expect "good" to be used more often by men (29 times) than by women (22 times). This finding is different from those in Figure 3.2 that suggest that "good" is used equally by both men and women, By standardizing the data, we discover that there is a gender distinction that we would not have discovered otherwise.

Our standardizations in Table 3.2 tell us that fathers use the words "school," "good," "lack," "student," "enjoys," "independent," "extremely," "like," "ability," "own," "wants," "high," and "interested" more than do mothers. On the other hand, mothers use the words "friends," "creative," "time," "honest," "uses," "talented," "respect," "lots," "kid," "goes," "difficulty," "average," and "adult" more than do fathers. Men and women, however, are equally likely to use the words "great," "mature," "humor," "times," "attitude," and "caring."

Notice the differences between the standardized measures in Table 3.2 and the rank orders (and frequencies) shown in Figure 3.2. The rank-order data tell us about the relative priority of words within each gender, while the standardized data let us compare use rates across genders. For instance, the word "good" was the most-used word for both women and men. When we compare across genders, we find that men tend to use the word more often. In contrast, men and women are equally likely to use the word "caring" in their descriptions, but the simple rank order for the word is higher for women than it is for men. The next question we might want to ask is why do such gender differences and similarities occur?

Our findings are similar to other research on gender differences. On many measures, men and women, boys and girls show substantial overlap in behavioral tendencies. Although mean or modal differences often are relatively small, specific measures (in our case, emphasis on different concerns in describing teens) are quite constant and are found cross-culturally (Best et al. 1994).

The word-counting techniques described here don't require complex and expensive text analysis programs. These simple methods help researchers concentrate often confusing data into a more manageable form and are relatively bias free. The techniques can be used for exploring central themes and for systematically comparing within and across groups.

Of course, these are just the first univariate, exploratory steps in a more detailed qualitative analysis. We still want to examine the context in which these words occur and how key words are related to each other. For example: How does the sex of the teen as well as the parent influence word use? We also want to explore some of the hypotheses that we have formed in this simple first step. Treating words as units of analysis offers researchers a simple way of exploring text and confirming hypotheses.

QUESTIONS

1. How were the sample of texts selected? (Where did they come from? How many texts were analyzed? What percent were from mothers? What texts were not analyzed?)
2. What are the advantages and disadvantages of analyzing words instead of the whole text?
3. What do we learn about the difference between men and women when we look at the statistics associated with the total number of words, sentences, average word length, and average words per sentence?
4. How did the authors standardize men's in Table 3.2? Why did they do this?
5. How are men and women different in the words they use to characterize their children? How are they similar?

NOTES

1. The Family Lifestyles Project (FLS) started in 1974 when investigators contacted 200 mothers during their third trimester of pregnancy. Mothers were involved in conventional and nonconventional living arrangements. Nonconventional arrangements included single mothers, social contract couples (not legally married), and mothers in communes or group living situations. Members of the research team have followed the mothers, their mates, and their child ever since. Over the years, **attrition** has been remarkably low. In 1992–1994, the FLS researchers conducted a follow-up study of the adolescent children and reached 100% of the mothers, 98% of the teenagers, and 48% of the fathers or other mates. The central question of the adolescent follow-up was: How did these "children of the children of the '60s" turn out? To find out, investigators mailed parents a written questionnaire in which they asked parents about their child's performance in school, personal relationships, political attitudes, gender identity, drug use, and other characteristics. (See Eiduson and Weisner [1978], Weisner [1986], Weisner and Garnier [1992], and Weisner et al. [1994] for reviews and key findings from the project.)

2. To do this in WordPerfect for Windows 6.1: Select Tools/Sort from the menu. When the menu for sorting appears, tell WordPerfect to sort by paragraph. (Note: WordPerfect assumes that paragraphs are separated by *two* hard returns.) Make sure that the appropriate settings are marked as follows: Type = Alpha, Sort Order = Ascending, Line = 1, Field = 1, and Word = 4. After making the changes, select OK. WordPerfect will put all the fathers' responses on top of the file and all the mothers' responses on the bottom. To do this in Word 6.0: Select Table/Sort Text. Select Options. In the "Separates fields at": dialogue box, select "Other" and fill in the box with a single period. Select OK. In the "Sort by" dialogue box, select "Field 4." Select OK.

3. Similar statistics can be obtained in Microsoft's *Word. Word*, however, doesn't automatically count the number of sentences in a document. To do so, you need to build a macro, as follows:

```
Sub MAIN StartOfDocument Count = 0 While SentRight(1, 1) <> 0 If
Right$(Selection$(), 1) <>Chr$(13) Then count = count +1 Wend MsgBox "Number
of sentences in document:" + Str$(count) End Sub
```

4. WORDS 2.0 was created by Eric Johnson and is distributed by TEXT Technology, 114 Beadle Hall, Dakota State University, Madison, SD 57042–1799. Email: langners@columbia.dsu.edu. For information on other programs that Johnson has created, check out the website http://www.dsu.edu/~johnsone/ericpgms.html.

5. The total number of words identified by WordPerfect 6.0 for the MOTHERS.WP file (1,692) differs from the total number of words identified by WORDS 2.0 (1,721). For the same file, Word 6.0 counts 1,731 words. Discrepancies occur because each program has a slightly different definition of what counts as a word. In our case, single hyphens (-) are the leading culprits. WordPerfect 6.0 counts the hyphen as a word, while WORDS 2.0 and Word 6.0 do not. Since most of our calculations use the total number of words as a fixed denominator and this denominator tends to be quite large, slight increases or decreases have little effect on the overall analysis. Be aware, however, that these differences do exist—and are rarely documented.

6. In WordPerfect 6.0, this is found under Format/Line. In Word 6.0, it's located under File/Page Setup/Layout.

MARK S. FLEISHER
JENNIFER A. HARRINGTON

Four

Freelisting: Management at a Women's Federal Prison Camp[1]

In October 1994, the Federal Bureau of Prisons (hereafter, Bureau) opened a new minimum-security prison camp for female offenders at Pekin, Illinois. We were asked by Bureau officials to do research on how these female inmates felt about the quality of life at this new prison, known as the Federal Prison Camp, Pekin.

FPC Pekin does not fit the stereotype of a prison. This one resembles a small college campus. No guard towers overlook drab cellhouses; no concrete wall or anchor fence topped with razor wire keeps inmates on prison grounds. A large grassy central compound is cross-cut with sidewalks that lead to classrooms, recreation buildings, and offices where inmates work. Inmates reside in two dormitory buildings. (Each building is divided into smaller areas that are partitioned by 5'-high cinder block walls into living cubicles.) The visiting room is bright and airy and has an outdoor playground dotted with toys and climbing apparatus for inmates' children who come to visit (Coyne 1997).

Inmates' perceptions of **quality of life** are important for two reasons. First, Bureau staffers are trained to be attentive to the inmates' needs and then staff are evaluated on performance. Thus, for Bureau staffers to move ahead in their careers, they must be judged capable of creating and sustaining a good quality of life within an institution.

Second, inmates' adjustment to daily life in a brand new prison has not been studied in either a state or federal prison before this FPC Pekin research. Federal prison facilities must operate by a set of policies that ensure that the prisons conform to legal and ethical guidelines. Among these guidelines are standards for high-level confinement conditions for inmates. It is, therefore, incumbent on Bureau staffers to ensure positive inmate adjustment. The federal prison system has been opening dozens of new prisons all across the United States. We assumed that inmates' life inside a new prison would be different from daily life in an existing one. Data collection would give us some idea about the nature of inmates' adaptation to a new prison. We use the term "existing prison" for one that has been operating for many years. We invented the term "start-up" to denote the initial period, say, the first 12 months of operation of a new prison.

We collected inmate data using the freelisting technique (Weller and Romney 1988). Freelisting asks informants (inmates, in this case) to list the names of things that compose a category, or domain of cultural knowledge. For example, a researcher might begin exploring a new culture by asking informants to "name all the plants you can think of," "name all the dirty words you can think of," "name all the foods people eat for breakfast." While anthropologists have used freelisting to explore domains of kinship, plants and animals, and foods in many different cultures, freelisting previously had never been used to explore inmates' knowledge of prison life.

We decided to use freelisting for three reasons. First, we needed a simple, inexpensive way to gather from inmates a lot of data about the quality of life at FPC Pekin. We didn't have the time and money to develop, pretest, distribute, and analyze data gathered with a survey instrument.

Second, we wanted a technique that would reduce the time used to collect a lot of data from inmates. Years of experience with inmate interviews has shown that face-to-face interviews between "outside" researchers and prisoners often turn into little more than long-winded gripe sessions that allow inmates to complain about staffers, food quality, sentencing guidelines, and so on (see Fleisher 1989, 1996). We didn't want to be trapped by this type of interview, because we had absolutely no control over anything inside this prison camp and no way of verifying the truthfulness of inmates' complaints. Nevertheless, inmate interviews were important because they would help us understand the general context and meaning of items reported on the freelists.

Third, freelisting in a prison setting was an experiment in data collection. Freelisting with inmates required that informants work alone and write down lists on notepads. We didn't know if inmates would respond well to such a task, given that most of these female inmates had relatively little education and were inexperienced at expressing their ideas in writing.

Background

The Federal Bureau of Prisons became a federal agency in 1930. Today, it houses more than 100,000 inmates in some 90 prisons across the United States. At the Bureau's inception, the population of federal inmates was nearly all male. As a result, federal correctional culture evolved with male inmates in mind. Thus, prison security, medical care, recreation, vocational training, styles of verbal interaction, discipline procedures, shakedowns (searches), and other daily operations and programs are oriented toward male inmates.

The Bureau's male-oriented model of federal corrections began to change as the number of female inmates increased. In 1980, 1,300 (5.4%) of all federal inmates housed in federal prisons were women. By March 1997, the number of female inmates rose to 6,813 (approximately 7.5%) (Federal Bureau of Prisons 1997). The incarceration of thousands of female offenders forced construction of new federal prisons for women (see *Butler et al. v. Reno et al.* 1984). In March 1997, 65% of federal female inmates were housed in minimum-security prison camps like FPC Pekin. The increased number of female inmates meant that it was important to learn their perspective on the quality of prison life.

Start-up has special significance.[2] In an existing prison, inmates are added one by one to an established social structure and quickly blend into daily life. In a new prison, inmates must learn how to live together while the institution develops its system of daily operations. Start-up is also when prison staff first meet the new inmates; in a real sense, staffers and inmates have to learn how to work together to accomplish the daily tasks expected of them in a federal prison.

Finally, start-up is the initial phase in an institution's organizational maturation. In a sense, start-up may be the infancy and adolescence of an organization. Like infancy and adolescence, organizational growth is sensitive to external factors (funding levels, politically influenced correctional fads) and internal factors, such as a warden's leadership skills, the formal and informal styles of interaction between staffers and inmates, and the proper balance of internal control mechanisms. Researchers may find that the character of a prison's mature organizational culture was influenced by what happened during its infancy and adolescence.

Freelisting as a Method

Freelisting elicits from members of a culture relevant items specific to categories of knowledge. We expected that freelisting questions would yield information about inmates' shared perceptions of their new prison environment. We developed questions along four dimensions of knowledge, or subthemes within the domain of knowledge, that inmates have about life in a new prison camp. These questions and dimensions are a result of Fleisher's 20 years of work, administrative, and research experience inside minimum- to maximum-security state and federal institutions. The four dimensions are: (1) commitment to a new institution; (2) adjustment to a new institution; (3) adjustments to a new population; and (4) relationship to staff. In correctional management vocabulary, commitment doesn't refer to a relationship, nor does it mean how loyal these inmates are to the institution. Commitment refers to an inmate's placement at an institution; we couldn't have used the term "admission," because that word refers to a place in a prison where inmates are photographed and fingerprinted. If we had used the term "admission" instead of commitment, the question would have been ambiguous to inmates. Table 4.1 lists these dimensions and each dimension's specific freelist questions, along with the brief designation, or code, we used for each question.

Pretesting Freelist Questions

Freelist questions were pretested in three phases. The list of freelisting questions had to be long enough to be comprehensive and include key items but short enough to hold an inmate's interest and be completed within 60–90 minutes, thus limiting disruption in camp activities. A panel of three inmates, selected at random, was asked to discuss the clarity, importance, and content of each question. Inmate panelists were also asked if there were important issues that were not covered in these questions. Using these suggestions, the list of freelist questions was rewritten. A second panel of three inmates was similarly questioned about the second set of freelist questions. The freelist questions were modified a second time. The process was repeated a third time with a new inmate panel. These inmates had no complaints about or suggestions for modifying the freelist questions. These questions were our final list.

Sampling Procedure

FPC Pekin quickly filled with inmates. By October 31, 1994, 76 women were housed there; 60 more arrived in November and another 60 in December. By December 31, 1994, there were 196 inmates. There were 295 inmates by July 1995; that number was then lowered to 268 to reduce overcrowding in the dormitories.

To develop our sampling strategy, we assumed there would be a difference in inmates' opinions about the camp's quality of life according to when they arrived. "Early arrivals" entered the camp sometime in the first quarter of operation. These inmates would, we assumed, experience unique advantages in camp life, as well as disadvantages. Early arrivals would have appreciated a relatively empty prison camp and would have had more opportunities to use its facilities. On the other hand, early arrivals would also feel, more so than later arrivals, the pressure of a continuously increasing inmate population. Short food lines would get longer, access to recreation equipment would become more difficult, privacy in dormitories would be somewhat lost, washers and dryers would be used nearly nonstop.

Early arrivals would, we assumed, experience the pressures of start-up more so than later arrivals. In our sampling design, time of commitment to the camp was a key variable. One hundred inmates were selected in a stratified random sample (a simple random sample might have undersampled first-month, or first-quarter,

TABLE 4.1
Freelist Questions by Dimension and Question Code

Dimension/Code	Freelist Question
Dimension: Commitment to a New Institution	
COMTOUGH	List the tough things about a commitment to a new institution
COMBEST	List the best things about a commitment to a new institution
LIVTOUGH	List the tough aspects of living in a new inmate population
LIVBEST	List the best aspects of living in a new inmate population
WOMANTOU	List the tough thing about being a woman in a new prison camp
WOMANBES	List the best things about being a woman in a new prison camp
Dimension: Adjustments to a New Institution	
CHANGE	List the things about the institution that you would change
ADJUST	List the adjustments you've had to make since you've been here
BENEFITS	List the benefits you've experienced since transferring here
PREVIOUS	List the ways that FPC Pekin is different from the institution you transferred from
Dimension: Adjustments to a New Population	
QUICK	List the things that happened to you when inmates were admitted too quickly
QUALITY	List the ways that the quality of life in the institution changed as the inmate population increased
Dimension: Relationships to a New Staff	
BOSSTOUGH	List the tough things about working for a new boss
BOSSBEST	List the best things about working for a new boss
STAFF	List the staff members by type of job (case manager, counselor, and others) who you talk to most frequently every day
TALK	List the things you talk about to the staff member you identified as your most frequent staff contact
REACH	List the ways that staff reached out to you in an effort to assist in your adjustment

arrivals). The stratification variable (see Bernard 1994:84–86) was "arrival month": 60% were drawn from October 1994, 30% from November–December 1994; and 10% from January–June 1995. Twenty-five women declined to participate. In the end, 75 inmates participated.

Collecting Freelist Data

Freelists and semistructured interviews (see below) were collected in May and June 1995. After inmates read and signed an informed consent statement (literacy was not a problem), each was given a notepad and pencil and asked to read the 18 freelist questions and to respond. Respondents spent between 45 minutes and two hours answering. When they were finished, we had a stack of notebook pages, one page of responses for each freelist question. We divided the freelist response pages into 18 freelist question piles, each pile had 75 freelists to one question.

Coding Freelist Data

Freelists have to be coded. Why? Coding is the process of building a "dictionary," or doing a minilinguistic analysis of each question's freelist. To build this dictionary, responses to each freelist question have to be assigned a common designator, or code. A **code** is a shorthand that refers to a larger set of items or meanings. For example, word-processing file names are codes for a text. A code is a substitute for the actual responses of the respondents.

Before showing you how we coded data, there are a number of points to keep in mind. First, in this case, coders had to be familiar with federal prisoners' jargon, and generally speaking, federal correctional jargon, as well. Why? Undergraduate students at Illinois State University talk about being "closed out of classes" and needing an "override." This is college jargon. Coders of inmate freelists must know the meaning of terms such as "programming," "AWs," "closer to home transfers," "security reduction transfers," "UNICOR jobs," and dozens of other terms and expressions unique to federal correctional institutions.

Second, coders must also be aware of synonyms in the jargon. To overlook synonyms would result in lists that are unnecessarily long with many terms that actually refer to the same things. On the other hand, to create too many codes would divide inmates' speech, or knowledge about the prison camp, adding too much complexity to this category.

Third, coders had to be able to link inmates' jargon to dominant themes in the culture of a federal prison camp. This point is important for this reason. Our research was designed to offer federal prison officials practical insights into inmates' perceptions of camp operations and quality of life. We had to ensure that our codes were consistent with not only inmates' perceptions but also with the management categories federal prison officials use in their interpretation of inmates' quality of life. Thus, our codes had to bridge the gap between inmates' and staffers' view of the prison camp, so we did not get a mixture of "apples" and "oranges."

Creating Freelist Codes

Create codes carefully. Before we built our code book, we read and reread the freelists for each question. When we fully understood the range of freelist responses on each question, we began to create codes. As we already noted, our freelist codes had to be consistent with federal prison managers' view of the prison environment; if codes were foreign to them, the analysis wouldn't be useful as a management tool. But coding the data into practical categories was easy, because as we discovered, inmates tend to perceive the prison environment in terms similar to those used by federal prison managers. Table 4.2 shows six inmates' verbatim responses to the question, "List the best things about a commitment to a new prison camp."

TABLE 4. 2
Inmates' Freelist Responses

Inmate	Verbatim Freelist Responses
#1	"fresh start with staff and inmates on new jobs; food is better; new staff start out friendlier"
#2	"cleanliness"
#3	"is cleaner"
#4	"closer to home so it's easier for your family to visit you and the place is clean"
#5	"there are few inmates, easy access to recreation, and the food is great"
#6	"clean, able to bring up ideas with staff without getting shot down"

Inmates made four references to the cleanliness of the new prison camp ("cleanliness" [inmate 2]; "is cleaner" [inmate 3]; "the place is clean" [inmate 4]; "clean" [inmate 6]); a dominant theme in federal correctional management is maintaining a clean facility. References to the cleanliness of the prison facility were coded FAC (facility).

Food quality appeared on two lists ("food is better" [inmate 1]; "food is great" [inmate 5]). We didn't code references to food quality as a separate category. Why? We know that in federal correctional culture, food quality is categorized as an "inmate program," along with other services and activities designed for inmates, such as recreation, commissary, visiting, education, religion, law library, and so on. We chose to lump inmates' statements about food quality with other freelist items relating to inmate programs, such as "easy access to recreation." Freelist items referring to inmate programs were coded QOL (quality of life).

Inmate 4 cited "closer to home" as a benefit of being committed to FPC Pekin. Keeping inmates close to their families is a priority in what federal prison officials call "inmate population management." In fact, all inmates at FPC Pekin were placed there because it put them closer to their home residences. Because we knew that proximity to home is important to inmates and to federal prison officials, we set up the code, HOM, and used it to classify all such references.

Other freelist items were more difficult to code. Consider the responses of inmate 1 ("fresh start with staff and inmates on new jobs"; "new staff start out friendlier"). These comments refer generally to inmates' opinion that in a new prison inmates can establish fresh social ties with inmates and staff. Remember, prisons are closed, confined, social communities, where inmates and staffers see one another every day for years or even decades. And when social relations sour, they tend to remain that way. In a new prison, inmates can wipe clean the social slate. A reference to new social ties was coded NST.

We know that constructive communication between staffers and inmates is a key management issue in federal prisons (Fleisher 1996). Thus, the reference made by inmate 6 ("able to bring up ideas with staff without getting shot down") is important, and such references were coded with RAP (rapport).

How Data Were Coded

The actual process of coding data took time and patience and required careful organization, because we had a lot of data. If we made mistakes early on in the coding, then we would probably have to go back and recode data again. We didn't begin to code data until we felt familiar with every freelist for each informant and had a sense of the types of information inmates were conveying.

We took the freelists and put them into 18 piles (one for each question). Each pile had 75 freelists (one freelist for each informant). We numbered each freelist, 1–75. Our numbering scheme was consistent from informant to informant, from pile to pile; that is, informant 33 in pile 3 was the same inmate as informant 33 in pile 15. Being so careful about data management ensured that if we or other analysts wanted to do more than freelist analysis later, the data would be clearly arranged.

We read the freelist given by, say, informant 1 to question 1 and coded each item on informant 1's freelist with a code, such as RAP, QOL, FAC, and so on. We wrote the codes next to each item on the freelist itself, in red pen. We kept a log of codes, what each code meant, verbatim statements that fit that code, and coined a three-letter acronym for each code, which would later be used to create the dataset. As we encountered a new freelist item, we added it to our running code list.

These verbatim descriptions are the equivalent of definitions listed for an entry in a standard dictionary. For example, we used the code DEV (institution development) to include inmates' statements relating to development of the prison camp as an organization that accomplishes its goal of delivering services and maintaining a positive climate for inmates and staffers.

To readers not familiar with federal correctional culture, the DEV code is probably fuzzy, but to us, to federal officials, and to federal inmates, it marks an important category. Inmate statements, such as "inmates helped with changes in camp operations as the institution increased population," "staff cooked for inmates,"[3] "getting to know staff was helpful," "gave inmates an opportunity to help develop their programs," refer to inmates' feelings that staff as well as inmates were contributing to the development of positive rapport and constructive communication.

Statements such as those above are examples of the "voice" of female inmates in a federal prison camp. Researchers who specialize in studying the organizational culture of federal institutions spend years learning how to understand the nuances of inmate and staff speech. And as their understanding of these nuisances improves, so will the coding of inmates' freelists. Table 4.3 is a portion of our actual codebook, which shows codes, code explanation, and code content.

TABLE 4.3
Three Freelist Codes in the FPC Pekin Codebook

Code	Code Explanation	Code Content
DEV	Institution Development	inmates helped with changes as institution increased population; staff cooking for inmates; getting to know staff was helpful; opportunities to develop new programs
FAM	Separation from Family	leaving family members and friends from home, being away from children, distance from home
HOM	Close to Home	more visits; see children often

We kept a running list of these preliminary codes and created new codes when we needed them. Some items, such as those relating to cleanliness, are easy to code; other items are difficult. For example, a number of inmates mentioned that they "aren't permitted to dress up and show off nice clothing." As it turns out, this item has to do with inmates' feeling that they aren't permitted to express themselves as women, but must remain within the role of prison inmate. Thus, we chose to code such references as DWN (deprived of women's needs).

We coded question 1 freelists for all 75 informants before moving on to question 2 freelists and so on. By coding the data in this way, we were forced to review a large corpus of data reported for the same question. This review process let us see the range of responses and cued us about items that appeared repeatedly versus those that were idiosyncratic or reported by a few informants. In the end, we created 109 codes. If you think of each freelist given by each informant for each question as a "chunk" of data, these 109 codes classify 1,350 data chunks (75 informants multiplied by 18 freelists). That's a lot of data to code.

Semistructured Interviews

Some freelist items, DEV codes, were mentioned frequently and deserved attention. But there were also infrequently mentioned but culturally interesting items, such as those coded DWN. We used our close familiarity with the data, and with federal prison camp culture, to develop a series of questions for semistructured interviews (see Bernard 1994:209). These interviews gave us some explanations of freelist items and helped us interpret inmates' freelists.

As we coded freelist data, we kept a running list of potential interview items. On that running list were questions such as, "Discuss the ways that inmates feel deprived of their needs as women," "Discuss how being closer to home has influenced your relationship to your family," and "Discuss the difficult adjustments you made since transferring here."

When we collected freelists we asked each inmate if she would volunteer for an interview. Fifty-two inmates (69.3% of the 75 inmates who gave us freelists) agreed to be interviewed; some even asked us to interview them. About half of the interviews were conducted one-on-one, that is, Fleisher and an inmate, Harrington and an inmate, or Fleisher and Harrington and an inmate. With the other half, Fleisher and Harrington worked together to interview 2 or 3 inmates at a time. Sitting around a conference table, we asked a question and inmates discussed it. Initially, we decided to do small group interviews because one-on-one interviews were so time consuming; we didn't have 80–100 hours to invest in interviewing inmates. To save time, we did small group interviews; only inmates who volunteered for a small group interview participated in these. These interviews were, in fact, especially productive, because inmates fed off each other's comments. One-on-one and small group interviews lasted between one and two and a half hours.

Creating Datasets

We now had codes for each freelist item, for each question, and for each informant. Recall that we wrote the codes in red ink next to each item. This would make the next step—creating a dataset for freelists—simple and straightforward. When each freelist dataset had been prepared, each one would be analyzed with ANTHROPAC (Borgatti 1992).

ANTHROPAC requires that datasets be written in the standard computer language known as **ASCII**. There are a number of ways to write an ASCII file. You can write the dataset in ANTHROPAC, which will automatically save the data as an ASCII file. If you use WordPerfect or Word, consult your manual for instructions on saving the text you create, that is, the freelist dataset, as an ASCII file. Be careful at this step; if you don't save the datasets correctly, ANTHROPAC can't read them and you won't get your analysis. If you use the hard drive, copy the datasets from the word-processing program into a subfile in ANTHROPAC created to house your freelist data. We created an ANTHROPAC subdirectory called FPCPEKIN. If you use a disk to store your freelist datasets, you'll use that data disk in conjunction with ANTHROPAC. ANTHROPAC's manuals give you detailed instructions about creating datasets and doing the freelist analysis.

Freelist analysis is based on two ideas: (1) Things most familiar or most important to people will be mentioned before things that are less familiar or less important; and (2) People who know a lot about a subject, in this case, the environment of a prison camp, will have more to say about it than people who know less. "More to say" means that their freelists will be longer.

ANTHROPAC reads a freelist dataset, counts the number of separate codes listed (frequency), determines the percentage of informants who used each code (response percentage), notes the place on each freelist and yields the average rank for each code (rank), and uses the frequency and rank to produce a score called salience. (The formula for salience is given in the ANTHROPAC guidebooks.) Generally, salience is a measure of how much knowledge informants share and how important that knowledge is to them. ANTHROPAC's freelist won't interpret the salience scores. That's left to the anthropologist.

To show you a portion of a freelist analysis, we chose to look at data for the question, "List the best things about a commitment to a new institution" (COMBEST). Table 4.4 shows the highest salience scores on this question.

TABLE 4.4
COMBEST: Highest Salient Scores

Code	Frequency	Response Percentage	Average Rank	Salience
FAC	38	51	1.368	0.388
DEV	21	28	1.952	0.154
HOM	18	24	1.389	0.205
QOL	10	13	1.750	0.043

There are several interesting things to note about this analysis. We listed the codes by frequency. But note the relationship between frequency and salience: The most frequently cited codes are *not* always the most salient items. Why? Because the placement of an item on a freelist in the first, second, third position, and so on, influences salience. In Table 4.5, DEV is cited more often than HOM, but HOM has higher salience, because its average rank is 1.389, as compared to DEV at 1.952.

TABLE 4.5
Highest Salient Items

Freelist Question Code	Freelist Item Code	Frequency	Response Percentage	Average Rank	Salience Score
Benefit	HOM	43	57	1.186	0.504
Talk	BND	46	61	1.261	0.460
Staff	COU	45	60	1.511	0.423
Womanbes	NO	31	41	1.000	0.413
Bosstough	BEX	34	45	1.118	0.413
Combest	FAC	38	51	1.368	0.388
Reach	HPS	27	36	1.519	0.360
Change	PGM	41	55	1.659	0.350
Livtough	ANI	29	39	1.172	0.327
Adjust	PRV	31	41	1.387	0.287
Bossbest	BNW	21	28	1.048	0.267
Quality	SUP	24	32	1.667	0.238
Comtough	ANI	25	33	1.520	0.236
Livbest	ANI	18	24	1.056	0.227
Womantou	FAM	21	28	1.429	0.211
Previous	ANE	19	25	1.632	0.164
Quick	CON	10	13	1.000	0.133

Now you understand why coding raw freelist data is a vital procedure: If the coding of the raw data changes, salience changes too. And if salience changes, the interpretation of data will be affected, as well.

On FAC, the salience score was interpreted to mean a consensus among inmates that the best part of a commitment to this new prison was that it is clean. Interviewees told us that by "clean" they mean not only newness of the physical facility itself but also the newness of clothing issued to them, brand new bed sheets, towels, and so on. We take for granted the freedom to buy new clothes and sheets for our beds, but inmates rarely have the opportunity to wear clothes that aren't hand-me-downs.

HOM (home) is the most salient item. Interview data explain inmates' attitudes about being closer to home: Inmates with children may visit with them more often, and inmates without children may be visited by parents and friends. In the end, we were able to tell federal prison officials that, according to sampled inmates, the material benefits of being in a new facility do not exceed the social benefit of being close to home.

Interpreting Freelist Data

Our research had a specific purpose: to uncover inmates' perceptions about the quality of life at FPC Pekin. There was one fiat, however: The analysis had to be in a form that would be useful to federal prison officials (see Kania 1983). We think we have accomplished our task. We coded the freelist data into categories that correspond to management issues important to operating a federal prison camp. Without a thorough knowledge of federal corrections, it would not have been possible to code the data in this way.

After analyzing the 17 questions, we isolated each question's highest ranking freelist item. Table 4.5 shows these highest salient freelist items, one from each list (except for the leftmost column showing freelist question codes, the columns in Table 4.5 mirror the output of a freelist analysis). We assumed these highest salient items denote inmates' most important perceptions. Let's see what these items tell us about the quality of life at FPC Pekin.

The single most important issue to sampled inmates was to be close to home, and it turns out that federal prison officials are sticklers for keeping inmates as close to home (HOM) as possible. Thus, the federal prison policy and the needs of the inmates are well matched. The least important issue is the conflict (CON) that is inevitable in the initial months of operation of a new prison. New prisons, like many new businesses, need time to work out the kinks in delivering services to customers. Inmates understand that there will be service delivery problems, so do staff, and this finding seems to show that inmates are willing to be patient with staffers.

Between the extremes represented by HOM and CON are a number of interesting management-related issues. Use Table 4.5 as you follow along in our discussion. BND (basic needs) refers to inmates' perception that staffers provide for inmates' basic needs; along with this issue, we find that COU (counselors), more so than other staffers, reach out to inmates. Indeed, this is exactly what the federal prison officials expect from counselors, and inmates confirm they are doing it. Sampled inmates also agreed that there are NO good aspects of being an imprisoned woman.

Inmate employment in the federal prisons isn't optional. All inmates must work. So we might expect that inmates, like citizens in the community, would feel anxiety when changing jobs and dealing with a new boss. And bosses' expectations (BEX) are reported to cause inmates anxiety. We've already noted that inmates feel the best part of being in a new prison is access to new building, beds, sheets and clothing, and so on (FAC). And the next item verifies, in another way, that staffers do reach out to inmates and are helpful as staffers are expected to be (HPS, helpful staff).

When a new prison opens, it takes months for all inmate programs to be fully operational. Inmate programs include such things as education, general reading library, law library, commissary, religious services, and the like. Because nearly every inmate in our sample transferred to FPC Pekin from a well-established prison, we expected these inmates to be disappointed with the array and development of program options at the new camp. And we were correct. We coded such references to programs with PGM. Our analysis shows that inmates perceived a lack of fully operational programs.

Anyone who has moved to a new community or gone to college for the first time and has had to give up a known physical and social environment for one unknown senses a bit of anxiety at first while adjusting to a new environment. Inmates experience these feelings too, as they become acquainted with new staffers, institution procedures that may be different from those in their previous institution, and new jobs and bosses. Responses referring to such adjustments were coded ANI (adjustment to a new institution). We had a problem with this code and discuss that problem below.

Most FPC Pekin inmates transferred from an institution where they resided in rooms or cells. At this new camp, inmates live in dormitories, where they have less privacy than they did in single or double cells. Adjusting to this lack of privacy is noted with the code PRV. As mentioned above, another adjustment was working for a new boss. While that situation created some anxiety (BEX), it also gave inmates a "fresh start." Inmates' positive responses to beginning a new job were coded BNW. Yet another adjustment to living in a new prison is running out of dormitory cleaning supplies in the commissary. It takes time for staff to learn what quantities to order and at what rate. Inmates noted that supplies (SUP) ran out too quickly.

The next responses are confusing. That's because we miscoded the data. We asked inmates to identify "the best aspects of living in a new institution," as well as "list the tough things about a commitment to a new institution." But we used ANI to code positive responses to the first question and negative responses to the second. We made a mistake that we didn't catch until the data were analyzed. Were we to do it again, we would use two codes, one for positive (best aspects), a second for negative responses (tough things), and we'd make sure that these codes were different from ANI.

FAM refers to family. Because relatively few sampled inmates had children, this item has low salience. It's interesting to note that HOM and FAM appear at different ends of the salience score continuum. These items aren't synonyms. Interview data tell us that being close to home and being among inmates who come from the same area is a psychological comfort; however, being close to home doesn't mean necessarily that inmates will receive frequent visits. FAM, however, has a specific referent (family members) and, in the context of the life course of women in our sample, interviewees told us that these inmates were estranged from family members most of their lives. Thus, FAM has low salience.

ANE refers to adjustment to a new environment. We wanted to distinguish the regional "environment" of central Illinois from life at the prison camp. Many inmates transferred to FPC Pekin from places that are quite different from the flat, wind-blown landscape at Pekin. We thought that a dramatic shift in physical environment from, say, the FPC Alderson, West Virginia, to FPC Pekin would negatively influence inmates' adjustment. It seems, however, inmates agree that a shift in physical environment is not overly important to them.

CON (conflict) is the final item. A nonviolent criminal history is a prerequisite to a commitment to a federal prison camp, for men or women. This means that FPC Pekin's inmates have not been convicted of a violent act, sex offense, or firearms violation. Interviewees told us that inmates worried about conflict, such as theft from living cubicles, as the inmate population increased over the first six months, but given the low salience of CON, it seems to be a minor worry.

Conclusion

Research is serious business. If you are working with officials of a private corporation, or a government agency as we did with the Federal Bureau of Prisons, be sure that you carefully read that organization's research policy and follow each of its stipulations. If you're collecting data as a student working on a senior paper or a thesis or dissertation, consult your university's research policy on human subjects and be sure to meet with the university research administrator (if you collect data in a state prison, there will be human subjects requirement that must be met). You will undoubtedly be required to secure the approval of your college or university's Institutional Review (or Human Subject Review) Board.

Be patient and meticulous in data organization. Good research takes time and relies on careful data management. Think through each step of data collection and data management well before you begin your project. If you work with others, be sure everyone knows what's going on before you start. Work with colleagues who are willing to invest the energy and time necessary to do a meticulous job. Pretest your freelist questions. Don't be afraid to modify your questions if they don't work well. Study the freelists once you've collected them and lay out possible codes before creating the ANTHROPAC dataset, or you may commit an error as we did. Don't be afraid to say you made a mistake, and correct the mistakes you make.

QUESTIONS

1. How can a researcher use freelisting to better understand the nature of a complex cultural system?
2. What are the pitfalls of coding freelist data?
3. Why must an anthropologist doing collaborative research with a criminal justice agency be mindful of agency needs?
4. How can freelisting help agency officials to better understand the needs of their clients?
5. Research with English speakers can be as challenging as research overseas. In what ways did research at FPC Pekin pose cultural and language difficulties to the researchers?

NOTES

1. We thank Warden David W. Helman, FCI Pekin, for his cooperation on this research. We are grateful to Chief Gerald Gaes, Office of Research and Evaluation, Deputy Chief William Saylor, and ORE staff who offered valuable comments and opinions about our project. This study was approved by the Federal Bureau of Prisons. The opinions expressed here are those of the authors and do not reflect the policies or the opinions of former or current employees in the U.S. Department of Justice, Federal Bureau of Prisons.

2. We hesitated to coin the term "start-up" because we didn't want to create more jargon. However, the federal prison system doesn't have a special term for the initial period of operation of a new institution, and we feel this period is worth denoting because of its significance to staff and inmates and to the development of a new prison's institutional culture.

3. In a fully operational prison, inmates cook meals and staff supervise meal preparation, but in the early weeks at FPC Pekin, staff cooks prepared meals.

JULIANA FLINN ∎

Freelists, Ratings, Averages, and Frequencies: Why So Few Students Study Anthropology

A Statement of the Problem

Why are enrollments in Cultural Anthropology low at UALR (University of Arkansas at Little Rock)? Since Cultural Anthropology satisfies one of the general education requirements for undergraduate students, our department expects to have enrollments comparable to those in other general education courses. Enrollments in Cultural Anthropology have been low even when factoring in an over-all decline in enrollment at the university.[1] Why? This was the question I set out to investigate.

Student evaluations are consistently very good; clearly the students taking our classes value Cultural Anthropology. The problem didn't appear to be that the faculty or courses were acquiring a bad reputation. However, without other data I was working with uncertain assumptions about student awareness and interest. It seemed foolish to plan strategies for raising our enrollments unless we first acquired some solid evidence about the reasons for the decline.

I already had evidence of some student misconceptions about anthropology. As a project in several of my upper-level anthropology classes, students interviewed other students (and nonstudents) about their understanding of anthropology. Those interviews revealed that most students viewed anthropology as the study of *other* people, *other* times, and *other* places. Anthropology excludes *us* as the subject of study. I assume that this contributes to a sense that anthropology is irrelevant and impractical compared to other social science options.

With these students' studies in mind, I decided to conduct a more systematic study.[2] According to the university's new core curriculum, students choose two courses from a list of eight to satisfy the "Individual, Culture, and Society" graduation requirement and fulfill what is called the "social and cultural awareness competency." Those eight courses are Criminal Justice, Cultural Anthropology, Gender Studies, Cultural Geography, Sociology, Mass Media and Society, Psychology and the Human Experience, and Religious World Views. When students have to decide which two courses to take, I wanted to know: (1) What criteria they use; and (2) How anthropology rates on each **criterion** compared with the other seven options.

I clearly needed two linked projects. First, I had to conduct interviews with students asking them their reasons for selecting courses. From a list of elicited reasons, I could generate a survey in which students are asked to rate each of the social science courses according to each of the criteria. For example, "interesting" turned out to be the most common reason cited for taking a class, and from this I generated the survey question asking students to rate each of the eight course options in terms of how interesting they thought it to be.

Freelisting: Uncovering Criteria for Selecting Social Science Courses

The first step was to discover the course selection criteria students use. I enlisted the aid of two UALR anthropology majors, Dee Dee Green and Tera Horsey, for this project. We conducted several pilot interviews to determine the most effective way of phrasing our questions.[3] My research assistants interviewed students in the student union, while I interviewed students who came to the department and were willing to participate in this project.

We used a **freelisting** format (see Bernard [1994:239–242] and Weller and Romney [1988:9–20] for more extensive discussions of freelisting). Students coming through the student union at various times of the day were stopped and individually asked to discuss their reasons for selecting courses satisfying the social science graduation requirement. They were told they could list as many reasons as they wanted. We wrote down their answers in the order they were given, and we also wrote down, to the extent we could, further comments students made about their answers. We stopped after 37 respondents, because we were no longer receiving significantly different criteria.[4] In effect, we weren't receiving any new reasons for selecting certain courses.

We ended up with 87 total responses. Responses such as "major/minor dependent," "required/core," "I didn't know what else to take," "wanted to graduate," "needed the hours," and "I was encouraged to get the basics out of the way" didn't provide information about the reasons for choosing *a particular* course and were eliminated.

By examining the list and recalling student comments on their answers, we realized that many of the answers were semantically identical in content and that we could collapse them together. Instead of focusing on the exact wording students used, we concentrated on the meanings of their reasons and their comments on those reasons. In looking at and discussing the student's responses, we concluded that the 87 total responses actually represented seven semantically distinct selection criteria.

Clearly, there are some potential problems with this type of reducing procedure. It's a necessary part of organizing freelist data as the freelisting task allows students to respond both with phrases and single word answers. Semantically equivalent criteria can easily be expressed differently. We also wanted to keep the number of criteria to a minimum because we didn't want to burden students with long survey forms in the second phase of this research. "Brainstorming" may not be the best or most systematic technique for accomplishing our task, but we felt confident in our collective ability to judge the similarities between the students' responses and in creating these seven categories.

Believing that a course is "interesting" is clearly a distinct criterion as it was the most frequently elicited response. Having an adviser or instructor suggest the course was another criterion. Responses in this category included "suggested by instructor," "advised," and "suggested by professor." A third category was having a friend recommend a course. The fourth category was composed of responses such as "easy professor," "easy class," and "easy course." "Useful" emerged as a fifth criterion (or category) from answers such as "useful later or on the job," "topic seemed more practical," "appeared to be a little more useful," and "I eliminated courses that seemed totally irrelevant for the job market." The sixth criterion was a concern for understanding others and oneself, as revealed in comments such as "I wanted to make myself a better person," "I wanted to get a better understanding of people," and "I wanted to understand others better and myself." The seventh (and last) criterion was prior knowledge of the course material. Students noted a reluctance to select courses they knew nothing about.

Preparing and Administering the Survey Questionnaire

With these criteria, we prepared a written questionnaire to survey students at the university. We turned each criterion into a question and asked students to **rate** each of the eight social science courses. Although we were interested in how Cultural Anthropology fared compared with the other seven options, we didn't mention this to the students. We constructed the following questionnaire and listed the eight courses under each question.

We worded the questions so that we could provide specific, verbal labels to each end of the rating continuum: "1" was the most negative rating and "5" was the most positive rating. We assumed that students completing the questionnaire would expect the scale to remain consistent across the set of questions. We deliberately chose a 5-point scale so that students could make a neutral choice ("3"; see Figure 5.1).[5]

---

1. Rate each of the following courses according to how easy you think they are (on a 1 to 5 scale). (1 was "very difficult" and 5 was "very easy.")
2. How interesting do you think these courses are (on a 1 to 5 scale)? (1 was "very uninteresting" and 5 was "very interesting.")
3. How useful do you think these courses are for later on (such as in a job, on a 1 to 5 scale)? (1 was "very useless" and 5 was "very useful.")
4. To what extent do you agree that these courses will give you a better understanding of others and yourself (on a 1 to 5 scale)? (1 was "strongly disagree" and 5 was "strongly agree.")
5. To what extent do you know what the courses are about (on a 1 to 5 scale)? (1 was "no idea" and 5 was "great extent.")
6. To what extent has an adviser or professor encouraged you to take each of the following courses (on a 1 to 5 scale)? (1 was "strongly discouraged" and 5 was "strongly encouraged.")
7. To what extent has a friend encouraged you to take the following courses (on a 1 to 5 scale)? (1 was "strongly discouraged" and 5 was "strongly encouraged.")

Figure 5.1. Questionnaire for selecting one of the eight required social science courses.

We administered the questionnaire to students least likely to have already taken their social science courses. Therefore, we distributed questionnaires in some required classes that tend to be full of first- and second-year students: World Civilization and Speech Communication. These are required freshmen-level classes, whereas the social science options are sophomore-level classes. Our sample size was 183 students. We would have preferred about 300 in order to be more confident that we could generalize from our sample to the entire student population.[6]

The demographics for our sample were as follows: 52% males and 35% females[7]; 54% white, 35% African American, 7% Asian, 1% Hispanic, and 3% Other; 25% freshmen, 29% sophomores, 28% juniors, and 16% seniors. We had a range of ages from 18–52; 32.4% were 19 or 20 years old.

Questionnaire Results

Although we had hoped to be able to single out one or two reasons for the low enrollments in Cultural Anthropology, the results showed that our course rated low on all seven criteria. This may indicate that the criteria are not independent from each other. A course perceived as "difficult" may simultaneously be "uninteresting" and "useless." Cultural Anthropology had the lowest ratings on five of the seven criteria ("no idea what it is," "not suggested by an adviser," "not suggested by a friend," "not useful," "difficult"). It was second lowest in terms of being "interesting" and third lowest in terms of "leading to a better understanding of others and oneself." Examining the **mean** or **average** ratings (on the 1–5 scale) for each criterion for each course, we found the following (remember that the higher the number, the better a course rated, so the courses toward the end of each list did the best, those toward the beginning the worst):

MEAN	COURSE

1. "EASY"

2.66	*Cultural Anthropology*
2.89	Religious World Views
2.97	Mass Media and Society
3.01	Gender Studies
3.02	Cultural Geography
3.06	Psychology and the Human Experience
3.08	Criminal Justice
3.25	Sociology

2. "INTERESTING"

2.58	Cultural Geography
2.65	*Cultural Anthropology*
2.85	Mass Media and Society
2.90	Gender Studies
2.98	Religious World Views
2.98	Sociology
3.28	Psychology and the Human Experience
3.34	Criminal Justice

3. "USEFUL"

2.45	*Cultural Anthropology*
2.86	Cultural Geography
2.88	Mass Media and Society
2.88	Gender Studies
3.01	Sociology
3.02	Religious World Views
3.24	Criminal Justice
3.32	Psychology and the Human Experience

4. "GIVE A BETTER UNDERSTANDING OF SELF AND OTHERS"

2.79	Cultural Geography
2.89	Mass Media and Society
2.96	*Cultural Anthropology*
3.10	Criminal Justice
3.32	Religious World Views
3.38	Sociology
3.40	Gender Studies
3.60	Psychology and the Human Experience

5. "KNOW WHAT THE COURSE IS ABOUT"

2.60	*Cultural Anthropology*
3.09	Gender Studies

3.10	Religious World Views
3.16	Mass Media and Society
3.44	Criminal Justice
3.55	Cultural Geography
3.65	Sociology
3.84	Psychology and the Human Experience

6. "ADVISER OR PROFESSOR ENCOURAGED"

2.46	*Cultural Anthropology*
2.50	Religious World Views
2.51	Gender Studies
2.58	Mass Media and Society
2.69	Cultural Geography
2.73	Criminal Justice
3.03	Sociology
3.17	Psychology and the Human Experience

7. "FRIEND ENCOURAGED"

2.45	*Cultural Anthropology*
2.55	Cultural Geography
2.55	Mass Media and Society
2.55	Religious World Views
2.69	Gender Studies
2.94	Sociology
2.95	Criminal Justice
3.16	Psychology and the Human Experience

Figure 5.2 is a visual representation of these descriptive statistics in a bar graph. The bar graph clearly shows that anthropology is consistently ranked at or near the bottom on all seven selection criteria.

We also examined the data as **frequency** data (expressed as percentages) by counting the number of students who assigned each rating (1–5) for each of the courses on each of the criteria. Since we had eight courses and seven criteria, we ended up with 56 sets of frequencies and percentages to analyze. We decided that for maximum comparative impact we would graph all the courses in terms of the frequencies of their end ratings, "1" or "5," respectively. We did this because the frequency with which a course is rated "1" on each criteria presents a vivid portrayal of its "negativity" quotient and, conversely, the frequency of "5" ratings portrays its "positive quotient" relative to the other courses (see Figures 5.3 and 5.4 below).

Probably the most revealing criterion is that mentioned in question 5: To what extent do you know what the courses are about?" Over 27% of respondents said they had "no idea" what Cultural Anthropology was about; for the next lowest rated (Gender Studies), only 12.6% said they had "no idea." For Psychology (the highest rated), only 6.0 % said they had "no idea," but 43.2% said they knew what it was about to a "great extent." For Sociology, the second highest-rated course on this criterion, 7.7% said "no idea," and 36.8% said "great extent."

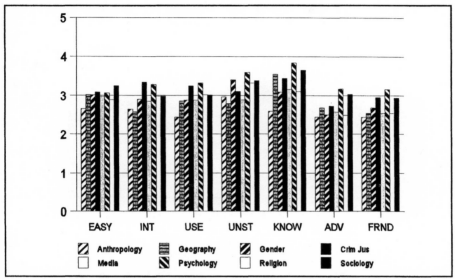

Figure 5.2. Bar graph of the mean ratings of selection criteria for each social science course option.

For criterion five, the average for Cultural Anthropology (2.60) was 1.24 lower than the average for Psychology (3.84), or 25% lower! In addition, the difference between Cultural Anthropology's average rating (2.60) and the second lowest (Gender Studies at 3.09) was greater than for any other criterion. This spread difference of anthropology was almost half a level (on a 5-point scale) below the second-lowest course. Consistent with these figures, the percentage of students who rated Cultural Anthropology a "1" (that is, said they had no idea" what it was) was the highest percentage for a "1" for any course and any criterion in our survey. Conversely, the 43.2% rating Psychology a "5" was the highest any course received for any criterion.

Cultural Anthropology was also perceived as the least useful (in terms of being practical after graduation or on the job), with Psychology considered the most useful. Among respondents, 24.0% said Cultural Anthropology was "very useless"; only 6.0% said it was "very useful." Faring somewhat better than Cultural Anthropology was Geography; only 18.8% labeled it "very useless." At the high end, 21.3% thought Psychology was "very useful," and only 9.3% said it was "very useless."

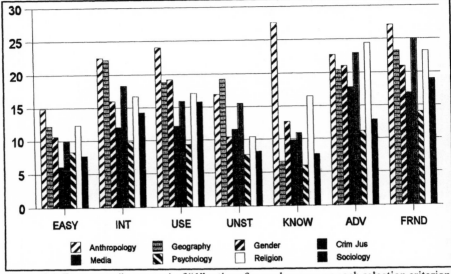

Figure 5.3. Frequency (in percent) of "1" ratings for each course on each selection criterion.

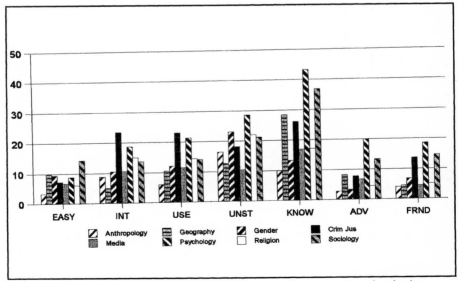

Figure 5.4. Frequency (in percent) of "5" ratings for each course on each criterion.

Results for this criterion show the second biggest spread between the average rating for Cultural Anthropology, the lowest ranking (with an average rating of 2.45), and Psychology, the highest (at 3.32), a difference of 0.87. Results also showed the second-largest spread for any criterion between Cultural Anthropology and the next-lowest course (2.86), a difference of 0.41, close to half a level on the rating scale. Cultural Anthropology's 2.45 rating was the lowest for any course on any criterion.

Another result that may be related to student lack of knowledge about the field is the perceived difficulty of the Cultural Anthropology course: 14.9% said it was "very difficult," and only 3.3% said it was "very easy." Students probably make no distinction between cultural anthropology and the field as a whole, which they view as being about evolution, fossils, ancient times, and "exotic" peoples. These are topics that are unfamiliar to most students so it's not surprising that they would think that the course would be more difficult than courses with which they have more a priori familiarity.

The results suggest, however, that Cultural Anthropology isn't quite as different as the other courses in an assessment of its easiness (or difficulty). The average ratings for this criterion represented the smallest spread: Cultural Anthropology averaged 2.66, and Sociology averaged 3.25, a difference of only 0.59 between the lowest and the highest of the eight courses. This also indicates, however, that there is not much variation in assessments of the "easiness" of a course among students. This was also the criterion for which the smallest percentage of students (14.9%) gave the rating of "5" (in this case "very easy"). Furthermore, a fairly large percentage (from 36.1% to 48.3%) of students chose the neutral "3" for this criterion. In other words, not many students judge any of the courses to be "very easy"; they tend to rate them all as "average." Easiness doesn't seem to be a significant factor in course selection among the eight options, though it is probably a signficant factor in specific contexts (for example, if a professor has a reputation for being "easy").

Cultural Anthropology was lowest ranked in terms of being recommended by friends, advisers, or instructors: Only 2.8% said that advisers or faculty had "strongly encouraged" them to take the course, and 22.7% said that advisers or faculty had "strongly discouraged" them. Psychology again ranked the highest: 11.1% said "strongly discouraged," and 20.0% said "strongly encouraged." These results may be related, in part, to perceived usefulness of a course. Many advisers lack a good understanding of what cultural anthropology is. One student, for example, who followed a friend's advice and took Cultural Anthropology told me that when he asked an adviser what social science course to take if he were interested in international relations, the adviser mentioned only Cultural Geography but not Cultural Anthropology. Consequently, I now make sure that advisers receive a flyer and course description each semester in the hope of improving this situation.

Perhaps because large numbers of students are not taking Cultural Anthropology and therefore not suggesting it in large numbers, Cultural Anthropology ranked lowest on the criterion "suggested by a friend," with Psychology again at the top. Only 4.0% said that a friend "strongly encouraged" them to take Cultural Anthropology, compared with 18.5% for Psychology.

The two criteria in which Cultural Anthropology didn't rank at the bottom of the ratings was on the criteria "interesting" and providing a "better understanding of others and yourself." Cultural Geography was rated as less interesting than Cultural Anthropology, while Criminal Justice was judged most interesting. Among the respondents, 22.5% said Cultural Anthropology was "very uninteresting," and 8.8% said it was "very interesting," whereas 12.0% said Criminal Justice was "very uninteresting," and 23.5% said it was "very interesting."

In terms of a perceived ability to help students understand themselves and others, Cultural Anthropology was the third lowest, with Psychology the highest and Cultural Geography the lowest (the media course was the second lowest). Only 16.9% said that they "strongly disagree" that Cultural Anthropology will give them a better understanding of themselves and others, and 16.4% "strongly agree," whereas for Psychology, 7.7% said "strongly disagree," and 28.6% said "strongly agree."

Conclusion

Although it was discouraging to find out how poorly Cultural Anthropology fared on so many of the criteria, at least we now have valuable information to use to address our problem. We can now focus our efforts and prioritize our problems and presumably be more successful in attracting students. The simple descriptive statistics provide us with vivid portrayals of how anthropology ranks in relationship to other social science course options on a number of important selection criteria. Considering the dramatic differences between the lowest- and highest-rated courses on the criterion "know what the course is about" and the knowledge that students were reluctant to take a course they knew little about, it's clear that the anthropology department at this university, and perhaps throughout the United States, needs to make more efforts to inform students about Cultural Anthropology before the students decide *not* to take the course.

In part, these survey results have motivated us to try to solve this particular problem. For example, the department has installed a bulletin board in a prominent location, and we have been posting information, photographs, and articles about the field and what we are doing. We now display and distribute flyers about our course offerings, especially where students are likely to sit and wait for advising. These flyers offer information about Cultural Anthropology and the topics we cover (such as marriage, religion, family, and politics).

Given that many students don't know what cultural anthropology is, and considering how earlier student surveys revealed the perception that anthropology was only about other people, places, and times, the perceived "uselessness" of anthropology isn't surprising. To help change the students' perceptions of anthropology's "uselessness," we have publicized the value students have found in it. For example, graduates have been asked to describe how anthropology has helped them with their lives and careers, and the results of these discussions have been published in a flyer for all students, a handbook for majors,[8] and a twice-yearly newsletter.

We should concentrate on combating ignorance about what anthropology is and ignorance about its possible usefulness. This should also improve students' perceptions about how interesting the field is and its value for understanding ourselves and others. Although we shouldn't ignore advisers, efforts to change the other criteria are less likely to have a strong effect considering how the scores cluster around "average" and how few students find any of the courses to be "very easy." With limited time and resources, our efforts to publicize the discipline and what we and our graduates do with anthropology appear to be the most fruitful avenues to pursue. In a few years, I hope to repeat the survey to see if Cultural Anthropology fares any better than it did this last time. Another way, meanwhile, to check on the effectiveness of our efforts, is to compare our average enrollments again with the average enrollments of the other social science options.

QUESTIONS

1. When obtaining a freelist, what is the value of recording comments as well as the answers?
2. What is at least one indicator that the researcher has enough respondents for freelists?
3. What is the value of being consistent with the positive and negative ends on rating scales?
4. What is a major difference between using an even-numbered versus an odd-numbered rating scale?
5. Why collect information on a survey form that does not directly relate to the specific research question being addressed?

NOTES

1. For example, this semester (Spring 1997), 1,431 students are enrolled in social science courses, an average of 178.9 for each of the eight choices students have. Cultural Anthropology enrolled 86, considerably less than one-eighth of the total.

2. I thank Anita Ianucci for her invaluable suggestions about how to conduct this investigation.

3. See Weller and Romney (1988:11) for a discussion of pretesting questions to examine how appropriately they are worded.

4. According to Weller and Romney (1988:14), 20–30 informants are usually enough.

5. See Weller and Romney (1988:41) for a discussion of the advantages and disadvantages of using an odd or even number of options and for a discussion of how many options to offer.

6. According to the formula recommended in Bernard (1994:77–79), a sample size of 366 would have been ideal for a sample of the entire student body. For the population of students who haven't taken the social science courses, the number is probably closer to 300.

7. These don't add up to 100% because of a number of missing values. A number of students failed to supply this information. Any analysis we make of differences according to gender is therefore likely to be suspect since we don't have gender information for almost 13% of the students who participated in the survey.

8. The handbook for majors probably has only a minimal impact on students selecting Cultural Anthropology. It is, nonetheless, on display in the department, and students— including Sociology students who haven't yet taken both of their social science courses—look through it. A number of students have come by the office with questions about our courses and stop to look at the handbook. And we've given advisers of undeclared majors copies so that they can help students see the value of anthropology. Finally, we hope that word of mouth about the utility of the field will have an impact as well.

Six

Pile Sorting:
"Kids Like Candy"

Food and eating are biocultural phenomena; we eat to get energy and nutrients for growth and body functions, but what, when, where, how and with whom we eat is influenced by food availability and a variety of sociocultural factors (for example, Fieldhouse 1995; Counihan and Van Esterik 1997). In most cultures, there are rules for combining foods and for associating particular foods and meals with particular social events, times, places, individuals, and social contexts (Goode 1989). For example, many people in the United States cannot eat Thanksgiving dinner without turkey, cranberry sauce, sweet potatoes, and pumpkin pie.

Each society or group has its own classificatory categories, and foods may be classified according to sensory characteristics (for example, taste, texture, color) and cultural factors including gender and age (Messer 1989). The way people classify foods reflects the various meanings associated with them, which vary intraculturally. In contemporary Western societies, women are often associated with eating vegetables, salad, and sweet foods whereas men are linked with eating red meat (Lupton 1996).

I am interested in how preadolescent girls and boys in the United States perceive gender through food. The general aim of my research is to describe children's food-related activities, the meanings of food and gender in children's lives, and the interaction between them (Roos 1995a, 1995b). Specific questions related to meanings include: How do children classify and organize foods? Are there differences in food classifications between girls and boys? Are adults' food and gender associations apparent in children's views of foods?

To answer these questions, it was necessary to collect information on food categories and meanings. Data on food meanings are usually gathered by a combination of observations and interviews (Messer 1989). In ethnographic studies, **pile sorting** has been used to collect descriptive information and judged similarity among large numbers of objects (Weller and Romney 1988). Michela and Contento (1984) used pile sorting in nutrition education to examine children's spontaneous food classifications and the dimensions underlying them. Their results suggest that most children categorize foods based on traditional food groups used in nutrition education (for example, fruits and vegetables), sensory characteristics (for example, sweet versus nonsweet foods), and how a food item is related to meal structure (for example, dinner entrées versus drinks and breakfast foods).

In this chapter, I describe how I used pile sorting to examine how children classify food and whether their classification systems reflect gender differences. I present the main results of the data analysis to illustrate the type of information pile sorting can provide.

The Sample

This chapter reports on data that I collected for a qualitative study of children, food, and gender in an urban community in central Kentucky in the spring of 1994 (Roos 1995a, 1995b).[1] When I started to plan the study, I contacted the principals of a few representative public elementary schools in the community. One of the principals showed interest and gave his approval to do the study. However, before I could begin, I had to get permission from the County Public School System and the University Institutional Review Board (IRB). Because I was working with underage children, the IRB required written consent from parents or guardians. I distributed letters to the children and those who returned a written permission were included in the study. (I had to exclude two boys from the study because they didn't return the form even though they were given a reminder to return the permission.)

The total study population consisted of 24 children (13 girls and 11 boys) in a fourth-grade class (9–11 year olds). The majority of the children came from Euro American households with two parents and one or two siblings. Most of the parents had gone to college, and many of them had professional or managerial jobs. All of the children were given the opportunity to take part in individual interviews and the pile sorting task. Participation required another written permission from parents or guardians, and 15 children (6 girls and 9 boys) volunteered for this part of the study. This sample size is rather small for pile sort data (20 or more is recommended), but when there are pile sorts with an equal number of piles per informant (constrained sorting), comparisons can be made (Weller and Romney 1988).

Selection of Research Methods

Nutritional scientists are mainly concerned with the relationships between diet and health. Methods frequently used in dietary studies are **quantitative** and based on self-reported food intake, for example, dietary recall, food frequency surveys, dietary history, food diary, and weighed intakes (Thompson and Byers 1994). In contrast to nutritional scientists, social scientists have traditionally focused on the meaning of food and eating in a specific culture or context. Sociocultural studies of food, such as the study presented here, usually rely on **qualitative** methods characteristic of ethnographic research such as observation and interviews (Bernard 1994; Denzin and Lincoln 1994).

Doing research with children influences the selection of methods. One reason I decided to work with preadolescent children was that they are capable of providing information on food consumption and food meanings. Children at the age of ten assert some influence over their eating and they are competent at communicating thoughts, feelings, and behaviors (Fine and Sandstrom 1988; Weber et al. 1994). However, it's important to remember that children think in concrete terms and may interpret questions quite literally. What children think a question means may be quite different from what an adult researcher means by a question (Holaday and Turner-Henson 1989). One reason for using pile sorting among children is that it's a more concrete task than answering interview questions. It's probably easier for children to have specific food items on cards instead of being asked more abstract questions such as, "What do boys eat?" This type of task also gives participants an opportunity to use their own terms and to take a more active role in the research.

Pile sorts alone don't mean anything because they aren't part of everyday food-related activities. Therefore, along with the pile sorts, I used a mix of ethnographic research methods to gather information on both actual behavior and ideal rules. The methods were chosen to be complementary, and I collected qualitative information by observation, group discussions, individual interviews, freelisting, writing and other assignments (see Bernard 1994; Denzin and Lincoln 1994; Weller and Romney 1988).

I first visited the school, observed class activities, and participated in school lunches to get to know the children and to establish rapport. After a few weeks, I arranged small group discussions to get more insight into what the children think is interesting about food and eating. To gather information on what foods and drinks are important, I asked the children to do a freelisting task (more of which later). A creative writing assignment provided knowledge of their ideas of foods and the contexts they associate with foods. I conducted semistructured, **open-ended** interviews in the school with 15 children. The interviews, which lasted approximately one hour each, covered a wide range of topics related to food, eating, and gender and included a pile sorting task. Although this study primarily relied on qualitative methods, a food frequency questionnaire[2] on which eating habits are quantified was also included.

Pile Sorting

In addition to observation and interviews, pile sorting provided data on food classifications and meanings of food and gender among children. I next describe the different steps I used in collecting pile sort data: First, I chose what and how many items to use; second, I decided what types of pile sorts to include; and third, I conducted the pile sorts.

From Pizza to Candy

When I selected foods and drinks for the pile sort assignment I considered earlier studies (Michela and Contento 1984; Thompson and Byers 1994), the children's freelisting of foods, and discussions and observations in school.

To make sure that I included a wide range of foods, I started with the list of 104 foods I used in the food frequency questionnaire (Thompson and Byers 1994). Second, I used freelisting (Weller and Romney 1988) because I wanted to include foods that were relevant for the participating children in their own language. In the beginning, I used ten minutes of class time for the **freelisting** task. I asked the children to write down for me as many foods and drinks as they could remember. The lengths of their lists varied from 9–51 items (mean = 31) and included more than 200 different food items and brand names ranging from more common foods, such as pizza, to horseradish and oysters. More than half of the children mentioned pizza, french fries, hamburgers, apples, tacos, donuts, Coke, corn, fish, hot dogs, milk, spaghetti, and potato chips, and I made sure to include all these in the pile sorting. Because many of the children mentioned Coke, I mentioned this brand name on the card for soda: "regular soda, for example, Coke." It's important to note that the freelisting was done right before lunch and expectations of what the cafeteria would serve may have **biased** the list.

In the next step, I compared the two lists (the one based on food frequency questionnaire and the one based on freelisting) and eliminated some of the foods. Michela and Contento (1984) had children aged 5–11 years old group 71 items, and I decided to use 60 items in my study. When eliminating foods, I made sure to include foods representing different food groups (for example, fruits, vegetables, and dairy products), drinks (for example, milk, orange juice, water), snacks (for example, fruit roll-ups, chocolate bars, candy), foods prepared in different ways (french fries and mashed potatoes, cooked carrots, and raw carrot sticks), and choices with different fat content (whole milk and skim milk). As a result, I created a list of 60 foods and drinks (Table 6.1A). I decided to use text cards instead of pictures, since ten-year-old children can easily read the text.

After I tested the 60 cards with one of the girls in the class, I reduced the number of cards to 40 (Table 6.1B). The main reason I did this was because handling and categorizing 60 cards was troublesome and took over 30 minutes, more than half the time I had planned to use for individual interviews. I was concerned about the length of the interview and about students losing too much class time because I didn't want to jeopardize my working relationship with the school. Therefore, I left out one–five cards from each food group: main dishes, cereal products, fruits, vegetables, drinks, and snacks (Table 6.1). I omitted more cards from larger groups. I didn't want to leave out foods or drinks that were important to the children, so, in addition to the criteria described above, I consulted my field notes and the results from the freelisting task and discussions.

TABLE 6.1

A. *Food Cards Initially Created for Pile Sorting*
(60 Items, *20 Items Eliminated)

pizza	cereal (e.g., Cheerios)	french fries	skim milk
hot dogs	PBJ sandwich[3]	mashed potatoes	whole milk
hamburgers	crackers	cooked carrots	*fruit punch
chicken nuggets	*biscuits	raw carrot sticks	chips
fish	*cornbread	green beans	ice cream
steak	cheese	*baked potato	donuts
spaghetti	apple	*lima beans	Poptarts
tacos	orange	*tomato	fruit roll-ups
vegetable soup	watermelon	*spinach	snack cakes
*fried chicken	*grapes	*broccoli, fresh	cookies
*turkey	*grape jelly	*broccoli and cheese	chocolate bar
*chili	*canned peaches	water	candy
*macaroni and cheese	corn	orange juice	*Jello
*eggs	peas	reg. soda (e.g., Coke)	*Popsicles
bread, white	tossed salad (lettuce)	diet soda	*yogurt

B. *Food Cards Used in Pile Sorting (40 Items)*

pizza	cereal (e.g., Cheerios)	french fries	whole milk
hot dogs	PBJ sandwich	mashed potatoes	chips
hamburgers	crackers	cooked carrots	ice cream
chicken nuggets	cheese	raw carrot sticks	donuts
fish	apple	green beans	Poptarts
steak	orange	water	fruit roll-ups
spaghetti	watermelon	orange juice	snack cakes
tacos	corn	reg. soda (e.g., Coke)	cookies
vegetable soup	peas	diet soda	chocolate bar
bread, white	tossed salad (lettuce)	skim milk	candy

Three Pile Sorts

I was interested in children's food culture and their own criteria for classifying foods as it reflects their meanings associated with food. One of the aims of my study was to explore if adults' food and gender associations were apparent in children's views of food. Therefore, I decided to use three types of pile sorts—one **unconstrained** and two **constrained**: one by age and one by gender (Figure 6.1).

I. Pile sorting based on children's own criteria (40 text cards)
        - unconstrained
II. Pile sorting based on age (40 text cards)
        - constrained
        - three piles: 1. Children's foods
                        2. Adults' foods
                        3. Both children's and adults' foods
III. Pile sorting based on gender (40 text cards)
        - constrained
        - three piles: 1. Girls' foods
                        2. Boys' foods
                        3. Both girls' and boys' foods

Figure 6.1. Pile sorting procedure.

In the first unconstrained pile sort, children were given the freedom to decide what to base their sort on and how many piles to create. To random order the cards, I handed them a shuffled stack of 40 food cards. I asked them to look through the cards and sort the cards into as many piles as they wished, based on how they thought the food items should go together. When they had sorted all the cards, I asked them to name the piles and to explain why certain foods appeared in the same pile. If children only had two–three piles, I asked them if they could think of some other way of sorting them. Each card was numbered on the back, and before we continued I asked the children to read the numbers as I took notes (the interviews were also tape recorded). Between the sorts, I shuffled the cards before I gave them back to the children.

The second and third pile sorts were constrained; the number of piles in each of these sorts was restricted to three. The second sort was by age. I asked children to sort the cards into three piles based on whether they thought that children, adults, or both children and adults mainly eat the food. I mainly wanted to learn if there are foods that children consider to be typical among only themselves and not adult food. The "both" category was included because I expected that some foods are not associated specifically with different age groups. To make the task easier, I put small labels ("children," "adults," and "both") on the table in front of the children. The children were again asked to explain their categorization, for example, why they think that children mainly eat candy. The third pile sort was similar to the second but this time on the basis of gender. The children were asked to sort the cards into three labeled piles: "girls", "boys," and "both" based on who mainly eats the food. I included this sort to make gender more explicit and to explore whether children associate certain foods with girls and boys.

Most of the children were interested in participating in the study and many volunteered for interviews. The children seemed to like the freelisting task; the class was very quiet, and the lists were often long. The ones who participated in the pile sort assignment also seemed to have fun sorting the cards. They had heard about the assignment from their classmates because each individual interview including the pile sorts was done separately on different days. To minimize bias, I decided to place the pile sorting task in the beginning of the interview so that interview themes and questions would not influence the assignment. In testing the interview I had asked questions related to meals right before the assignment, and many of the piles formed turned out to be examples of meals.

Data Analysis

Data from the pile sorts were analyzed in three different ways. First, the various food categories formed by the children in the first pile sort and foods included in the piles in the second and third pile sorts were tabulated. Second, the reasons given by the children for why they placed specific foods in particular groups were arranged into tables. Third, to judge similarity among the children, data were analyzed using ANTHROPAC (Borgatti 1992). Based on the instructions in ANTHROPAC, I entered the data and applied Johnson's **hierarchical clustering** to identify groups of foods that go together. The outcome was a cluster diagram (Figures 6.2 and 6.3) in which the food items are columns and the levels of clustering are the rows.

Children's Food Classifications

There were as many ways of classifying foods as the number of participating children. The number of groups the children formed varied between two and ten (median six). When one girl formed two groups that she named "what I like" and "what I don't like" I asked her if she could think of any other way of grouping the cards. She created four new groups based on eating events and called these "break-fast," "lunch," "dinner," and "in-between snacks." However, most of the children

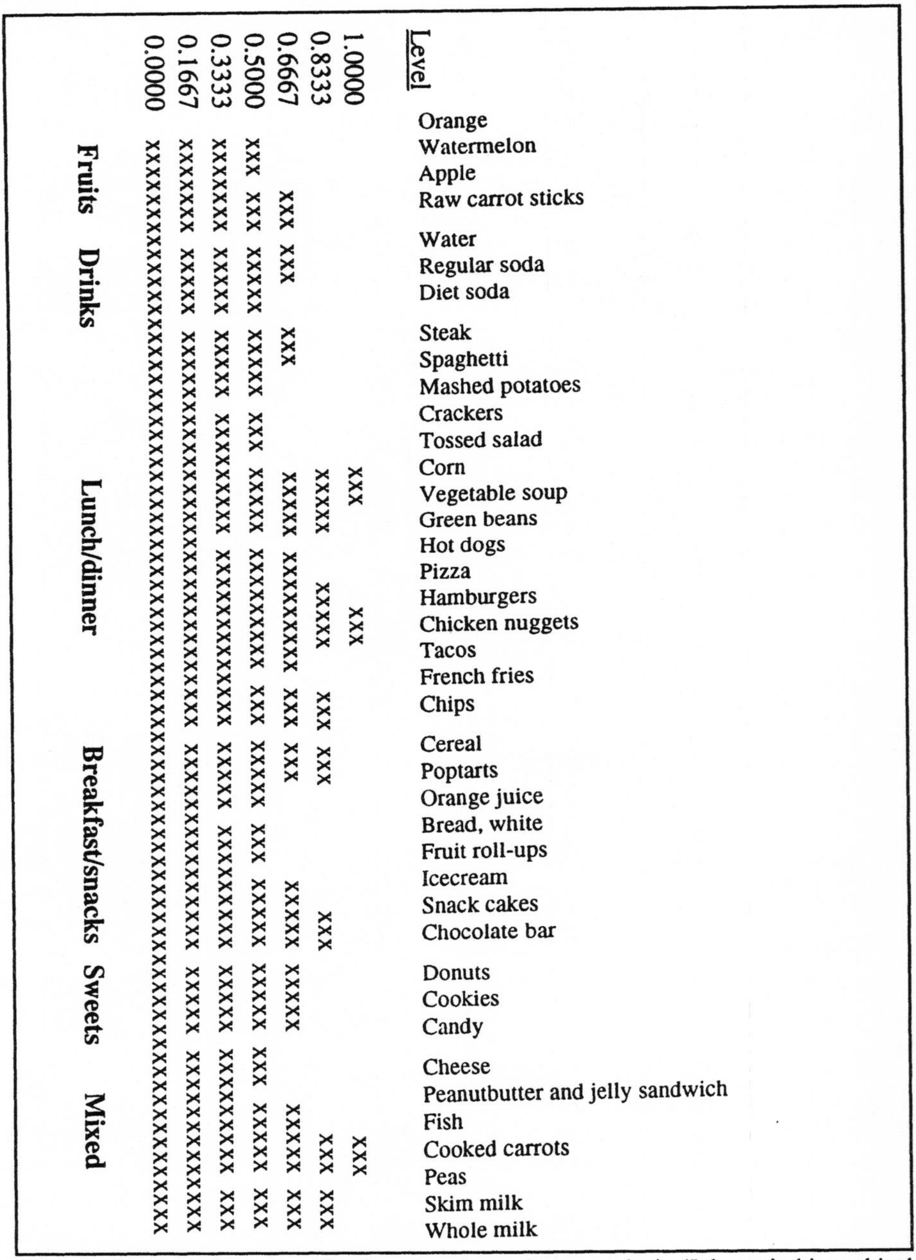

Level

1.0000		Orange
0.8333		Watermelon
0.6667		Apple
0.5000		Raw carrot sticks
0.3333		
0.1667		Water
0.0000		Regular soda
		Diet soda

Fruits   Drinks   Lunch/dinner   Breakfast/snacks   Sweets   Mixed

Orange
Watermelon
Apple
Raw carrot sticks

Water
Regular soda
Diet soda

Steak
Spaghetti
Mashed potatoes
Crackers
Tossed salad
Corn
Vegetable soup
Green beans
Hot dogs
Pizza
Hamburgers
Chicken nuggets
Tacos
French fries
Chips

Cereal
Poptarts
Orange juice
Bread, white
Fruit roll-ups
Icecream
Snack cakes
Chocolate bar

Donuts
Cookies
Candy

Cheese
Peanutbutter and jelly sandwich
Fish
Cooked carrots
Peas
Skim milk
Whole milk

Figure 6.2. Girls' food classifications based on cluster analysis (Johnson's hierarchical clustering; see Borgatti 1992).

```
Level
1.0000                                                       Orange
0.8889                                                 XXX   Apple
0.7778                                           XXXXX XXX   Watermelon
0.6667                                     XXXXX XXXXX XXX   Vegetable soup
0.5556                               XXXXX XXXXX XXXXX XXX   Corn
0.4444                         XXXXX XXXXX XXXXXXXXXXX XXX   Tossed salad
0.3333                   XXXXX XXXXX XXXXXXXXXXXXXXXXX XXX   Raw carrot sticks
0.2222             XXXXX XXXXXXXXXXX XXXXXXXXXXXXXXXXX XXX   Cooked carrots
0.1111       XXXXXXXXXXXXXXXXXXXXXXX XXXXXXXXXXXXXXXXX XXX   Mashed potatoes
0.0000 XXXXXXXXXXXXXXXXXXXXXXXXXXXXX XXXXXXXXXXXXXXXXX XXX   Peas
                                                       XXX   Green beans

                                                       XXX   Hot dogs
                                                 XXXXX XXX   Hamburgers
                                                 XXXXX       Spaghetti
                                                 XXXXX XXX   French fries
                                           XXX   XXXXX XXX   Fish
                                           XXX   XXXXX XXX   Chicken nuggets
                                           XXX   XXX   XXX   Steak
                                     XXX   XXX   XXX   XXX   Pizza
                               XXX   XXX   XXX   XXX         Tacos
                               XXX   XXX   XXX               Crackers
                         XXX   XXX   XXX                     Cheese
                   XXXXX XXX   XXX                           Bread, white
                   XXXXX XXX                                 Peanutbutter and jelly sandwich
                   XXXXX XXX                                 Chips
             XXXXX XXXXX XXX                                 Poptarts
             XXXXX             XXX                           Cereal
             XXXXX             XXX                           Donuts

                                     XXX                     Fruit roll-ups
                                     XXXXX             XXX   Icecream
                               XXXXX XXXXX             XXX   Cookies
                         XXXXXXXXXXX XXXXX                   Snack cakes
                         XXXXXXXXXXX                         Chocolate bar
                         XXXXXXXXXXX                         Candy

                                           XXX               Water
                                     XXX   XXX   XXX         Orange juice
                               XXX   XXX   XXX   XXX   XXX   Regular soda
                               XXX   XXX   XXX   XXX   XXX   Diet soda
                         XXX   XXX   XXX   XXX   XXX         Skim milk
                         XXX   XXX   XXX   XXX               Whole milk
```

Fruits/vegetables   Breakfast/lunch/dinner   Sweets   Drinks

Figure 6.3. Boys' food classifications based on cluster analysis (Johnson's hierarchical clustering; see Borgatti 1992).

were not as systematic and they simultaneously had groups based on various criteria. For example, one boy categorized the cards into the following ten piles: "Eat for snacks most of the time," "Things I like to get at McDonald's," "Like together sometimes," "Like to put in mashed potatoes," "Like for breakfast," "Usually served at normal nights," "My brother's two favorite foods," "My dad likes pretty much," and "Usually what I like for dessert sometimes."

Table 6.2 summarizes the main criteria the children used in their classifications. The most prominent food classification scheme involved distinctions based on the role food plays in terms of eating events: meals (breakfast, lunch, or dinner) or snacks. Many children based at least part of their classification system on food groups similar to those used by nutrition educators. Sweets (not really considered a food group in dietary recommendations) was the group that the children used most often. Four girls and eight boys had some form of group called "sweets," "candy," "snacks," or "junk food." Other commonly formed groups were drinks, fruits, and vegetables. The children often talked about food in terms of preferences and tended to categorize foods into foods they or somebody else in the family likes or dislikes.

TABLE 6.2
Food Categories Formed by Girls and Boys

Groups formed	Girls N = 6	Boys N = 9
Eating events:		
Breakfast	5	6
Lunch	3	3
Dinner	2	6
Snacks	4	7
Food groups:		
Sweets, candy	4	8
Fruits	5	6
Vegetables	4	6
Drinks	4	7
Meat	2	4
Dairy	2	4
Breads	1	3
Cereals, wheat, grains	2	–
Preferences (e.g., I like)	3	5

To identify recurrent food groupings used by the children, cluster analysis was performed using data from the first unrestricted pile sort separately for girls and boys. In the cluster diagrams (Figures 6.2 and 6.3), subgroups of food items with a higher degree of similarity within than between groups are displayed. In Figure 6.2, the most proximate groups are corn and vegetable soup, hamburgers and chicken nuggets, and cooked carrots and peas. At the next step, more food items are joined. There were six recurrent food groupings used by girls: fruits, dinner/lunch foods, snack foods, sweets, drinks, and a mixed group (this group contained, for example, dairy products, dislikes, and peanut butter and jelly sandwich) (Figure 6.2). Boys used somewhat different food groupings: fruits and vegetables, breakfast/lunch/dinner foods, sweet snack foods, and drinks (Figure 6.3).

By performing **cluster analysis** separately for boys and girls, I learned that boys grouped vegetables and fruits together whereas girls had a fruit group but they included vegetables in the lunch/dinner group. This might suggest that girls perceive vegetables as components of meals and think of foods in terms of eating events more than boys. Girls had more subgroups (that is, possess more detailed knowledge, perhaps because food is a feminine domain [for example, Bordo 1993; Lupton 1996]), and food, diet, and figure are already becoming important.

"Kids Like Candy" and "Adults Eat More Vegetables"

The children didn't express any difficulties in classifying foods based on age. When asked to sort food cards based on what mainly children or adults eat, they often put fruit roll-ups, peanut butter and jelly sandwiches, and candy and other sweetened or snack foods in the children's pile (Table 6.3). In contrast, adults were associated with cooked carrots and other vegetables, fish, and steak (Table 6.4).

The results from the constrained pile sorting were used to support data obtained by observing and talking to the children. Foods associated with children were often referred to as "junk" and said to be unhealthy. Children reported that they mainly ate these foods for breakfast, lunch at school, and snacks without the presence of parents or other adults. Foods associated with adults correspond with what children considered to be components of proper meals. Because meals are usually family occasions at which parents provide the food, children may have classified foods adults serve at meals as foods mainly adults eat. Some of the children explained that they did put foods they do not like in the adults' pile.

"Most Girls Like to Eat Healthy Stuff" and "Boys Go Fishing"

Gender did not seem to be an important criterion in classifying foods because when the children were asked to sort the cards by gender, some said that the task was difficult and that there were no differences. Therefore, the pile "both" turned out to be the largest and two of the boys ended up with all cards in this pile. On the other hand, the pile sort results suggest that the children associated girls with vegetables and salad and boys with fish or steak (Tables 6.5 and 6.6).

TABLE 6.3
*Foods that Girls and Boys (>50%) Included in the Pile of Foods
that Mainly Children Eat*

Girls N = 6		Boys N = 9	
fruit roll-ups	6	fruit roll-ups	8
PBJ sandwich	6	PBJ sandwich	7
candy	4	candy	6
chips	4	snack cakes	6
Poptarts	4	cereal	5
snack cakes	4	whole milk	5
chicken nuggets	3		
chocolate bar	3		
cookies	3		
pizza	3		
regular soda	3		

TABLE 6.4
*Foods that Girls and Boys (>50%) Included in the Pile of Foods
that Mainly Adults Eat*

Girls N = 6		Boys N = 9	
cooked carrots	6	cooked carrots	6
fish	6	steak	6
green beans	5	tossed salad	6
		fish	5
		vegetable soup	5

TABLE 6.5
*Foods that Girls and Boys (>50%) Included in the Pile of Foods
that Mainly Girls Eat*

Girls	N = 6	Boys	N = 9
tossed salad	4	tossed salad	5
vegetable soup	4		

TABLE 6.6
*Foods that Girls and Boys (>50%) Included in the Pile of Foods
that Mainly Boys Eat*

Girls	N = 6	Boys	N = 9
fish	4	steak	5

The children couldn't easily express reasons for their classifications. When asked why they had sorted the way they did, the children often said that they didn't know or they referred to preferences and observations, for example, that they had seen more boys eat steak or that boys go fishing. Girls were said to eat healthy, avoid fat, and worry about their weight. Analysis of gender based on the interview data showed that the children expressed connections between boys being active and needing more food and girls eating to enhance their appearance. Gender-based classifications may reflect the idea that meat and fish are male because they contain protein, which is necessary for building up muscles (Bourdieu 1984; Fiddes 1991), whereas vegetables are female because they are healthy and components of diets for women, who are expected to be thin (Bordo 1993; Lupton 1996).

Conclusion

In this chapter I've sketched the different steps in using pile sorting as a technique to get information on meanings of food among children. First, a decision about which foods to include has to be made. The number of cards, what items to include, and in which form (text or photograph) depend on the goal of the research and the participants. These choices ultimately influence the results. I decided to include several foods associated with school lunches because I conducted the study in a school setting and many of the children included such foods in their own lists. However, the children might have listed different foods and sorted the food cards differently in another environment.

The types of pile sorts used depends on the research questions. I first used an unconstrained pile sort because I was interested in children's own criteria for classifying foods. I also wanted to learn if adults' food and gender associations were apparent in children's food classifications. Therefore, I used two constrained pile sorts and asked children to categorize foods based on age and gender. I tabulated the data for frequencies (percentages) and applied cluster analysis. The results showed that although children's food classifications vary, most of them categorize foods based on food events, food groups, and preferences. When asked to group foods based on their own criteria, none included groups that referred to age and gender. So, if I hadn't included the two constrained sorts based on age and gender, based on the pile sorting data, I wouldn't have been able to conclude if the children associate some foods with children/adults or girls/boys.

The results of these two pile sorts reveal that some of the children had difficulties distinguishing girls' and boys' foods, but they all recognized children's foods. These results suggest that food may play a role in age differentiation among children, whereas gender is not expressed through types of food (although it might be expressed in other ways, such as quantities eaten). The children indicated that they eat certain foods because they are children (for example, sweets but no vegetables), whereas gender differences in eating (for example, women dieting and eating healthy) were mainly an adult issue. The results from the constrained pile sorts were used to support results obtained by other methods.

An advantage of using pile sorts is that they are easy to administer and meaningful within children's own frames of reference. Children are used to playing different games and doing different assignments in school. The active participation may facilitate data collection. If, in addition, children are asked to label the different groups and to give reasons for their groupings, more information is attained. When children are asked to sort cards into already labeled groups, that also needs to be taken into account in interpreting the results. However, pile sorting is a theoretical or noncontextualized task that is different from children's actual food-related behavior. This study has shown that pile sorting can be used successfully to elicit food-related meaning systems among children—especially when it is used in combination with other methods such as observation and interviewing.

QUESTIONS

1. What kind of information can you get by using pile sorting? Give examples of research questions.
2. What methods can you use to complement pile sorting?
3. What are the possible advantages or disadvantages of using constrained compared to unconstrained pile sorting?
4. What do you need to take into account when you plan to use pile sorting among children? Give examples of special considerations.
5. How can pile sort data be analyzed?

NOTES

1. This qualitative study of children, food, and gender was funded by the Academy of Finland and the graduate school of the University of Kentucky.

2. I used the "Harvard Food Frequency for children" (Thompson and Byers 1994) as the basis for the food frequency questionnaire. The questionnaire included 104 foods. Children were asked to cross out foods they never eat and then mark the others with five different colors in frequencies ranging from several times per day to one–three times per month.

3. PBJ = peanut butter and jelly.

Seven

Guttman Scaling: An Analysis of Matsigenka Men's Manufacturing Skills[1]

Introduction

Guttman scaling is a method for discovering whether a series of measures on a set of individuals (or groups) belong on a unidimensional continuum (McIver and Carmines 1981:40; Bernard 1994:292–297). For example, it's probably true that in many developing economies people acquire some possessions or attributes (for example, Western dress) before others (for example, secondary education). Still others (for example, motor vehicles) would come only after the first two have already been acquired. We would therefore expect anyone with a motor vehicle already to have a secondary education and wear Western dress.

Of course, there will be exceptions. But if most cases conform to this expectation, then an underlying dimension, call it "modernization," would account for the differences between individuals (Bernard 1994:296).

Matsigenka Skills

In the present example, I'm interested in whether "skill" is a single dimension for Matsigenka men of the Peruvian Amazon. On the one hand, we wouldn't be surprised to learn that some men are more skilled than others. On the other hand, there is no reason that the skills they possess should form a cumulative scale, such that a man with more skills than his neighbor will always possess all his neighbor's skills plus one or more additional skill, as implied by a unidimensional continuum.

On the face of it, it would seem just as likely that some men would master some skills and other men master others. For example, one might make excellent bows and arrows while another is a master house builder. Such differences in individual skills could become the basis for economic specialization and exchanges or, in an egalitarian society like the Matsigenka, we might expect that all men would share all the basic skills in order to be self-sufficient. If the possession of skills among Matsigenka men does reflect a single underlying dimension, therefore, it's a somewhat counterintuitive result calling for explanation.

In working up the data on 12 Matsigenka men's manufacturing skills for an ethnography, I began to suspect that the possession of skills might be **scalable** in the sense just described. By simple inspection, it was clear that some men have more skills than others, but is it also true that some skills are likely to be widely shared, while others represent more specialized skills? If that were true, then it might also be the case that "skill" is a dimension along which:

1. men can be distinguished from each other, that is, from more skilled to less skilled, and
2. skills can be distinguished from each other, that is, from more common to less common.

Scaling the Data

Before I say anything more about the Matsigenka or the kinds of men and skills included in this analysis, I will examine formally the raw data and the way I created **Guttman scales** from such data. I began by setting up a table in which 12 individuals (named here 1–12) were the rows and 23 skills were the columns.

By moving rows and columns mechanically, I came up with a raw data set that appeared to show that men's skills represented a scalable domain (Table 7.2). (When you have a large number of informants and items, it's better to let the Guttman scaling routine in **ANTHROPAC** do this column- and row-arranging for you, but with a small data set it's instructive to try and do the rearranging by hand just to get a feel for what's in the data.)

The 23 skills are listed in Table 7.1 and the distribution of those skills among the 12 Matsigenka men is shown in Table 7.2.

In this initial version of the scale we can see that the individuals closest to the top possess the most skills, and the skills closest to the left margin are those possessed by the most individuals.

Table 7.3 shows the results of running these data in ANTHROPAC's Guttman scaling program (Borgatti 1992). The program identifies "errors" in the data. In Guttman scaling, a person lower on the scale should not possess any skills not possessed by someone higher, and a skill farther to the right should not be possessed by anyone who does not possess all the skills to the left. To be more precise, an

TABLE 7.1
Matsigenka Men's Manufacturing Skills

1 *tsegontorinsi*, coded TS. Bird arrow (game birds)
2 *kapiro*, coded KA. Big game arrow (e.g., peccaries)
3 *pankotsi*, coded PA. House
4 *tivana*, coded TI. Twine
5 *tyonkarintsi*, coded TY. Blunt arrow (small birds)
6 *kurikii*, coded KU. Monkey arrow
7 *shintipoa*, coded SH. Balsa raft
8 *komarontsi*, coded KO. Oar
9 *iviri*, coded IV. Trap
10 *tsivogo*, coded TV. Cane box
11 *piamentsi*, coded PI. Bow
12 *tseoki*, coded TK. Net bag
13 *kishirintsi*, coded KI. Comb
14 *shiriti*, coded ST. Women's fishnet
15 *shimamentotsi*, coded SM. Fish arrow
16 *timasiamentotsi*, coded TM. Barbed arrow (small birds)
17 *konoritsa*, coded KN. Y-slingshot
18 *varakatsa*, coded VA. 3-string (bolo) slingshot
19 *patsikorintsi*, coded PK. Arrow (other-1)
20 *inchakii*, coded IN. Hardwood-tip arrow
21 *katsarorintsi*, coded KT. Arrow (other-2)
22 *kitsari*, coded KR. Men's fishnet
23 *pitotsi*, code PS. Canoe

TABLE 7.2
Skills Possessed by Individuals
["1" Indicates the Individual Possesses the Skill;
"0" Indicates He Does Not.]

	T S	K A	P A	T I	T Y	K U	S H	K O	I V	T V	P I	T K	K I	S T	S M	T M	K N	V A	P K	I N	K T	K R	P S
	1	2	3	4	5	6	7	8	9	10	11	12	13	14	15	16	17	18	19	20	21	22	23
1	1	1	1	1	1	1	1	1	1	1	1	1	1	1	1	1	1	1	1	1	1	1	0
2	1	1	1	1	1	1	1	1	1	1	1	1	1	1	1	1	1	1	1	1	1	0	0
3	1	1	1	1	1	1	1	1	1	1	1	1	1	1	1	1	0	1	1	1	1	1	0
4	1	1	1	1	1	1	1	1	1	1	1	1	1	1	1	1	1	1	1	1	0	0	0
5	1	1	1	1	1	1	1	1	1	1	1	1	1	1	1	1	0	1	1	1	0	0	0
6	1	1	1	1	1	1	1	1	1	1	1	1	1	1	0	1	0	0	0	0	0	0	0
7	1	1	1	1	1	1	1	1	1	0	1	0	0	0	1	1	1	0	0	0	0	0	0
8	1	1	1	1	1	1	1	1	1	1	1	1	1	0	0	0	0	0	0	0	0	0	0
9	1	1	1	1	1	0	0	0	0	1	1	1	0	1	0	0	0	1	0	0	0	1	0
10	1	1	1	1	1	1	1	1	1	0	0	1	0	0	0	0	1	0	0	0	0	0	0
11	1	1	1	1	0	1	1	1	1	1	1	0	0	0	0	0	0	0	0	0	0	0	0
12	1	1	1	1	1	1	1	1	1	1	0	0	0	0	0	0	0	0	0	0	0	0	1

individual with n skills should possess only the first n skills in the scale, no more or less.

For example, in Table 7.3 individuals 1, 2, and 4 show no errors. Individual 3 shows two errors. Possessing 21 skills, he should possess skill 16 but he does not (an **error of omission**). And he has skill number 22, which he should not (an **error of commission**). In Table 7.3, individual 12 has been moved by the program ahead of individual 11, because individual 12 has one more skill than does individual 11 (11 skills versus 10).

TABLE 7.3

First Guttman Scale

[A "−" Is an Error of Omission;

A "+" Is an Error of Commission]

	TS 1	KA 2	PA 3	TI 4	TY 5	KU 6	SH 7	KO 8	IV 9	TV 10	PI 11	TK 12	KI 13	ST 14	SM 15	TM 16	KN 17	VA 18	PK 19	IN 20	KT 21	KR 22	PS 23	Score
1	1	1	1	1	1	1	1	1	1	1	1	1	1	1	1	1	1	1	1	1	1	1		22
2	1	1	1	1	1	1	1	1	1	1	1	1	1	1	1	1	1	1	1	1	1			21
3	1	1	1	1	1	1	1	1	1	1	1	1	1	1	1	−	1	1	1	1	1	+		21
4	1	1	1	1	1	1	1	1	1	1	1	1	1	1	1	1	1	1	1	1	1			21
5	1	1	1	1	1	1	1	1	1	1	1	1	1	1	1	1	1	−	1	1	+			19
6	1	1	1	1	1	1	1	1	1	1	1	1	1	1	−	+								15
7	1	1	1	1	1	1	1	1	1	−	1	−	−	+	+	+								13
8	1	1	1	1	1	1	1	1	1	1	1	1	1											13
9	1	1	1	1	1	−	−	−	−	−	1	1	+		+			+			+			11
10	1	1	1	1	1	1	1	1	1	−	−	+				+								11
12	1	1	1	1	1	1	1	1	1	−												+		11
11	1	1	1	1	1	−	1	1	1	1	1	+												10

Total # of errors: 28; coefficient of reproducibility: 0.899

The degree to which data match the assumption of an underlying single dimension is measured by the **coefficient of reproducibility, CR**:

$$CR = 1 - (\#\text{errors}/\#\text{total responses})$$

where the numer of total responses is the number of cells in the table. In this case, $CR = 1 - (28/276)$, or 0.899. By convention, a Guttman scale analysis is considered to be significant evidence for an underlying single dimension if the coefficient of reproducibility is 0.90 or greater, so our result, by rounding to two decimals, is marginally significant.

Improving the Scale

The next stage in the analysis of the data is to ask if there are any obvious ways to improve the scale represented in Table 7.3. Two points immediately stand out. First, we note that all 12 men in the sample possess skills 1–4. Since there is no variation in possession of these skills, they add nothing to the scale analysis and can be removed.

The other immediate issue concerns skill number 23 (making a canoe). Only one individual in the sample possesses this skill, and he is far from being the most skilled man. This skill, then, appears to be an **outlier**—an oddity that may not belong on the dimension of skill we are attempting to analyze. Below, I will provide an ethnographic interpretation of the data that will place skills 1–4 and 23 in fuller perspective.

If we remove skills 1–4 and 23 and rerun the program, we get Table 7.4.

TABLE 7.4
First Revised Guttman Scale

	T	K	S	K	I	T	P	T	K	S	S	T	K	V	P	I	K	K	
	Y	U	H	O	V	V	I	K	I	T	M	M	N	A	K	N	T	R	
						1	1	1	1	1	1	1	1	1	1	2	2	2	
	5	6	7	8	9	0	1	2	3	4	5	6	7	8	9	0	1	2	Score
1	1	1	1	1	1	1	1	1	1	1	1	1	1	1	1	1	1	1	18
2	1	1	1	1	1	1	1	1	1	1	1	1	1	1	1	1	1		17
3	1	1	1	1	1	1	1	1	1	1	1	–	1	1	1	1	1	+	17
4	1	1	1	1	1	1	1	1	1	1	1	1	1	1	1	1	1		17
5	1	1	1	1	1	1	1	1	1	1	1	1	–	1	1	+			15
6	1	1	1	1	1	1	1	1	1	1	–	+							11
7	1	1	1	1	1	–	1	–	–	+	+	+							9
8	1	1	1	1	1	1	1	1	1										9
9	1	–	–	–	–	1	1	+		+			+				+		7
10	1	1	1	1	1	–	–	–				+							6
11	–	1	1	1	1	1	+												6
12	1	1	1	1	1	1													6

Total # of errors: 26; coefficient of reproducibility: 0.880.

By removing the first four skills and skill 23 we have reduced the total number of responses by 60 while removing just two errors, so the coefficient of reproducibility has actually decreased. We would have to say that these data now fail to meet the criterion of significance for Guttman scaling.

From a strictly mechanical point of view, we could try to reduce the number of errors simply by removing individuals or skills that produce a lot of errors. For example, the most error-producing individual is 9, with eight errors, and the most error-producing skills in the original data set are 12, 16, and 17 (three errors each). As an experiment, we could remove them to see what happens (Table 7.5).

TABLE 7.5
The Revised Gutman Scale
with Skills 12, 16, and 17, and Person 9 Removed

	T Y 5	K U 6	S H 7	K O 8	I V 9	T V 1 0	P I 1 1	K I 1 3	S T 1 4	S M 1 5	V A 1 8	P K 1 9	I N 2 0	K T 2 1	K R 2 2	Score
1	1	1	1	1	1	1	1	1	1	1	1	1	1	1	1	15
3	1	1	1	1	1	1	1	1	1	1	1	1	1	1	1	15
2	1	1	1	1	1	1	1	1	1	1	1	1	1	1	1	15
4	1	1	1	1	1	1	1	1	1	1	1	1	1	1	1	15
5	1	1	1	1	1	1	1	1	1	1	1	1	1			13
6	1	1	1	1	1	1	1	1	1							9
8	1	1	1	1	1	1	1	1								8
7	1	1	1	1	1	−	1		+							7
12	1	1	1	1	1	1	−									7
11	−	1	1	1	1	1	+									6
10	1	1	1	1	1											5

Total # of errors: 5; coefficient of reproducibility = 1−(5/165) = 0.970

As we can see, the second revision, in which error-prone cases were dropped, produced a major increase in the coefficient of reproducibility. It's now 0.970, well above the 0.90 convention. Now we must bring in ethnographic evidence to ask what the Guttman scale has taught us to this point and whether the simplifications of the data to produce the higher coefficients of reproducibility were justified.

Interpretation of the Scale

At the time of this research (1972), the Matsigenka were tropical forest forager-horticulturalists with no appreciable involvement in the market economy. Individual households lived separately and were largely self-sufficient, although extended family hamlets were also common (A. Johnson and O. Johnson 1988).

An extreme division of labor by sex meant that men depended either on themselves or their wives for the manufactured goods on which their livelihood depended, just as women depended on themselves and their husbands. If a man did not know how to make a given item of men's manufacture, for example a bow, he either had to do without or obtain it from another man. Possession of skills, therefore, was a matter of basic importance to a man and his family.

As we saw earlier, four of the skills in Table 7.1 are shared by all 12 men in the sample: bird arrow, big game arrow, house, and twine. The two arrows on this short list are among the three most important for hunting, the monkey arrow (skill 6) being the other.

Given their self-sufficiency and the likelihood that they will live in widely scattered individual homesteads, it is also meaningful that everyone knows how to build a house. And the twine referred to is a basic element of manufacture in traps, fishnets, and carrying bags—all basic to subsistence activities. Skill with twine can be generalized readily to making similar products (from other materials) used in bowstrings and in other useful items.

Although these four skills were removed in the Guttman scale analysis, they belong ethnographically to the category of widely shared skills, which we might say, somewhat arbitrarily, includes the first 12 skills, shared by from 9–12 individuals.

The removal of skill 23, making a canoe, is an opposite case. That only one man knows this skill is ethnographically significant: The study population occupies a montane forest zone where rivers are small and swift. Canoes in this setting, by contrast with the light and maneuverable balsa raft, are cumbersome and generally ineffective. Few men own canoes and even fewer know how to make them. Removing this skill from the Guttman scale analysis, therefore, is reasonable on the grounds that it is an extraordinary one.

The reduction of the data set to produce Table 7.4, therefore, appears justified ethnographically, though it produces a worse scaling of Matsigenka men's manufacturing skills than just leaving the original data alone.

The further steps we took to produce Table 7.5, however, are more problematic. True, the removal of individual 9 does make a kind of sense: This individual is something of a loser, a whiner and a stingy man who is the frequent butt of others' jokes. That his repertoire of skills is odd may well reflect his marginal position: He lacks such key skills as making balsa raft (7) and oar (8), while possessing the unusual skill of making a bolo slingshot (18). We would not want to take this too far, though: two of his errors of commission are for men's (22) and women's (14) fishnets, which are valued and useful skills.

It does not make good ethnographic sense, however, to remove the "error-prone" skills of making net bag (12), Y-slingshot (17), and bolo slingshot (18), even if doing so raises the coefficient of reproducibility. These are skills that have a moderate value, since they are used frequently: net bags serve a variety of important functions, and some men carry slingshots with them everywhere, hoping for a chance encounter with some small prey. There is no ethnographic reason to consider them any less an important part of the male package of skills than say, cane boxes (10) or combs (13).

Because, with eight errors, individual 9 accounts for 30% of the errors in Table 7.4, I think it makes sense to remove him from the analysis. This amounts to saying that his range of skills does not reflect the pattern common to other Matsigenka men, which is, in fact, my conclusion from the ethnographic evidence. Removing skills 1, 2, 3, 4, and 23, along with individual 9 produces Table 7.6, which I consider to be the best attainable Guttman scale consistent with ethnographic evidence.

TABLE 7.6

The Best Revised Guttman Scale Consistent with the Ethnographic Evidence

	T Y 5	K U 6	S H 7	K O 8	I V 9	T V 1 0	P I 1 1	T K 1 2	K I 1 3	S T 1 4	S M 1 5	T M 1 6	K N 1 7	V A 1 8	P K 1 9	I N 2 0	K T 2 1	K R 2 2	Score
1	1	1	1	1	1	1	1	1	1	1	1	1	1	1	1	1	1	1	18
2	1	1	1	1	1	1	1	1	1	1	1	1	1	1	1	1	1		17
3	1	1	1	1	1	1	1	1	1	1	1	−	1	1	1	1	1	+	17
4	1	1	1	1	1	1	1	1	1	1	1	1	1	1	1	1	1		17
5	1	1	1	1	1	1	1	1	1	1	1	1	−	1	1	+			15
6	1	1	1	1	1	1	1	1	1	−	+								11
7	1	1	1	1	1	−	1	−	−	+	+	+							9
8	1	1	1	1	1	1	1	1	1										9
10	1	1	1	1	1	−	−	+					+						7
11	−	1	1	1	1	1	+												6
12	1	1	1	1	1	1													6

Total # of errors: 18; coefficient of reproducibility: 0.909

Further ethnographic information can help us understand why Matsigenka men's skills constitute a significant Guttman scale. In Table 7.3 there is a natural break between individuals 5 (with 19 skills) and 6 (with 15 skills). If we look at the two groups formed by this division, an interesting pattern emerges: The most-skilled men (1–5) are generally "loners," in the sense of being highly individualistic men who, with their families, choose to live apart from other groups either permanently or for extended periods of time.

By contrast, most of the men in the less-skilled category (6–12) live in extended family hamlets. This means that, for example, individuals 10 and 12, who do not know how to make bows (skill 11 in Table 7.2), can get their bows from other individuals, like 6 or 8. Men who would live autonomously must acquire more skills in order to be able to do without the reciprocity of the hamlet. In this sense, the underlying dimension might best be labeled not "skill," but "autonomy."

There are several skills, however, that none of the men in the less-skilled group have, such as knowing how to make three kinds of arrows (19–21). These I would see as secondary skills, elaborations on the main arrow types that nearly everyone knows how to manufacture. They might best be thought of as idiosyncratic, or micro-local, variations in material culture resulting from individual inventiveness and style. They may be the stuff of which cultural selection is made (Boyd and Richerson 1985), but they probably do not make a very big difference in the daily lives of the men or their families. If the underlying dimension is "autonomy," then we would say that autonomous men are also likely to be idiosyncratic, or perhaps experimental, in the unusual skills they acquire.

In sum, the Guttman scale analysis of Matsigenka men's skills indicates that there is a single dimension along which men can be arrayed according to the skills they possess. All men possess four basic skills, and most possess another eight skills. Men who possess more skills tend to possess all the skills the less skilled men possess plus some additional ones. The most skilled men tend to be the most individualistic or self-sufficient. Either they have additional skills because they do not plan to trade for manufactures with other men, or because they also are the kind of people who like to experiment with or acquire unusual skills that most men do not master.

QUESTIONS

1. What does it mean to call "modernization" a unidimensional continuum?
2. Why is it counterintuitive that Matsigneka men's skills should fit a Guttman scale?
3. Why is it acceptable to remove skills 1–4 from the analysis?
4. What value is ethnographic evidence in deciding which table best represents the Matsigenka case?
5. In what sense could the dimension underlying the Guttman scale be called "autonomy" rather than "skill"?

NOTE

1. This article appeared in *CAM*, the *Cultural Anthropology Methods Journal*, Vol. 7(3), October 1995.

ROBERT C. HARMAN ■

Eight

Triad Questionnaires: Old Age in Karen and Maya Cultures[1]

Systematic research on the lives of older persons is a relatively recent phenomenon in ethnography. It dates back to the 1970s, and the work of Christine Fry (1980, 1981) is a landmark in the field. Valerie Fennell (1994), another pioneer contributor to the ethnography of the aged, has written about the ways that residents of a southern town in the United States think about the characteristics of old age. Fennell (1994:158) found that her subjects focused primarily on physical appearance. Her female subjects, in particular, worried about losing their youthful appearance, while men were more anxious about declining abilities to perform (pp. 162–169).

In classes I've taught on "culture and aging," each year approximately 20 students would each interview several different informants, mostly white Americans, in the area of Long Beach, California. There was considerable agreement among their informants about the characteristics of old age. The findings were quite similar to those described for the southern town, and my students, like Fennell (1994:162), found that younger informants were more negative about the conditions of advanced age than were the aged themselves. I questioned whether non-Western people had similar age-based discrepancies in their conceptualizations of old age. My concerns about cross-cultural perspectives on old age developed into a research project on conceptualizations of the aged in a tribal society of southeast Asia.

The research findings reported in this chapter represent a period of fieldwork in northern Thailand from October 1993 to January 1994. Data were obtained and analyzed through **formal ethnographic methods** that had been carefully tested for **validity** and **reliability** (see Weller and Romney 1988:69–85; Bernard 1994:38–39). The methodology combines qualitative and quantitative approaches, using systematic data collection.

I begin the chapter with a description of the Karen hilltribe people in northern Thailand, and my entrée into their society. In the next section, I address the systematic collecting and analysis of data on Karen old age. I will describe the ethnographic methods used in the Karen community, specifically the freelisting procedure and the use of triad questionnaires to obtain rank order data. Then I will analyze the findings. I conclude with a discussion that evaluates the methods I described and offer suggestions for future research.

The Karen People

The Karen are a hilltribe people of northern Thailand and Burma. Karen roots are in Burma, but several hundred thousand Karen have migrated eastward to Thailand, usually without any formalized, legal rights to cross the border. Those remaining in Burma, the vast majority of Karen, live under harsh sociopolitical conditions and suffer extreme human rights abuses.

In Thailand, the Karen do not actually comprise a single sociopolitical entity. Two large language groups are represented: Sgaw Karen and Pwo Karen. Most speakers of both languages live in autonomous villages in western and northern Thailand (Renard 1980:11). My research project was conducted with the Sgaw Karen.

Karen acculturation experiences with Thai people of the area vary considerably. Most Sgaw Karen are now Christian, having been converted during a period spanning over 150 years of contact with Western Baptist missionaries. Some of the Karen continue to live quite far from Thai cities and have minimal contact with non-Karen. They rely primarily on rice cultivation and a variety of other crops for subsistence, although yields have declined considerably in recent years. In some of the more isolated villages, particularly among the Pwo Karen, Buddhism, rather than Baptist Christianity, is the dominant religion.

The population of villages nearer the Thai cities tends to be predominantly Christian. Many Christian Karen, including a number of adult children of my village informants, now reside in urban areas such as Chiang Mai, the largest city of northern Thailand.

I arrived in Chiang Mai in October 1993, and by the end of the month I was in touch with the Karen. In this early contact stage some things went rather well, while others didn't go at all according to plan. On arriving in Chiang Mai, I immediately began to seek interpreters. I was looking for assistants to conduct field interviews, and I needed translators to transcribe taped interview data.

As a visiting professor at Chiang Mai University I had the benefit of an academic identification, in a country where teachers are highly respected and trusted, and I had a university telephone number for applicants to call. The chairperson of the sociology and anthropology department was supportive, and several of the faculty members, as well as neighboring Hilltribe Institute personnel, were very helpful. Even with those advantages, however, communication sometimes went awry.

A very accommodating faculty member, for example, befriended me and posted notices announcing my search for assistants. He put up announcements in the Thai language addressed to students passing through the Faculty of Social Sciences building. Days passed without any inquiries, and the days became weeks. I was very disappointed and surprised that nobody showed interest in the position for which my salary offer was competitive. I had no clue that an intracultural communication problem existed until one morning another faculty member told me that he had read a notice posted in the building that indicated that I was looking for assistance on an AIDS project. At that time, nobody in Thailand wanted to be associated with AIDS. It wasn't surprising that the ad went unanswered until it was changed to reflect the fact that the project actually focused on the topic of aging.

Shortly after that, a female student interviewed for and took the position of translator and transcriber of texts collected in the field; she was competent in Karen, English, and Thai. She couldn't accompany me to the field sites because of her class schedule and gender constraints, but male interpreters contacted through other sources became available for that task.

Through good fortune, I made another important initial contact with an American Baptist missionary couple who had served the Karen for over 20 years. They introduced me to S, a 40-year-old Karen mission teacher and lay preacher, who was quite fluent in English. S was widely known and well liked by Karen in the region. His good rapport with the people made it possible for me to get started with the systematic collection of a substantial amount of data on old age.

S knew how to drive and often had access to a pickup truck at the Baptist mission compound in Chiang Mai, not far from my residence. On days when the pickup was unavailable, we took a bus or a *silaw*, a modified pickup-for-hire, along the highway route between Chiang Mai and the city of Chiang Rai, approximately 100 miles to the north. The nearest of the three villages we researched was located 25 miles north of Chiang Mai, and the other villages were located within 3 miles to the north.

Karen Data Collection and Analysis

Freelistings

With the assistance of S, and later with other interpreters, I asked informants to **freelist** in response to the question, "What are the characteristics of the old Karen people?" The initial responses (in Karen) were actually too diverse to establish the existence of a single **cultural domain**. Some informants focused on pleasures, some on work, others on disabilities and illness, and yet others on worries of the aged.

At the suggestion of Kate Bond, an American anthropologist conducting research in Chiang Mai, I abandoned the original stimulus question on "characteristics" of the aged in favor of seeking freelistings on four narrower domains of the aged: pleasures, work, sufferings, and worries.

I went on to collect freelistings from 20 informants for each of the four domains of the aged Karen. For the pleasures domain we asked, "*pga sa' pga 'a-ta samu me m-nuleh?*" (What are the pleasures of the elder Karen?). Freelistings from individual respondents ranged in length from as many as 15 items provided by one informant to a low of 3 items. Each word or phrase in response to the stimulus question was considered an item of the domain, "pleasures of the aged."

Freelistings of each informant were entered into the ANTHROPAC editor (Borgatti 1992). The "pleasures" file was then brought into ANTHROPAC, which provided an aggregate output of 144 items mentioned by the informants. Items appeared in an order of those mentioned by the highest percentage of informants down to those of lowest frequency. At the high end, 8 informants (40%) identified "children and grandchildren being healthy," while at the low end are items listed by only one informant. The aggregated responses of the 20 informants are presented in Table 8.1, with the actual number and the percentage of respondents listing each item. Items mentioned by only one informant are omitted from the table.

The majority of the response items in Table 8.1 relate to the elders' children and grandchildren. Thirty–five percent listed "the children and grandchildren (from another village) making a visit" to the house of the elder, sometimes coming to stay for several days or longer. Thirty percent identified the "health" of the elder. The same number of respondents listed a group activity "gathering and hunting," "the children and grandchildren being correct," and "the children and grandchildren being united." Twenty–five percent of informants for the domain listed "the children and grandchildren being happy." Twenty percent listed "going to visit the children (in another community)," "having something to do," "people coming and conversing with them," and "telling stories and legends." Fifteen percent of the informants indicated that it brings pleasure to the elders when their "children are holding a good job." Ten percent said that "staying home" provides pleasure for the aged.

Karen informant responses to the question, "*pga sa' pga 'a-taphi tama me m-nuleh?*" (What kinds of work are done by the elders?) are presented in Table 8.2. The freelisting responses on the work domain cover a broad range, and a large majority of the 20 informants mentioned several items in the top half of the table; 6 items were listed by over 50% of the informants. The highest number of items listed by an informant was 12, and the lowest was 4. "Weaving bamboo objects" was listed by 80% of the informants, and "doing tasks at home" by 75%. Sixty percent said that "cooking," "raising pigs and chickens," and "childcare" are work activities of the elderly Karen. Fifty–five percent identified "weaving with thread." Forty percent of the informants listed "taking care of the house," and 30% listed "going fishing." Twenty–five percent placed on their lists "looking after grazing water buffalo" and "working in the yard." Twenty percent said the aged spend time "collecting wild food," while 15% named "looking after grandchildren" and "trapping animals."

TABLE 8.1

Freelisting Responses to the Question,
"What Gives Pleasure to the Elder Karens?"
n = 20 informants

Item—English gloss (and Karen response)	Frequency	Percent
children and grandchildren are healthy (*pho li ochu okhle*)	8	40
children and grandch make extended visit (*pho li heh ha' 'o 'aw*)	7	35
being healthy (*ochu okhle*)	6	30
gathering and hunting (*ha' xu 'aw kha' aw ta*)	6	30
children and grandchildren being correct (*pho li 'a-nalo*)	6	30
children and grandchildren being united (*pho 'ali oxu 'ophaw*)	6	30
children and grandchildren being happy (*pho li su khu sa khy*)	5	25
going to visit the children (*o s-kaw 'a-pho*)	4	20
have something to do (*pheh 'atama 'o*)	4	20
people coming and conversing (*pga heh k-tota daw 'aw*)	4	20
telling stories and legends (*teh ke ta luhkhi luh pluh*)	4	20
children are holding a good job (*'apho neba tama luh 'age*)	3	15
staying home (*'o luh hi*)	2	10

TABLE 8.2

Freelisting Responses to the Question,
"What Kinds of Work Are Done by the Elder Karen?"
n = 20 informants

Item—English gloss (and Karen response)	Frequency	Percent
weaving bamboo artifacts (*the ta*)	16	80
doing tasks at home (*ma ta luh duh pheh 'ama se*)	15	75
cooking (*phaw 'aw ta*)	12	60
raising pigs and chickens (*bu thaw bu chaw*)	12	60
childcare (*kwa pho sa*)	12	60
weaving with thread (*tha tha*)	11	55
taking care of the house (*kwa thweh duh*)	8	40
going fishing (*xu 'aw nya*)	6	30
looking after grazing water buffalo (*kwa p-na*)	5	25
working in the yard (*mata luh k-ruh pu*)	5	25
collecting wild food (*xu 'aw ta*)	4	20
looking after grandchildren (*kwa 'ali*)	3	15
trapping animals (*cheh ta pho xa*)	3	15

The third Karen old age domain is that of "sufferings." We asked, *"pga sa' pga ba tu wehne me m-nuleh?"* (What are the sufferings of the elders?) Slightly over 100 different items comprise the domain. The top 13 are listed in Table 8.3. All the items are directly related to poor health.

TABLE 8.3
Freelisting Responses to the Question,
"What Makes the Elder Karen Suffer?"
n = 20 informants

Item—English gloss (and Karen response)	Frequency	Percent
pain in the joints (*xi k-me' cha*)	17	85
being hard of hearing (*na t-'uh*)	11	55
having dim eyesight (*meh yu'*)	10	50
middle-of-the-back pains (*yaw de cha*)	10	50
losing teeth (*meh paw*)	8	40
aching body (*t-kiy t-ka*)	7	35
irritability (*sa' 'ene*)	6	30
insomnia (*mi t-ne ba'*)	6	30
tiring easily (*law bgi' nyaw*)	5	25
lacking appetite (*ta t-wi ba'*)	4	20
dizziness (*meh khi su*)	3	15
urinary problem (*chi tacha*)	3	15
mental illness (*kuh nuh to cha*)	2	10

Eighty–five percent of the informants said that "pain in the joints" is something that is suffered by the aged. Fifty–five percent indicated "being hard of hearing." Fifty percent listed "having dim eyesight" and "middle-of-the-back pains." Forty percent said that the aged Karen are concerned about "losing teeth," and 35% listed an "aching body." Thirty percent said the aged are characterized by "irritability" and 30 percent also listed "insomnia." Twenty–five percent said that an affliction of the aged is "tiring easily." Twenty percent mentioned the elders "lacking appetite." Fifteen percent said that "dizziness" and "urinary problem" are sufferings of the aged. Ten percent listed "mental illness."

Table 8.4 shows the freelisting responses to our question, *"pga sa' pga 'a-ta bayo babaw me m-nuleh?"* (What are the worries of the elders?). Sixty–five percent of the informants mentioned that elders worry about their "health." Sixty–five percent also had on their lists a preoccupation of the elderly about "lacking energy." Fifty–five percent listed a general "concern for children and grandchildren." Thirty–five percent listed a worry about having "insufficient things," and 30% indicated that the aged worry that their "children and grandchildren will become useless." Another 25% of the informants indicated that the aged are worried about "affording children's and grandchildren's education" and 25% suggested that the aged worry about "children and grandchildren not caring for them." Twenty percent said that the aged are concerned that their "children will quarrel with each other." Fifteen percent of informants listed as worries of the aged "wanting to die," "children and grandchildren abandoning traditions," "insufficient inheritance for children" and "having to maintain themselves." Ten percent of the informants said that the aged are preoccupied with "having to work with much difficulty," "fear of dying," "children's health," and "having a severely difficult life."

TABLE 8.4

Freelisting Responses to
"What Are the Worries of the Old Karen?"
n = 20 informants

Item—English gloss (and Karen response)	Frequency	Percent
health (*ochu 'okle*)	13	65
lacking energy (*leh ta t-ke luh ba'*)	13	65
concern for children and grandchildren (*'a-pho 'a-li 'a-gaw*)	11	55
insufficient things (*ta t-luh t-pgeh ba'*)	7	35
children and grandchildren will become useless (*a-pho a-li ha' gaw*)	6	30
affording children's and grchildren's education (*chaw thweh pholi 'atamalo*)	5	25
children and grchildren not caring for them (*pho li kwa thweh 'aw sga*)	5	25
children will quarrel with each other (*a-pho 'elaw 'a-sa'*)	4	20
wanting to die (*'ehdaw si*)	3	15
children and grchildren abandoning traditions (*pho li t-hi' xa' 'alu 'a-laba'*)	3	15
insufficient inheritance for children (*'-ata t'o naw t-mi luh 'a-pho a-gawba'*)	3	15
having to maintain themselves (*'a-ta phi' 'aw ma 'aw*)	3	15
having to work with much difficulty (*ba phi' 'aw ma' 'aw*)	2	10
fear of dying (*'a-k-si*)	2	10
childrens' health (*pho 'ochu 'okle*)	2	10
having a severely difficult life (*ta 'omu na'*)	2	10

Table 8.4 has 16 items listed whereas Tables 8.1, 8.2, and 8.3 each had 13 items. The reason for the difference has to do with the next step of the project, which was the administration of **triad** questionnaires. This was carried out first with the top 16 items of the "worries" domain. Because using 16 proved too cumbersome, I administered triad questionnaires for only the top 13 items of the other three domains.

I had ANTHROPAC construct the triad questionnaires. One option for constructing the triad questionnaire was to construct a complete triad design that would have each item appear with all other items in every possible combination for sets of three (Weller and Romney 1988:32). I did this first with the 16 items, but the resulting questionnaire was unmanageably long. Even with 13, it was too extensive:

The **complete triad design** for a 13-item questionnaire consists of 286 triads. Informants would likely find the length of such a questionnaire to be onerous as it is approximately ten pages long.

I used a **lambda-2 design**, which was carefully tested by Burton and Nerlove (1976), instead of a complete triad design. In a lambda-2 design, each item is paired only twice with each of the other items in the triad questionnaire (Weller and Romney 1988:49–55). Using the lambda-2 design reduces the length of the triad questionnaire considerably.

My objective was to get a ranking of the importance of items in each of the four domains of the aged Karen. I wanted to have informants **rank order** the Karen old age items that pertain to each domain. I used triads because those who are illiterate, the vast majority of my informants, would find the ranking task more manageable with 3 items at a time, rather than 13, to keep memorized. Triads had been used previously for that purpose (Weller and Romney 1988:31).

Four separate Karen triad questionnaire sets were constructed; one for each of the old age domains. Due to space considerations, I will describe the findings from the triad questionnaire technique for only two of the four domains—those of the "pleasures" triad questionnaire and the "work" triad questionnaire. (I'll address the "sufferings" and "worries" triad questionnaires in another publication.)

The "pleasures" triad questionnaire was prepared with the 13 freelist items that had been identified by the largest number of informants (Table 8.1). I made an **ASCII file** of those items and ANTHROPAC made the triad questionnaires, using a lambda-2 design (Borgatti 1992). Each questionnaire in this phase was designated KHAP, an abbreviation for Karen pleasure or happiness, and had the triad items on each questionnaire appear in a unique order as randomized by ANTHROPAC. When each item is paired twice with all the other 12 items, the total number of triads on the questionnaire form is 52. The Karen KHAP triad questionnaire consisted of two pages. Sample size for the pleasures questionnaire was 60.

Interpreters were instructed to inquire of the informants, "Which of the three items brings the most pleasure to the old people?" After the first choice was established, a follow-up question was asked, "Which of the two remaining items brings the most pleasure to the old people?" The item named ranked second. The unnamed item in the triad ranked third and last.

The ranking of the 13 items that comprise the domain of "pleasures" is found in Table 8.5. The triad questionnaire results show that, according to the 60 Karen informants, what gives the most pleasure to the aged Karen is to have their "children and grandchildren being united." That reflects a core value of Karen culture, which is to establish and maintain harmonious relations among relatives. A close second in the ranking is "children and grandchildren being healthy." That concern for the well-being of succeeding generations is ranked higher than the elder's own "health," which is the third item. The next item in the rank order is the happiness brought by the "children and grandchildren being correct." That concern has been a strong theme of the Baptist church, and most of my Karen informants are Baptists. Next, the aged Karen are believed to be quite pleased about their "children holding a good job." The Karen, especially those living near Chiang Mai city, are relying more and more on salaried employment as farm production declines and their needs for goods from outside rises (Phothiart 1989). At the time of my field research, a severe drought, which for several years had adversely affected farming in northern Thailand, increased the young adults' desires for good jobs.

TABLE 8. 5

Results of Triad Questionnaire Rankings of the
Pleasures of the Aged Karen

Scores represent the totals from separately scoring each protocol and assigning a value of 3 to the item ranked highest in each triad, 2 to the second-highest-ranked item, and 1 to the item ranked lowest for contributing to the pleasure of the aged.

Item	Rank	Score
children and grandchildren being united	1	1,967
children and grandchildren being healthy	2	1,917
health (of the elder)	3	1,806
children and grandchildren being correct	4	1,714
children holding a good job	5	1,704
children and grandchildren making a visit	6	1,555
children and grandchildren being happy	7	1,362
going to visit children	8	1,237
gathering and hunting	9	1,198
people coming and conversing with them	10	1,161
having something to do	11	1,082
telling stories and legends	12	1,077
staying home	13	922

The next highest item in the rank ordering of pleasures of the old Karen is "children and grandchildren making a visit" from outside the village. Following that is "children and grandchildren being happy." The next item concerns visits once again, in this case the elder "going to visit the children." It is customary among elderly Karen to make extended visits of weeks or longer to children residing in other villages. Many of the elders spend a few weeks at the home of one child, and then move on to spend time at the home of another child. Older Karen also enjoy festive outings where they carry out organized group "gathering and hunting." Elder Karen enjoy "people coming and conversing with them." This particular item, unlike most of the others, does not specify that the interaction is with relatives. Ranking somewhat lower, but still important to the aged Karen, is "having something to do." A 70-year-old woman who, contrary to the wishes of her son, continued to spend several hours a day on household tasks, told me that to live without work is not really being alive. The next item in rank is "telling stories and legends." Of the 13 items, the one that ranks a distant last is "staying home."

After the rank order data were collected and the first, second, and third choice frequencies tabulated, the next step was to systematically score the choices by assigning three points for every first place count, two points for second place, and one point for third place. The highest possible score for a pleasure item when there are a total of 13 items in a lambda-2 triad questionnaire design, with three points allocated for each highest selection in a triad, is 2,260. The lowest possible score, which could occur if any item were chosen last in every triad in which it appears is 720. Table 8.5 shows that no item reached either extreme, but some came close. The top-ranked item, "children and grandchildren being united," with a total of 1,967 was selected as first choice by more than 50% of the informants for every triad in which it appeared. It was a third and lowest choice in only 44 of 720 triad choices made by the 60 informants. At the other extreme, "staying home," wasn't considered by informants to have a great deal of appeal to the elders. It received only 44 (of 720) first-place selections and well over 50% of third-place selections by the 60 informants. Remember, every triad gets counted three times: for first, second, and third place choices.

The procedures for the "work" domain, abbreviated KWORK, triad questionnaires were exactly like those for the pleasures set of questionnaires. Sixty informants responded to the KWORK questionnaire. Informants for the "work" questionnaire were instructed to pick from each triad the work that is most prominent in the lives of the old people. The resulting rankings are found in Table 8.6.

The most prominent work activity of the elderly Karen is "looking after grandchildren." It is not as dominant as the highest-ranked item of the happiness domain and, indeed, the work items ranking shows that aside from the very low score of the bottom item, "trapping animals," work items are more closely clustered. The second-ranked item, "weaving with thread," is not far behind the first item. The third item again involves "childcare," and it differs from the top-ranked item in that it is not limited to the elder's own grandchildren. The fourth-ranked item is "taking care of the house." When younger members of the household are away at work, school, and elsewhere the elder household members often stay at home alone. The next-highest-ranked item is "doing tasks at home." Able elders can be found carrying out numerous light tasks in the vicinity of the house. Next in rank is "weaving bamboo objects." Elders spend many hours a day making a variety of bamboo objects. The older women continue "cooking" as long as they are able to do that, and they often work in the kitchen with younger female members of the household. The next-highest-ranked work item of the elders, according to informants who worked on the triad questionnaire, is "looking after grazing water buffalo," and that is followed by "going fishing." The next item in the rank order is "raising pigs and chickens." The next-highest-ranked item is "collecting wild food." "Working in the yard" is ranked 12th. As mentioned previously, "trapping animals" is in a distant last place.

TABLE 8.6

Results of Triad Questionnaire Rankings of the
Work of the Aged Karen

Scores represent the totals from separately scoring each protocol and assigning a value of 3 to the item ranked highest in each triad, 2 to the second-highest-ranked item and 1 to the item ranked lowest for work participation of the aged.

Item	Rank	Score
looking after grandchildren	1	1,797
weaving with thread	2	1,766
childcare	3	1,658
taking care of the house	4	1,653
doing tasks at home	5	1,488
weaving bamboo objects	6	1,452
cooking	7	1,443
looking after grazing water buffalo	8	1,368
going fishing	9	1,343
raising pigs and chickens	10	1,326
collecting wild food	11	1,285
working in the yard	12	1,157
trapping animals	13	950

Procedures for the Karen "sufferings" and "worries" domains were the same as those for "happiness" and "work." Sixty informants responded to the sufferings triad questionnaire, and 48 informants to the worries triad questionnaire. Since the "worries" triad questionnaire was a page longer than the other three questionnaires, it took longer to administer, and we ran out of time before we could get 60 respondents. In all, 226 Karen adults responded to the four triad questionnaires. The results of eliciting and ordering the data, using systematic data collection techniques, provide some understanding of what it means to be aged in Karen society.

Summary and Analysis

Analysis of the data begins with the considerable amount of concern for family that informants ascribe to Karen elders (Tables 8.1–8.4). Children and grandchildren occupy a prominent position among the freelisted items pertaining to "pleasures" (Table 8.1). Their presence in the "worries" domain is likewise notable (Table 8.4). In Table 8.1, 8 of the 13 most frequent items specify children and grandchildren. In Table 8.4, 9 of the 16 items (8 of the top 13) do so. Some of the worries are clearly the opposite of the pleasures; for example, worrying that "children will quarrel with each other" as opposed to the pleasure brought from "children being united."

Table 8.2, on the kinds of work done by Karen elders, shows more agreement among informants, especially in the top half of the table, than for the other Karen aged domains. Eighty percent of the informants freelisted "weaving bamboo objects," and 75% listed "doing tasks at home." Over 50% of the informants also listed "cooking," "raising pigs and chickens," "childcare," and "weaving with thread." All of those are carried out inside or near the home.

In Table 8.3, the majority of informants listed as sufferings "pain in the joints," "being hard of hearing," "having dim vision," and "middle-of-the-back pains." Pain in the joints, which one interpreter unequivocally stated is arthritis, was listed by 85% of the informants. Pain in the joints may be a major complaint of older persons in all societies.

Tables 8.5 and 8.6 contain the same items presented earlier in Tables 8.1 and 8.2 on conceptualizations of aged Karen pleasures and work. In Tables 8.5 and 8.6, however, those items have been subjected to another level of testing. Those triad questionnaire results inform us of Karen informants' rankings of the most prominent Karen pleasures and work items in the lives of the aged. The order of items in Tables 8.1–8.4 is established by frequency counts during freelisting. One might think that items mentioned most frequently in freelisting will also rank highest in triad questionnaire results. That is clearly not the case, nor should it be. The order of items in Tables 8.5 and 8.6 is a refined measure of exactly how triad question-naires informants rank the items when they are forced to choose which ones con-tribute more to the domain tested.

The triad questionnaire rankings add to our knowledge about the lives of the aged Karen. The Karen ranking of pleasures (Table 8.5) shows that nearly all of the highest-ranked pleasures are associated with children and grandchildren. Seven of the top eight items involve children and grandchildren. The Karen clearly have a high degree of positive concern for their lineal descendants.

The top-ranked work item is "caring for grandchildren" (Table 8.6). Work activities that center on the home are the higher-ranked ones, while subsistence activities that take the elder away from home are at the bottom.

Discussion

Freelisting elicited the basic terms and phrases of advanced age concerns in the Karen culture. Freelisting, by itself, captures much of what it means to be a Karen hilltribe elder. The informants, 20 each for pleasures, work, suffering, and worries, are experts on those domains because they are Karen hilltribe people themselves, having been born into Karen society and enculturated as Karen. There can be no better source for knowledge about the Karen characteristics of advanced age.

The meanings of advanced age for the Karen are not exactly the same for everyone. If they were, each item would represent the views of all informants. Since 85% for "pain in the joints" is the closest the informants came to unanimity, complete homogeneity of knowledge about advanced age is lacking among the Karen. There is relatively high agreement, however, with a substantial number of items in the four domains listed by over 50% of the informants.

Systematic data collection findings are influenced by implicit cultural values and social institutions that are not being measured. Karen freelisting and triad questionnaire results quite clearly show that the aged Karen are intensely concerned about relationships. They live in a world where the major pleasures derive from satisfactory relations with kin and fellow villagers. Aged mainstream Americans, in contrast, may operate in a context of individualism, which is associated with independence and self-reliance (Kaufman 1986:167). The Karen "pleasures" freelisting doesn't mention anything remotely related to independence and self-reliance. Differences between aged Karen and aged Americans is, perhaps, even more obvious when considering the domain of work (Table 8.2). Most of the aged Karen work items are not even available options for Americans. How many American elders weave bamboo objects?

The infirmities that are listed under "sufferings" provide some insight into what the aged Karen endure in the Thai countryside. Some of the same afflictions are, of course, familiar to older Americans also, but most of the Karen items are apt to be replaced by other concerns on an aggregate freelisting of North American sufferings. Social and cultural differences promote different concerns.

In looking at Karen conceptualizations compared to those of Americans, many other differences stand out. The Karen have positive cultural images of the aged. The Karen do not dwell upon the physical appearance of the aged. And elderly Karen are well integrated with other age categories of their society.

Beyond the Karen freelistings, the triad questionnaire rankings add further to our knowledge about the lives of aged Karen. They tell us what Karen informants consider the highest to the lowest contributing items for pleasures, work, sufferings and worries. Family involvement, especially prominent in the "pleasures" domain is of paramount importance to the aged Karen.

Their helpfulness notwithstanding, the triad questionnaire interviews were difficult for my subjects. Most Karen informants complained that working with the three 13-item triad questionnaires was too laborious. Their opinion of the 16-item worries questionnaire was even more negative. One answer to this problem is to use fewer items and a shorter questionnaire. The drawback to having a triad questionnaire with fewer items (than 13, in this case) is that a substantial amount of knowledge about the domain gets omitted. Besides, in addition to struggling with large numbers of triads, the illiterate informants had difficulty with the instructions on what they were supposed to do to begin with. Most informants had no formal education, and they were unaccustomed to the kind of concentration required of a triad test.

When I return to Thailand, I may use a pair comparison method instead of triads for future ranking tasks with the Karen. In pair comparisons, only two items are opposed. I have had previous experience using the pair comparison technique, with a literate population on an unrelated ranking topic, and I got satisfactory results (Harman and Briggs 1991).

In any case, I am planning to conduct research with the Karen to obtain **similarity data** through the use of pair comparisons or triad questionnaires. If I use triad questionnaires, they will look the same as they did for the rankings research, but the informants will be instructed to indicate which item of the triad is most different from the other two rather than to rank the items. I may use a lambda-1 design to get a shorter questionnaire, although that would involve a trade-off, sacrificing some reliability and validity for a more user-friendly instrument.

As I consider alternative methods, I am leaning toward a pair comparison similarity measure. Instructions should be easy for informants to comprehend. Subjects rate pairs of items for similarity on a three-point scale (Weller and Romney 1988: 64–65; Brazill et al. 1995:362). From the responses, a similarity matrix or table in which each cell displays the degree of similarity between two cases (see Table 14.3 in Clark et al., this volume) can be constructed just as is done with triad data.

Another technique I'm considering for future research on characteristics of the Karen aged is the **pile sort**. Some cultural domains lend themselves well to the use of pile sort cards (see Roos, this volume). I have used pile sort cards with Maya subjects, including illiterates, for a domain of "activities of the aged" (Harman 1996). Each card had a drawing of an activity above the written word for the activity. I believe that the items in the Karen domain of work of the aged will lend themselves well to pile sort card drawings. Even pleasures and sufferings may be amenable to the use of pile sort cards with drawings. A domain like worries, on the other hand, might not be possible to pursue with the pile sort technique.

Using formal ethnographic procedures makes it possible to collect a large body of sound data in a relatively brief period of fieldwork. Students should be advised, however, that the planning period prior to field research will be more intense and more time consuming than the preparatory period for more conventional ethnographic fieldwork. During the planning period, the student needs to master the theoretical principles of the various formal data collection and analysis procedures (see Weller and Romney 1988) and, if ANTHROPAC or another computer program is to be used, to get a good grasp of the computer operations.

The potential of using systematic data collection procedures for cross-cultural research is enormous. The formal procedures used with the Karen attest to the power of the techniques that are available.

QUESTIONS

1. Should an anthropologist go into the initial fieldwork situation with the cultural domains to be studied already well defined? Argue for and against this statement.
2. What are the differences between data collection and analysis?
3. How can an anthropologist systematically collect data in a society when he or she is not fluent in the local language?
4. How could the data collected in the Karen project be used to resolve practical issues of concern to applied anthropologists in Thailand?
5. What are the advantages and disadvantages of using triad questionnaires?

NOTE

1. California State University, Long Beach, reduced my course load in Fall 1995 so that I could analyze the Karen data. I am grateful to Robert Trotter for introducing me to the recent advances in systematic data collection. I thank linguist Emilie Ballard for her work on the presentation of Karen words and Timothy Brazill for his consultation on statistics.

More Advanced Means to Model Culture

CAROLE E. HILL ■

<u>Nine</u>

Decision Modeling: Its Use in Medical Anthropology[1]

Introduction

Decision modeling is a method that allows researchers to discover the basic criteria people use to make decisions. Bernard (1994) defines ethnographic decision modeling as "qualitative, causal analyses that predict what kinds of choices people will make under specific circumstances" (p. 373). Models are constructed that are intended to mirror human decision-making processes. This approach further assumes that these models are predictive of future decisions on the same topic. Decision modeling is always used in conjunction with other data collection techniques. While its goals and analysis procedures are unique, the decision-modeling research process is framed within ethnographic methods.

The theoretical basis of decision modeling is cognitive science. There is a growing interest within anthropology to specify methods for linking human cognitive processes with behavioral systems. As D'Andrade explains, "a cultural model is the representation of what happens inside people—in their minds, or psyches—that results in their doing what they do" (1995:158). A model in the head when confronted with problems in the empirical world (external reality) enables one to "try out" alternatives, conclude which is the best solution for that situation, and record the solution for future use.

Models are initially "fuzzy." People are frequently unaware of the rules, conditions, and constraints that guide their decisions. Nonetheless, it is these

139

guidelines for action—for solving human problems—that the decision-modeling method attempts to discern by assuming that the human mind, within a specific cultural and social context, possesses a model for actively solving a problem. A model, however, is always changing—new parts (alternatives and solutions) are added and others subtracted. In other words, decision models are processual, not static.

A **decision rule** generally means the constraints and conditions placed on specific behavioral responses to a problem. These constraints and conditions are mainly due to learned ways of solving problems in daily living. The rules for solving problems change through time as people encounter new experiences with new constraints on their choices. Decision rules represent "both cultural knowledge and personal experience" (Mathews 1987:58). When conditions are added to or subtracted from the repertoire of possible seeking responses among a group of people, the rules will change. As the case studies in this paper will illustrate, rules don't imply static structures in the mind.

The Types, Contexts, and Research Questions in Decision Modeling

Descriptive Models

The methodological work needed to describe these rules involves a dialectic between discovering, systematizing, testing, and predicting cultural factors for decision making. Anthropologists generally study decision modeling in naturalistic settings, making their models descriptive rather than normative or statistical. Generally, economic, mathematical, and psychological models assume that individuals make "rational choices," allowing little room for variation and diverse rules of logic (Mingers 1989a, 1989b).

Naturalistic descriptive models, in contrast, begin with the assumption that groups of people don't necessarily use Western-based linear forms of logic when making decisions; they use diverse rationalities instead. Descriptive models delineate cultural and emotional reasoning as well as practical reasoning.

Garro (1982) explains that anthropologists who study decision making in naturalistic settings assume that in "recurrent choice situations, like that of illness, where people must regularly choose among alternative courses of action, the members of a given group often come to have a common set of cultural standards used in choice situations. These shared standards of choice can be discovered through examining how information is evaluated by individual actors and what considerations are involved in their choices of treatment" (p. 177). This chapter will focus on descriptive decision-modeling methods combined with **ethnography**, as used in the majority of **medical anthropology** studies.

Contexts and Constraints of Models

The first step in decision modeling is to determine what decisions you wish to model. You must also decide which parts of the complex social and cultural system of the group being studied will be included in the research questions. Smaller contexts tend to be more amenable to more formal research techniques. Broader contexts involve the interface of personal, social, and cultural factors. These extending contexts increase the complexity of the research and require additional types of research methods. Gladwin and Garis state that "because decision-making occurs at the interface between cognition and action, where what people think affects what they do, methods of understanding the whole decision process are crucially important" (1996:316).

Medical anthropologists have shown that groups and individuals are not driven by the same beliefs, constraints, goals, and structures to solve a health problem. People perceive symptoms and causes of illnesses in different ways. Decision modeling is a technique that describes how a group of people make decisions about illnesses in their daily lives. A model is "a formal representation of the considerations (involved in treatment choice) and represents an attempt to describe the standards of choice in an explicit and testable manner" (Garro 1982:177).

Decision-modeling studies conducted by medical anthropologists (that is, Young and Garro 1981, 1982; Mathews 1982; Stoner 1985; Garro 1986; Ryan and Martínez 1996; Weller et. al. 1997) reveal the tremendous variation of research methods.[2] Nardi (1983), for example, who didn't construct formal models, sought to delineate external and internal constraints on reproductive choices. According to her, internal constraints include beliefs, values, and attitudes, while external constraints broaden the context to include social structural issues, such as ethnicity, race, socioeconomic status, and political power. Some studies emphasize internal constraints; others focus on external ones.

Research Questions

The basic research questions of most studies of decision modeling in medical anthropology are the following:

1. What are the health care alternatives the members of the group under study consider reasonable responses to their health care problem?
2. What variation exists among the population being studied?
3. What are the criteria people use for selecting among the alternatives?
4. What are the internal and external constraints and conditions (perceived and/or real) placed on decision making?
5. What are the rule sets used to order criteria (that is, what are the principles whereby this information is used or manipulated in making a choice)?
6. How do decisions fit into the social and cultural context of the group under study?

Research Assumptions

The basic research assumptions are the following:

1. Knowledge, beliefs, and social context directly affect health behavior.
2. Individuals in a group share a cultural model for decision making.
3. Intracultural variation exists in the shared decision model.
4. Rules can be discerned and tested for predictability.

Decision Criteria

What information is used for solving health problems? How does a researcher discover this information and how is it modeled? Individuals make subjective evaluations about their health problems. These evaluations may or may not lead to action. At one time, health decision modeling assumed that an individual who suffered from an illness would seek help—that this was a given goal. Mathews (1987) places this assumption within the framework of single goal decisions, suggesting that groups of people select a course of action among alternative courses in order to reach that goal. People may, however, have several goals which are placed in a hierarchy. The hierarchy of goals are situation specific—decisions may be made to reach different outcomes, although the problem may be defined in a similar manner (Nardi 1983; Mathews 1987). Mathews clearly states that "goals determine criteria" used for making decisions (1987:54).

In addition to goals, perception and ordering of perceived symptoms also determine criteria for making treatment choices (Young 1980; Young and Garro 1981). Evaluating the significance of symptoms determines criteria for action (treatment choice). For example, several studies demonstrate that the two most salient aspects of symptoms that frame criteria for health decisions are: (1) the seriousness of symptoms; and (2) the ordering of symptoms.

It's usually assumed that people who live together and talk about their experiences with illnesses and with the health care options available to them will share standards for evaluating their symptoms and for making choices based on these evaluations. Sharing these experiences over time with one another adds information to their overall cultural model for specific illnesses and for choosing from health care alternatives. These choices are always ordered and, given their context, often lead to very different outcomes. Nonetheless, outcomes can be modeled and predicted when the limited set of multiple **decision criteria** are discovered and ordered.

The research process to find criteria requires using exploratory methods when interviewing a sample of people within the group being studied. Finding criteria involves a continual interplay between the researcher(s), respondents, and key informants. A brief description of four case studies using decision-modeling studies in medical anthropology will illustrate the methods and issues involved in applying this technique. Before discussing the case studies, an outline of the decision tree approach is appropriate.

Decision Tree or Rule-Based Modeling: Gladwin's Approach

Christina Gladwin, in substantial ways, laid the foundation for using decision modeling for data collection and analysis in anthropology. (Her work has concentrated on agricultural decision making.) Gladwin (1976, 1983) argues that people don't make complex calculations when choosing one alternative over others. Rather, they simplify their decision-making calculations, which can be represented in hierarchial models or trees with decision criteria at the nodes or branching points of the tree.

Decision tree modeling is based on a hierarchal theory of choice rather than a linear one. It assumes that an alternative is a set of characteristics or aspects (a dimension of an alternative) that come into play in the mind for the decision maker. Decision makers mentally manipulate these aspects in relatively simple ways to arrive at a choice. Because it uses an ethnographic approach, tree modeling also assumes a composite or aggregate model can be constructed from individual models. Lastly, this approach can be tested, which according to Gladwin, makes the method of decision modeling unlike ethnographic interpretations. She feels that "decision trees are testable cognitive models" (1989:13).

After deciding what decisions to model, the next step is to find the specific constraints and orderings used for decisions. Gladwin sets forth several steps for constructing a model:

1. Decide which decision you're studying.
2. Decide on the set of alternatives in the decision.
3. Conduct an ethnographic interview; find an informant in your cultural scene and practice on him or her. Don't worry about eliciting decision criteria in this step.
4. In addition to ethnographic interviews, do some participant observation.
5. Decide on the sample of decision makers to use to build the model. Decide when and where to interview them.
6. Discover the decision criteria.
   a. Using one informant, look for contrasts over decision makers, over space, and over time.
   b. Elicit criterion for contrasts (using "why" questions).
   c. Construct first decision tree of first informant.
7. Build a composite decision model for the group from the individual decision trees of the sample interviewed.
   a. Direct method—build an individual model of each informant's decision process and put them together later into one composite decision model.
   b. Indirect method—build one "composite" decision model for the group during the interviewing of the first sample.

8. Combine all the different decision trees from all informants in the model-building sample; combine them in a logical fashion while preserving the ethnographic validity of each individual decision model.
   a. Look at the decision criteria in the individual tree models and identify the reasons for the behavior.
   b. Identify the "unless-conditions" or constraints on each branch that cause the decision maker to pick the other alternative.
   c. Stand back and see if the new tree is logical and complete.
   d. See if the new tree is still empirically correct and the informants still "go down" the path of the tree that they went down before.

After constructing the model, Gladwin sets forth several steps for testing it:

1. Construct a formal questionnaire to test the composite model using each decision criterion as a question in the questionnaire.
2. Decide on the sample of decision makers to test the model and decide when and where to interview them. This sample should include informants who participated in the model construction phase of the research.
3. Elicit quantitative data about what the informant is actually doing so that the choice is made before you ask the questions about why she or he is making the choice.
4. During the test interviews, know when the model is failing and identify the error of the model.
5. After the test interviews, calculate the error rate (and success rate) of the model(s).
6. Listen to what "the errors" say about why they do what they do, and devise an alternative model to predict choices by:
   a. Rephrasing or generalizing an existing criterion or,
   b. Switching the order of criteria or even whole paths of the tree.
7. After devising an alternative model(s) which might predict better than the original composite model, test the alternative model with the test sample data, and compare the two models.

Finally, Galdwin delineates six steps for constructing sequential decision trees:

1. Recognize the signs that there is more than one decision to be modeled in the decision context being studied.
2. Identify the other related decisions in the series. Figure out which decisions are logically prior to which.
3. Once the sequence of decisions is specified, model each decision by following the steps outlined above, including testing the model(s).
4. Once all decisions are modeled, check them for logical consistency and proper "fit" of the decision criteria.
5. Add feedback loops in models where they belong to allow decision makers to go back and forth between the related decisions, allowing for more flexibility and simultaneity between the models.

Gladwin is very specific about the steps involved in decision tree modeling and elaborates on each step, giving detailed examples for discovering criteria, constructing a model(s), and testing the model(s). After reading the case studies in this paper, it will become clear that she influenced, in varying degrees, the thinking of all decision-modeling researchers. The following case studies in medical anthropology reveal that, while the basic procedures are similar, significant variation in methods exists for collecting data in the field to construct and test decision models.

Case Study I: Illness Decision Modeling in San José, Mexico

A recent study in Mexico, conducted by Ryan and Martínez (1996), describes a decision model for predicting diarrhea management by mothers in the rural community of San José. The initial goal of their study was to understand how mothers decide to treat episodes of childhood diarrhea. Martínez had conducted previous studies to determine how mothers classify illnesses and what their beliefs were about causation, symptoms, and treatments of diarrhea. Unlike Young and Garro, Ryan and Martínez chose a research design that only delineated the order in which mothers started treatment; it didn't include their second choices or overlap of treatments. Ryan and Martínez built and tested their model using three steps: (1) asking open-ended questions to elicit decision criteria; (2) constructing a formal model (hypothesis about the relationship between decision criteria and reported illness behavior); and (3) testing the model's ability to predict behaviors.

First, Ryan and Martínez elicited decision criteria from a sample of women in San José (Sample A). To ensure variation in health beliefs and behavior, they constructed a true/false test of 45 questions about general medical knowledge using questions elicited from doctors, nurses, and nutritionists. They pretested 50 questions with 10 women from another village. Later they gave the test to 40 mothers living in San José who had children younger than five years old. Ryan and Martínez used cultural **consensus modeling** to analyze the data. This allowed them to ascertain if they, indeed, had cultural consensus and to identity women whose answers most closely matched that cultural consensus. Ryan and Martínez then selected a purposive sample of 20 women whose answers indicated variation in beliefs for developing their predictive model. Ryan and Martínez called this group Sample A.

After interviewing Sample A using **open-ended questions** and probing for criteria, Ryan and Martínez posited several decision rules after each interview and tested them on the next respondent. After 12 interviews, no new criteria were being elicited although Ryan and Martínez finished interviewing all 20 women. From these data, they created a formal **closed-ended** interview schedule that included questions about treatment preference. The analysis of these interviews allowed Ryan and Martínez to construct a tentative decision model that linked together the decision criteria representation of the aggregate behavior patterns. They modified the model using an expert system shell (Ryan 1991) to postdict the respondents' reported behavior. The women's decision model of sequential treatments is represented by a series of decision rules and constraints on remedies (see Figures 9.1 and 9.2).

Rule 1
IF   child has blood stools OR
           child has swollen glands OR
           child is vomiting
THEN   take child to the doctor

Rule 2
IF   diarrhea is caused by *empacho*
THEN   give physical treatment

Rule 3
IF   previous rules do not apply OR
           there is no cure with the *empacho* treatment
THEN   give the highest preferred curing treatment that meets constraints*

Rule 4
IF   previous treatment did not stop diarrhea
THEN   compare the two highest treatments of remaining options
           4.1   IF   one is a curing remedy AND meets its constraints
                    THEN   give this treatment
           4.2   IF   both or neither are curing remedies AND
                              each meet their respective constraints
                    THEN   give the highest-ranked preference

Rule 5
IF   the previous treatment did not stop the diarrhea AND
           the episode is less than one week long
THEN   repeat Rule 4

Rule 6
IF   the episode has lasted more than one week
THEN   take the child to the doctor

---
*Only sugar-salt-solutions or medications have constraints. These constraints are listed in Figure 9.2.

Figure 9.1. Overall decision model.

For their final step, to predict the decision model, Ryan and Martínez selected another sample, Sample B, comprised of 20 mothers from the same community who had not participated in the previous data collection phase, Sample A. After informally asking each respondent about their behavioral responses to their child's diarrhea, Ryan and Martínez used the same closed-ended interview schedule about decision criteria that had been administered to Sample A. This tested the predictive power of the model on 119 possible treatments (17 cases; 7 treatments per case).

Sugar-salt-solution
IF   you know how to make ORS AND
                your child will drink ORS
THEN   give ORS

Pill or Liquid Medication
IF   you know a medication that works for diarrhea AND
                you have it in the house
THEN   give the pill or liquid medication

IF   you know a medication that works for diarrhea AND
                it is cheap AND
                it is easy to obtain
THEN   give the pill or liquid medication

Figure 9.2. Constraints on remedies.

To try to avoid bias and to create ways to test the predictive value of the model using computers, Ryan and Martínez programmed a computer to classify cases in a "blinded" fashion, based on the decision rules of the model. It predicted a sequence of treatments for each woman that was compared to their reported responses. If the predicted sequence didn't agree with the reported sequence, the discrepancy was considered an error. In this process, they considered two types of error: (1) errors of omission (model failed to predict that the mother used a particular treatment); and (2) errors of commission (models predicted that the mother would use a treatment but in fact did not). To compare the measures of accuracy to some standard, Ryan and Martínez compared them with what they would expect to find by chance (Weller et al. 1997). They calculated the probabilities of correctly predicting treatments by constructing a measurement of predicted treatments by averaging the measures of chance across all modalities. A test of the model on Sample A found it made 13 errors or an accuracy rate of 89% while Sample B had a predictive accuracy rate of 84%, which was almost 1.4 times greater than chance.

The patterning of criteria lead Ryan and Martínez to conclude that the women of San José followed conditional rules and constraining rules. Conditional rules are those in which women chose treatments under certain conditions. For example, Rule

1 states that "*If* a child has bloody stools, swollen glands, or is vomiting, *then* a woman seeks medical advice," while Rule 2 refers to the condition of a belief. Constraining rules, on the other hand, set restrictions on women's treatment choices. For example, *if* the woman knows how to make ORS and the child will drink ORS, *then* the child is given ORS. The women are constrained by their knowledge and by their child's behavior (see Figure 9.3 for constraints on use of pills and liquid medication). Ryan and Martínez found that rule ordering is also important for predicting decisions. Women use treatments sequentially. Their faith in a treatment tended to be the basis for their ordering. Lastly, the model accounts for intracultural diversity. Thus, Ryan and Martínez state that "our research suggests that predicting lay behaviors depends on conditional rules, perceived constraints, ordering effects and intracultural differences" (1996:55).

The following case study uses different research techniques from those used by Ryan and Martínez for delineating decision rules. While there is some overlap between the data collection and analysis techniques, there are some significant differences. The search for criteria lends itself to a variety of traditional ethnographic methods.

Case Study II: Illness Treatment Choices in Costa Rica

The work of Hill (1985) and Mathews and Hill (1990) illustrate a slightly different research design for modeling treatment choices in two rural areas of Costa Rica. During the early 1980s, Hill collected data on health-seeking behavior among a sample of residents living in Caribe, a frontier area in Costa Rica. She developed a composite model for decision making among the West Indians living in the community. This area of Costa Rica had been isolated from the highly populated areas in the central plateau of the country. The population was made up of three ethnic groups: (1) Bribri Indians, who live on a reservation; (2) West Indians, who had settled in the area beginning in the late 1800s; and (3) white Hispanic immigrants from northern Costa Rica, Nicaragua, El Salvador, and Honduras. The area traditionally had very few medical care services; most people had to travel long distances for help.

Mathews and Hill decided to test the model built for the residents of Caribe and El Puente (studied in 1983 and 1984) in the community of Puerto Viejo, located 15 miles from Caribe. The make-up of its population and their culture paralleled those of the other two communities. Therefore, many of the variables would hold constant for testing the model. The test sample was selected in a nearby community rather than in the communities from which the model was constructed. Mathews and Hill collected data from a sample of households on perceived health needs, health behavior, and available health resources. They used the following techniques: (1)

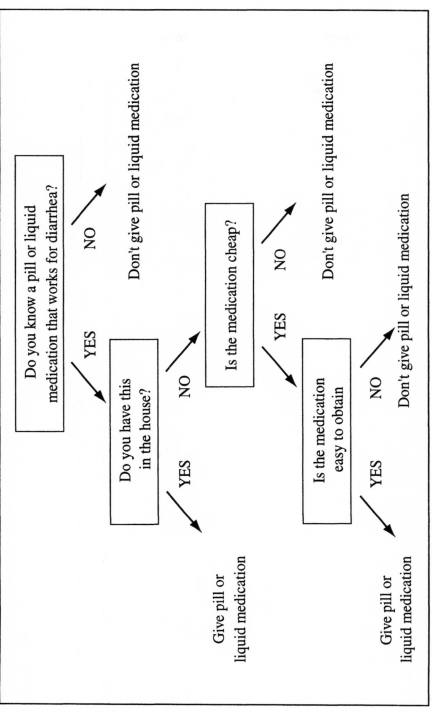

Figure 9.3. Constraints on pills and liquid medication (tree).

participant observation; (2) informal interviewing; and (3) formal interviewing based on a series of systematic elicitation techniques. The alternatives include: (1) bush medicine (self-treatment); (2) local health post; (3) Limón clinic (24 miles); (4) Limón physicians; (5) San José clinic 120 miles), and (6) San José physicians.

The formal decision model was constructed using the criteria and ordering indicated in the original model (see Table 9.1). It specifies the criteria used for deciding among the alternatives for treatment and the ordering of criteria the people used to arrive at the choice of each possible alternative health care option. Nine decision rules comprise the model, stated in the form of *If/Then* statements. For example, Rule 1 is read as "*If* an illness is judged to be nonserious or to be only moderately serious, and *if* the person has a greater belief in the efficacy of bush or traditional medicine than in Western medicine, *then* bush medicine (self-treatment) will be the option chosen. As in the other case studies, these rules are considered hypotheses, based on statements of the respondents, about which conditions will lead to the choice of a treatment option.

TABLE 9.1
Decision Model for Illness Treatment Choice

Rules:	1	2	3	4	5	6	7	8	9
*Conditions**									
Seriousness	1,2	1	2	2	2	3	3	3	3
Faith	B	W	W	W	W	B	W	W	W
Transportation			N	Y	Y		N	Y	Y
Financial Resources				N	Y			N	Y
Choices									
Bush medicine (self treatment)	X						X		
Local health post		X	X					X	
Limón clinic				X					
Limón physicians					X				
San José clinic								X	
San José physicians									X

*KEY:
Seriousness:
  1 = nonserious; 2 = moderately serious; 3 = very serious
Faith or orientation to treatment:
  B = greater belief in effectiveness of bush medicine
  W = greater belief in effectiveness of Western medicine
Availability of transportation and financial resources:
  Y = Yes, transportation is available and/or adequate financial resources are available
  N = No, transportation is not available and/or adequate financial resources are not available

The model was subsequently tested in Puerto Viejo using a random sample of 20% of all households. The sample included 14 West Indian, 6 Hispanic, and 2 mixed-race, and Native American households. A team researcher was assigned to each household who collected information, for over six months, on the illnesses they had suffered the past week, the symptoms of the illnesses, the treatments chosen, the perceived effectiveness of the chosen treatments, and the reactions of other family members to the illness. The project director didn't participate in the collection of illness diaries. This information was entered on a standardized illness diary form used by a family member for writing down all illnesses episodes occurring over the research period. A total of 204 illness episodes was recorded by the family members in the 23 sample households. This technique allowed the researchers to gather information in a time frame close to the illness episode rather than having the sample respondents recall illnesses that may have occurred weeks or months previous to collecting the data.

These data were scored using the same technique developed by Young and Garro (1981). The analysis process is as follows:

> When an illness episode was reported on a form, information was given about how serious it was perceived to be by informants and about what course of action was pursued. Initial interviews had solicited information about each occupant's overall greater faith in bush or Western medicine. The availability of transportation was assessed both by reference to our knowledge of existing resources in the town and to informants' statements about availability in the illness diary. Similarly, our assessments of financial resources were based both on financial data collected in original census interviews and on informants' report at the time of specific illness under consideration occurred. If all the criteria predicted in a decision rule in the original model were met. And if the predicted alternative [see Table 9.1] was indeed chosen, then the choice make was scored as a correct prediction by the model. However, if the criteria predicted to lead to one choice did not, then the choice was scored an error. (Mathews and Hill 1990:159–160)

The testing of the model resulted in a 62% prediction rate of all treatment choices (see Table 9.2), indicating that 62% shared standards for their treatment choices. This relatively low rate of predictive success was not unexpected given the cultural context of the research sites.

The final stage in this research was to analyze the errors. Reexamining the ethnographic data and the illness diaries, Mathews and Hill identified four sources of variation from group consensus, which, taken together, account for all the incorrect predictions made in the model (see Table 9.3). Two sources of error related to differential use of health resources, including new options, by ethnic group (West Indian and white Hispanics). In other words, ethnic differences were a major source of error. The final sources of error involved the experience of chronic illness and idiosyncratic beliefs. In order to account for the sources of error, the researchers used another research technique developed by Kleinman (1978), the **explanatory modeling** approach (EMs), which yielded data on the cultural context of the reported illness episodes. EM data include the respondent's believed-in cause of the illness, their perceived symptoms, their treatment(s), and their evaluations of the outcomes of their choices. These data allowed Mathews and Hill to explain the sources and nature of errors. They found it highly complementary to decision modeling in that eliciting more general information about illness beliefs and conditions brings in factors not generally collected in a strictly decision-modeling method such as similarities and differences between chronic illnesses and illness choices exhibited by diverse ethnic groups.

TABLE 9.2
Test Results for Total Population

	No choice	Bush cures	Local post	Limón clinic	Limón physician	San José SS clinic	San José physician	Other	Correct No.	Correct %	Wrong No.	Wrong %
Rules												
1		47	(8)					(5)	47	78	13	22
2		21		(6)				(4)	21	68	10	32
3	(2)	(4)	11					(3)	11	55	9	45
4	(3)	(2)	(3)	17	(1)			(3)	17	59	12	41
5	(2)	(3)		(3)	6			(3)	6	35	11	65
6	(3)	8							8	73	3	27
7		(2)	7					(4)	7	54	6	46
8	(4)	(5)			(2)	6			6	35	11	65
9					(2)		4		4	67	2	33
									127	62	77	38

[a]n = 204 illness episodes from 23 households over a six-month period..

TABLE 9.3
Analysis of Errors by Ethnic Group

	Type of error[a]				
	Differential ethnic Treatment strategy	Use of new treatment alternative	Subsequent choice for chronic illness	Idiosyncratic choice	Totals
West Indians	11 (31.4%)	0	18 (51.4%)	6 (17.2%)	35
Hispanics, mixed, and Indians	17 (41%)	9 (21%)	9 (21%)	7 (17%)	42
Totals	28 (36%)	9 (12%)	27 (35%)	13 (17%)	77

[a]n = 77 total errors.

Mathews and Hill, like researchers in the other case studies, collected their data in several phases over a relatively long period of time, using a battery of research techniques to develop and test a decision model. Unlike the other studies, they incorporated another frequently used technique in medical anthropology—explanatory modeling—to help contextualize their sources of error through ethnographically accounting for variation in the model. Mathews and Hill (1990) state that "that presence of error does not invalidate the decision process nor limit its utility. Rather, these errors highlight the ways in which individual behaviors deviate from group norms and point the way to more detailed investigations of sources of such variation" (p. 168). By combining decision modeling with explanatory modeling, Mathews and Hill could incorporate regional and group patterns and, at the same time, explore individual variation from these patterns. They were able to represent intracultural variation in treatment choice within the context of cultural and regional variation.

Case Study III: Modeling Mental Health Decisions in Rural Virginia[3]

Research for the final case study was conducted in rural Virginia by a research team consisting of three people directed by Hill. Unlike the previous studies, this one attempts to construct a decision model for mental disorders, rather than physical illnesses. Like the previous case studies, the researchers used several ethnographic and elicitation methods on separate subsamples to develop decision criteria and to test the model. Both decision trees and rules were constructed in the process of discovering how rural residents in Virginia make decisions about treatment for mental disorders. The research was carried out under the auspices of the Rural Mental Health Research Center, University of Virginia. The team collected data for six months in Jefferson County, making frequent return visits over a 12-month period. The objective of the project was to discovery the social and cultural factors that guided the residents' choice of formal and informal treatments of mental disorders.

During the initial field period, several ethnographic methods were used to collect information that would allow the research team to understand the mental health disorder domain (including the residents' mental health categories and their treatment options) and, secondly, to delineate their decision criteria for treatment choice.

Exploratory Interviewing

The research team lived in the county during the intensive data collection phase and participated in the daily activities of county residents. The purpose of this phase of the research was to establish rapport with different groups in the county and develop key respondents. The research team attended church, fairs, ate in different restaurants, and talked informally with providers. These interactions yielded textual data based on our observations and informal interviewing. Residents were asked their ideas about mental health disorders and their experiences with these disorders. These data gave the team their first clues concerning how residents think about mental health and their treatment choices. It didn't take long to learn that people didn't organize their cultural knowledge like mental health providers for mental health disorders do; rather, they talked about mental health problems. It also became clear early on that residents were reluctant to talk about mental health at all, making it fairly difficult to delineate the boundaries of their mental health knowledge system and the context for its operation.

Formal Interviewing

After getting to know people in the county, the researchers constructed a formal interview instrument. During this phase of the research, several formal interviewing techniques were used to determine the residents' cultural knowledge and mental health disorders and their criteria for treatment choice. Before direct attention was paid to finding decision criteria, structured interviews were used to ascertain the people's general beliefs and behaviors about mental health disorders. The sampling strategy for choosing whom to interview consisted of dividing the rather large county into five geographical sectors to assure that the sample was representative of the county's racial and cultural diversity. With one exception, all areas consisted of African American and white populations. The exception was an area adjacent to the Appalachian region with a predominantly white population. Each research team member spent time interviewing in each sector balancing the interviews in terms of race and gender. Four criteria, determined by the research center, were used for selecting respondents: (1) age (18 years or older); (2) income (at or below poverty line); (3) lived in the county at least ten years; and (4) experience with mental health problems (themselves, family, or friends). Using these criteria, a convenience sample was selected.

The research team conducted 61 **structured interviews**. The interview instrument included a set of short closed-ended questions and a set of open-ended questions. It also included a long illness narrative designed to ascertain all components of their explanatory model for a mental health problem. Each respondent was interviewed, in detail, about their experience or the experience of a family member or friend with a mental health problem. A section of the interview schedule also included questions that would permit the researchers to construct explanatory models (discussed in Case Study II).

In addition to using the structured interview schedule, the research team used the freelisting technique (see Fleisher and Harrington, this volume) to delineate the residents' mental health problem cultural domain. Analysis of the freelisting indicated that the rural residents have a rather loosely organized mental health problems domain consisting of the following items: (1) "drinking"; (2) "drugs"; (3) "depression"; (4) "nerves"; and "(5) "mental breakdown." The research team also asked the respondents to list their treatment options for each category. The most frequently reported items were: (1) family; (2) friends; (3) God; (4) minister; (5) hospital in Charlottesville; and (6) clinic (located in the county). The first four are informal treatment choices (nonscientific medical help); the final two are formal treatment choices. No mental heath facilities were listed as a treatment option.

Discovering Decision Criteria

The research team independently coded the informal interviews and narratives in an attempt to uncover the residents' shared standards for making decisions about treatment for "drinking," "drugs," "depression," and "nerves." The interview schedule asked residents to respond to questions pertaining to their beliefs about the causes of mental disorders, the symptoms, possible treatments, and their evaluation of treatments. Each case was analyzed for decision criteria. In this process, members of the research team asked their key respondents a series of questions to double check the tentative findings.

Analysis of the open-ended questions on the structured interview allowed the research team to develop "hunches" (hypotheses) about decision criteria. A short structured instrument was subsequently constructed consisting of a set of yes/no questions designed to elicit specific factors that led them or someone they knew to seek help. The factors we included for testing were cost, transportation, severity of problem, previous experience with problem, and treatment outcome. This short questionnaire also included space for recording their verbal responses to the questions. A convenience sample of 17 residents was interviewed. Data analysis indicate that only one factor, severity, "pushed" the residents into the formal mental health system. They prefer and rely on informal care if they seek treatment at all. At this time, the researchers decided that severity of the problem and its impact on the family is used by the residents as criteria for choosing formal help.

Discovering decision criteria required interfacing the ethnographic data with the findings of the structured interviews, and interviewing key respondents. The **triangulation** or combined use of these methods increased the analytical validity of the residents' reasoning about their behavioral responses to mental health disorders. The research team constructed its initial decision criteria for treatment choices from these databases. The initial criteria for seeking treatment consisted of: (1) family and/or friendship disorder: (2) family abuse/violence; (3) loss of job; (4) loss of family; and (5) confrontations with the judicial or social service system. Evaluation of symptoms for judging the existence of a mental health problem relied, almost exclusively, on the behavior of the individual with a problem and her/his impact on other people's lives. Symptoms become serious enough for the decision maker to seek treatment when there is significant disruption in the individual's social networks. This threshold was difficult to precisely measure. Nevertheless, the ethnographic data strongly indicated that neither family nor friends alone was a strong factor for seeking formal treatment. Some outside force was necessary for predicting treatment from the system (law, employer, or social worker).

Collection of Data from Two Additional Subsamples

Before finalizing the decision model for testing, the research team decided to collect two new data sets that would give them more precise information about the ordering of treatment choices for each mental health problem, their preferred treatment choice for each problem, and their ranking of choices for each problem. The team interviewed a sample of 15 respondents using a set of structured questions about the reasons they chose or did not choose a treatment modality. Each respondent was given a set of cards to sort. In the first task, respondents were asked to pile sort (see Roos, this volume) the cards of the major mental health problems in terms of severity (normal, moderately serious and very serious) and to sort the treatments in terms of effectiveness (very effective, sometimes effective, not effective, and don't know). The second task asked the respondents to choose a treatment option from a pair of treatments (**paired comparison**) for each problem. Each respondent was given a set of cards with the treatment options printed on them. They were asked to make piles of their first, second, and third choices of treatment for each problem. They were then asked to describe their reasons for selecting each treatment. Analysis of these data further clarified the rationale behind their decision criteria and allowed the researchers to delineate constraints and conditions on the residents' decisions. These data also indicated the ordering of treatment choices.

The research team was careful to select the sample to assure gender and race balance. These data were collected to further clarify the criteria used for mental health problem decision making. Not all these data were helpful for delineating criteria or for directly building a decision model. Taken together, however, they were invaluable for delineating patterns of choice, and, perhaps, more importantly, for looking at the data in different ways in order to make sense out of the residents' mental health decisions and for constructing a formal descriptive decision model. This topic is an extremely difficult one to model. Mental disorders are chronic problems, and rural residents believe that, for the most part, these disorders should be dealt with within the informal system. Their decisions are based on the immediate social situation and not on distinct and measurable criteria such as fever or bleeding.

The researchers interviewed another sample of 26 residents to clarify their treatment preferences, particularly in regard to formal and informal treatments. In this interview, we asked respondents about hypothetical situations. They also asked them to describe their sequencing of treatments using formal and informal systems and their reasons for seeking specific treatments at each decision point. The team designed a short interview schedule using open-ended questions to identify the constraints on making one decision as opposed to another. In addition, they asked respondents to pile sort a set of 20 treatment cards. They were asked to perform two tasks: (1) Sort the treatment options into three piles based on their evaluations of whether the treatment was effective, ineffective, or no opinion; and (2) Rank the set of treatments they would use for mental health problems in general and for drinking, drug, and depression (nerves was not included in this sample). They were then asked to explain their rationale for these rankings.

These data sets were analyzed using the microcomputer program ANTHROPAC. These data sets indicated that the respondents didn't believe that formal treatment was effective. In fact, they believed that when individuals enter the mental health system, they will never be free of it. They also indicated that they didn't want to use the formal system because they didn't want anyone in their community to know that they had received psychological treatment or counseling. Consequently, the major criteria for not using the formal system are its perceived ineffectiveness and the stigma associated with using it.

Constructing and Initial Testing of the Models

As discussed above, the research team began constructing a decision model for the four most frequently listed mental health problems in the data collection phase of the research. They built a tree model based on the early informal interviewing of respondents. Each member of the research team built a model for five residents (a total of 15 models). At this point, it seemed apparent that there was little variation in the models, with the exception of nerves.

These models were subsequently combined into a composite model for each problem and taken to key respondents for verification. The models were initially tested for their postdictive accuracy on 40 problem episodes using the narratives collected from the ethnographic part of the study. There were 12 cases of drinking, 10 cases of drugs, 12 cases of depression, and 8 cases of nerves. An independent researcher was hired to score the errors for each problem episode against the composite decision trees. All of the errors were based on gender variation, not race, particularly with regard to drinking and drugs. The 5 cases that deviated from the decision path were men who didn't seek informal help. Their ordering of decisions jumped from having problems with family and friends about their drinking or using drugs to getting in trouble with the law and being forced to seek formal treatment.

The final two data sets allowed the research team to refine the models—attempting to adjust it so that each respondents' experience fit on the tree paths. Once the adjusted models appeared to account for all cases, the models were converted into decision rules for formal testing. At that time, the researchers felt that a questionnaire based on decision rules was more appropriate for constructing decision rules. This was certainly a judgment call. Whatever the form—trees or rules—it models the same paths to treatment or no treatment.

Tentative composite decision rules (see Figures 9.4, 9.5, 9.6, 9.7) for depression, drinking, drugs, and nerves were constructed from these data sets. Since one of the main objectives of the overall study was to explain and distinguish help-seeking behavior that resulted in choosing formal treatments from those that result in informal treatments, the decision rules reflect this concern. A third option is an outcome of refusing to seek either formal or informal treatment even if the problem continues over a long period of time. In fact, for most mental health problems, the majority of residents did not choose to seek formal help. They were literally forced into the mental health system.

The decision models represent the ordered use of perceived treatment alternatives. As stated above, these models illustrated that residents rarely seek formal treatment on their own volition. They generally don't judge their problem as being serious enough to seek treatment. The impetus for getting treatment is based on interaction with a person or a representative of the system who regards the problem as serious. Until some kind of social threshold is reached that pushes individuals into the formal system, they will likely seek and maintain informal help, if they get help at all. The findings of this study suggests that individuals rarely make up their own minds to seek treatment. Making choices to seek mental health treatment is a household- or community-level decision. Since these mental health problems are chronic and thought to be a "normal" part of life, and, since residents generally don't seek formal treatment, the model accounts for how rural residents sequenced choices. Once an individual reaches the threshold, she or he is, in most cases, literally forced into formal treatment. Therefore, if the criteria for decisions are met in these decision rules, there's a high probability that a person will end up in formal treatment, although the decision may not have been made entirely by the individual with a mental health problem.

The researchers thought it irrelevant to specify the formal treatment choices although these options could have been included in the model. Since most residents don't choose to seek formal treatment, the specific alternatives would add little to the model. Likewise, since there are so few informal alternatives and because most residents choose family and friends as their first choice for help, these categories were grouped together as they are, for the most part, in the minds of the residents. The next most frequently sought help was from God or ministers. At this time, the specific formal and informal choices have not been modeled. That is certainly a next step in this study.

Rule 1
IF   I feel sad OR
            have a problem with everyday work
THEN   Seek no help (0%)

Rule 2
IF   Rule 1 applies AND
            I find it difficult to leave the house or visit friends and family
THEN   Seek informal help (25%)

Rule 3
IF   Rule 2 applies AND
            problems with family
THEN   Seek informal help (10%)

Rule 4
IF   Rule 3 applies AND
            problem continues for at least six months AND/OR
            problem at work
THEN   Seek formal help (25%)

Figure 9.4. Depression.

Rule 1
IF   Upsets family and friends
THEN   Seek no help (0%)

Rule 2
IF   Causes trouble at work OR
            fight with family and friends (violence)
THEN   Seek no help (20%)

Rule 3
IF   Rule 2 applies AND
            conditions continue for a year
THEN   Seek informal help (30%)

Rule 4
IF   Rule 3 applies AND
            gets DUI OR
            gets in other trouble with the law
THEN   Seek formal help (5%)

Figure 9.5. Drinking.

```
Rule 1
IF        Fight with friends and family (violence)
THEN      Seek no help (0%)

Rule 2
IF        Rule 1 applies AND
          trouble at work
THEN      Seek no help (15%)

Rule 3
IF        Rule 2 applies AND
          problems last over a year
THEN      Seek informal help (12%)

Rule 4
IF        Rule 3 applies AND
          employer recommends help
THEN      Seek formal help (12%)

Rule 5
IF        Rule 3 applies AND
          trouble with law
THEN      Seek formal help (5%)
```

Figure 9.6. Drugs.

Predictive Testing of the Decision Rules

The decision model was tested for its predictive power (predictive accuracy) on a sample of 25 respondents who had not participated in the project and who met the criteria for participation in the study cited above. The sample was chosen so that at least five respondents had experience with each of the mental health problems. They were asked 51 closed-ended questions (yes/no) designed to test each rule and the ordering of criteria for each model. Overall, the accuracy rate was 91%, which represents the correspondence between predicted outcomes and actual outcomes. Every error could be attributed to gender variation. Most men decide that no treatment or help is the preferred course of action.

The Strengths and Weaknesses of Decision Modeling

Decision modeling attempts to construct models that guide the choices people routinely make for solving a problem. The idea of routine is an important one in that it is the basis for predicting future behavior. From the cases presented in this paper, it's clear that this technique seeks to distinguish routine behavior from nonroutine behaviors. It's also clear that the type of illness sets different criteria for health care choices. For example, people respond to acute short-term illnesses very differently than they do to chronic illnesses or problems. The choices are much broader for chronic illnesses and the response time is generally longer. It appears that the daily routine for acute illnesses/problems is substantively different than that for chronic illnesses/problems.

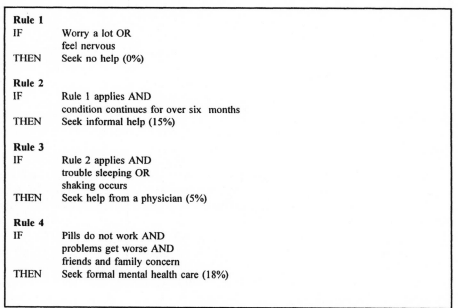

Rule 1
IF   Worry a lot OR
            feel nervous
THEN   Seek no help (0%)

Rule 2
IF   Rule 1 applies AND
            condition continues for over six months
THEN   Seek informal help (15%)

Rule 3
IF   Rule 2 applies AND
            trouble sleeping OR
            shaking occurs
THEN   Seek help from a physician (5%)

Rule 4
IF   Pills do not work AND
            problems get worse AND
            friends and family concern
THEN   Seek formal mental health care (18%)

Figure 9.7. Nerves.

Routinization of choices and behaviors must be considered carefully when designing decision-modeling research. The key issue related to routine choices and behaviors is the unit of analysis. Researchers need to make sure they are clear about who makes decisions (that is, are household choices being modeled or are individual cases being modeled?). One of the main weakness of decision modeling is that it generally assumes individuals, not household members, make choices. The literature in medical anthropology certainly demonstrates that most decisions are group based, not individual based. Another weakness is the narrow focus of the research, which often predicts the obvious routines. Hidden routines, routines that aren't readily apparent to researchers due to the stigma attached to the topic (as encountered in the mental health study), make it difficult to limit research methods to decision-modeling techniques. Where there are no routines or obvious choices and when the conditions are chronic and/or stigmatized, the focus must be expanded to larger social and cultural analyses. Lastly, decision modeling has a tendency to produce static models when, in fact, making choices about illnesses is a process, and people's decisions are constantly changing.

The strengths of decision modeling certainly make using this method worthwhile. First, it uses systematic data collection methods. Truly in-depth information is collected for a domain in a precise way. Second, it is a systematic attempt to explain choice making, linking behavior to thought. Driven by cognitive anthropology theory, decision modeling is one of the few methods that seeks to discover this linkage. And third, decision modeling enables hypothesis testing and prediction. The use of several ethnographic methods allows researchers in the field to make hypotheses about choices and immediately test them for their predictability. Consequently, decision modeling forces researchers to think deductively and inductively at the same time as they develop decision criteria and models.

The Importance of the Larger Context in Decision Modeling

Using decision modeling in the field is an on-going process of refining the model and placing it in a larger context. The everyday living experiences—the sociopolitical structures of the population—frame the decisions. The material world (that is, economic, ethnic) is an important context for the reproduction and transformation of cultural models and should be more fully explored in decision modeling.

Decision modeling simplifies ethnographic complexity while retaining predictive power. All the researchers in the case studies looked for decision criteria and rules throughout the research process. They were continually engaged in developing and revising formal rules from complex ethnographic descriptions of health problems. In the beginning, the rules may be elusive. In effect, researchers construct cognitive "sketch maps" of ethnographic worlds and refine them by collecting successive data sets and by using ethnography as a general gauge to test the model(s).

The use of *systematic methods*, such as freelisting and pile sorts, clarify hypotheses. Yet, it is the ethnographic data that give life to the rules. How are the decision rules used in everyday life? What are the larger social forces that place constraints and conditions on the rules? The local contexts in which decision making takes place and how these contexts are influenced by larger social systems provide answers to these questions. While the words of people tell researchers what they believe the constraints are, an ethnographic analysis combines their words with actions, truly circumscribing decision models with their daily behavior.

The choices people make are not the same every day. However, they follow a set of cognitive rules with contraints and conditions set by larger social systems. To understand their choices, they must be linked to broader context—to family, community, state, and nation. The people who live in rural Virginia, for example, certainly don't categorize their problems solely in terms of the local level alone. They link them to the larger political and economic systems that impact their lives. Broadening decision-modeling methods is an attempt to combine the study of culture and the political economy.

Conclusion

Decision modeling is an exciting method for determining and predicting health behavior. It is one method in the medical anthropologist's toolbox for discovering and explaining illness behavior. While the method is based on collecting data from individuals about illness episodes, decision modeling can go beyond the individual as the only unit of analysis. People's decision models for treatment and help-seeking choices are embedded in their everyday lives. Decision criteria are inextricably linked to social and political contexts that provide the background for solving health problems. These contexts must be ethnographically recorded and used as reality checks, if you will, for the processes involved in constructing decision models. It is imperative to understand how choices are socially constructed as well as culturally constructed within the on-going stream of social life. Treatment decisions and strategies are cognitively and socially organized within the context of uncertainty. Decision modeling in medical anthropology cannot afford to lose the people and their connections with their world.

QUESTIONS

1. What are the purposes of decision modeling? What are its assumptions?
2. What are the steps in decision-modeling research? What is the order of research?
3. What are decision criteria and how do you find them?
4. How do you build a decision model and how do you test it?
5. Why is it important to use ethnographic methods in combination with more focused methods in building models and testing them?

NOTES

1. I am grateful to the following people who read drafts of this paper: Holly Mathews, Christina Gladwin, Melissa Melby, Anne Geluade, Larry Brown, and Deborah Schwartz. A special thanks to William Dressler and Kathryn Oths for taking time over the past two years to discuss and critique decision modeling with me. Finally, I thank the editors of this volume for their critical review, patience, and editorial comments.

2. See Quinn (1975) for a historical account of studies that used decision modeling for analyzing social structure. She delineates earlier studies that were concerned with systematic retrieval and exhaustive listing of decision criteria from later modeling that was concerned with prediction. The latter models are divided into three types: information-processing models, retrodictive models, and models of cultural principles. There are also studies conducted by anthropologists using decision modeling within the contexts of economic decision making (Quinn 1978; Oths 1994) and agricultural decision making (Gladwin 1976, 1980; Barlett 1977).

3. The research conducted in Virginia was funded by the National Institute of Mental Health through the Southeast Rural Mental Health Research Center, University of Virginia, Charlottesville, Virginia. I thank the center's director, Dr. Jeanne Fox, for her guidance and support. The research team consisted of Libby Vann, Shawn Lucus, Gertrude Frazer, Rim Hendi, and Michael Blank. I am grateful for the time and effort they contributed.

W. PENN HANDWERKER ■

Ten

Consensus Analysis:
Sampling Frames for Valid,
Generalizable Research Findings

This chapter explains how to design and use sampling frames for ethnographic research. Social and behavioral research characteristically take the viewpoint of an observer looking in (at "subjects") from the outside. Ethnographers, by contrast, ask people to help dispel their ignorance and aim to see cultural phenomena from the viewpoint of the people who create and use them, looking out from the inside. To achieve this goal, ethnography requires distinctive methodological tools.

First and foremost, ethnographers must interact intensively and create personal relationships with the people they want to understand. Culture consists of the systems of mental constructions that individuals use to interpret and respond to the world of experience—more simply, of the knowledge they use to live their lives. Spending time getting to know someone opens the only door available for you to learn what that person sees, and what it means, when he or she looks out at the world.

Second, and no less important, ethnographers must address questions bearing on all research: (1) Have we gotten it right?; and (2) To whom, if anyone, can we generalize? The first question bears on the internal validity of a study and asks if we haven't misunderstood what our teachers (the people we talked with and observed over the course of our study) tried to make clear to us. The second bears on the external validity of a study and recognizes that, having studied with only a handful of teachers, we generalize to a community of hundreds, perhaps hundreds of thousands of people we never met. Careful design and use of sampling frames gives answers to both.

Sample Cultural Experts and Their Social Relations

All ethnographic research begins by collecting data from one person. When you go to the next person, you will always find something different, since each of us is a unique human being with a distinctive way of looking at and responding to the world. But you will also find some things much the same, since each of us is human, negotiating the way we look at the world by interacting with other people. You keep track of similarities, note variability, and keep at it until you no longer find significant cultural or behavioral variability. You construct a story from the inferential generalizations arrived at about the characteristics of the people. You write about their lives; about what those people think, feel, and do; about who agreed with whom about what and to what extent; about who is similar to whom and to what extent; and about how they differ from others and to what extent.

Begin with a Topic and Talk with People Who Know About It

Where do you begin? Who do you talk with? You begin, of course, with a topic you want to learn about. And you talk with the people who know about that topic—cultural experts and the people with whom they interact to construct their expertise.

If you want to know about farming, talk with farmers—and with the other people who make up farmers' key social relations: their parents, siblings, partners, children; their suppliers and their buyers; their friends; and others whose lives mesh with farmers, including farm workers, farm extension agents, bankers, tax assessors, and county planning commissioners. If you want to know about prostitution, talk with prostitutes—and with the other people who make up prostitutes' key social relations: their parents, siblings, partners, children; their suppliers (if any) and clients; their friends; and others whose lives mesh with prostitutes, including the police. If you want to know about parental involvement in their children's education, talk with parents—and with the other people who make up key social relations for parents, including their own parents, their children, and teachers. For many realms of life, nearly everyone is a cultural expert. All women are experts about being women; all men are experts about being men. Everyone living in the United States is an expert on life in the United States.

If They Don't Agree, Who's the Expert?

Everyone is an expert in what they know. When you begin your study, however, you can't know who knows what, or who is a cultural expert at what. People construct the way they look at the world by reflecting on events they experience at particular points in their life and by working through the meaning of those events through specific interactions with specific people. Don't expect all farmers or all prostitutes, all women or all men, to have the same points of view. Remind yourself that, at the beginning of your study, you're still looking in from the outside. People who look the same from an outsider's perspective—like farmers or prostitutes, women or men—may work with different, even conflicting, understandings about the topic you want to study. Remember: You are there to learn!

Track Life Experiences

Cultural differences reflect variation in internal processes of development and maturation, the time in human history people live, the region(s) in which life stories take place, their gender, and the details of the intergenerational and intra- and intergroup relationships in which they take part. Search for concrete events and circumstances in people's lives that may shape the understandings they now work with. What people think and do must reflect not only their individual life history, but broader regional and global histories of people, events, and social interaction into which they were born and in which they grew up. So try to identify events, circumstances, and processes that provide one set of choices to some people and a different set of choices to others. Ask individuals to identify life experiences that were significant to them and to help you understand why those experiences were significant. Keep track of life experience markers that people identify as important, as well as those that might be important.

The knowledge of older people will reflect their cumulative experiences, which will be very different from those of their grandchildren, and provide them a distinctive vantage point due only to age. The knowledge of men and women of the same age may differ solely because of gendered experiences. Men and women the same age may work with a common body of knowledge merely because they grew up in poverty or experienced privileges by having wealthy parents. Puerto Ricans, irrespective of age, gender, and class, may work with a common body of knowledge merely because they share an ethnic heritage that may differ in significant ways from the heritage of Connecticut Yankees.

Design Sampling Frames Using Key Life Experiences

It's important to design sampling frames that encompass regionally and historically situated life experiences. For example, a generic sampling frame might track age, gender, class background, and ethnic (and other pertinent) identities of informants. A fully nested sampling frame is designed to distinguish differences in knowledge for each combination of life experience markers. An example of a nested frame is shown in Table 10.1.

TABLE 10.1
Generic Nested Sampling Frame

Gender	Men				Women			
Age	Young		Old		Young		Old	
Class	Poor	Not Poor	Poor	Not Poor	Poor	Not Poor	Poor	Not Poor
Ethnicity	EA/AA	EA/AA	EA/AA	EA/AA	EA/AA	EA/AA	EA/AA	EA/AA

Key: EA=Euro American; AA=African American.

Informal and semistructured interviews should be designed to elicit information on the significance, if any, of these distinctions. To do so, ask informants if they know people who think differently and interview people who take different points of view. Actively search for sources of cultural difference and select informants who reflect knowledge you gain during the course of field research.

Talk with Anyone Who Will Teach You

Who should you select to interview and observe? Anyone willing to teach you. Social and behavioral scientists conventionally judge the **validity** and generalizability of findings by referring to classical statistical theory, which requires unrelated cases chosen without bias (that is, a random sample) for valid analysis and generalization. Cultural data, however, come from questions like: "How do you farm and how did you learn it?" or "What different kinds of clients do you have, what kinds of sex do they prefer, and how much do you charge them?" No one can respond to such questions without reference to the social interactions through which experience and knowledge was acquired.

To reiterate: Cultural data reflect the social (interactive) processes by which we construct our knowledge of each other and how social processes work. To select informants according to a random sampling procedure would defeat most the purpose of most ethnographers, which is to find people who know about the aspects of the culture that you want to learn. Among those people, what any one person knows can never exist independently of what other informants know or tell you.

Cultural Data Show Case Dependence

The problem of case dependence arose the first time an anthropologist used numerical methods. In the late 1800s, Edward B. Tylor, whose classic definition of culture still appears in textbooks, tried to explain the origins and distribution of kin avoidances (1889). One of the originators of classical statistical theory, Sir Francis Galton, asked Tylor how he knew his cases were independent, since the similarities he tried to explain by reference to individual needs and social functions might merely reflect social interaction—the similarities might have come about merely because the people lived near each other or because they shared common ancestors. Tylor had no answer.

Franz Boas—widely known as the father of American anthropology—addressed this problem with a cluster analysis of regional and historical social relationships bearing on the distribution of myths and stories found among tribes of the Northwest Coast of North America, the adjacent plateau, and three widely scattered communities (1894). Boas found that neighboring communities shared more than distant communities (for example, Northwest Coast tribes were more similar to each other than to tribes on the plateau) and people who share a common ancestral community (who spoke languages from the same language family) probably shared more than people who spoke languages from different language families.

Recent research extends Boas's findings about community case dependence to cultural data taken to characterize different individuals (Handwerker et al. 1997; Handwerker and Wozniak 1997). The socially constructed nature of cultural phenomena means that any person who knows about a particular phenomenon participates with other experts in its construction. Talking with any person yields data very much like that provided by any other. Although standard kinds of statistical tests won't give us the information needed for valid analysis of cultural data, Weller (1987) has shown that the Spearman-Brown Prophesy Formula can be applied to informants rather than items, allowing us to measure the reliability and validity of the cultural data we report. Ethnographic findings based on information from small numbers of informants (3–36, depending on the average level of agreement, see Table 10.2), can exhibit exceptional reliability (.90–.99) and validity (.95–~1).

Validating Your Findings

"Getting it right" refers to a correspondence between your findings and what your informants told you. During the course of research, you will find it helpful to use different means—different questions, different formats, a combination of questions and observations—to collect data about a given phenomenon. Taking different approaches to the same issue helps you triangulate to accurate findings. But explicit validation of key findings calls for numerical analysis of data collected (usually) through structured interviews bearing on agreements (or disagreements) concerning ratings or similarities among the components of the cultural domain you study.

Numerical methods are nothing more than explicit tools for assessing similarities and differences of the kind you ask about and track while you're in the field. They allow you an independent check on the accuracy of your inferential generalizations about the characteristics of the people, lives, and life stories you studied, about what those people think, feel, and do, about who agreed with whom about what and to what extent, and, so, about who is similar to whom and to what extent, and how they differ from others and to what extent. They also help you evaluate a source of variability you might not have even thought about: the role of chance—random variation—in what people tell you and what you see.

TABLE 10.2
Reliability and Validity Estimates for Cultural Data

Number of Informants	Average Level of Agreement	Reliability	Validity
9	0.5	0.9	0.95
18	0.5	0.95	0.97
36	0.5	0.97	0.99
6	0.6	0.9	0.95
12	0.6	0.95	0.97
24	0.6	0.97	0.99
4	0.7	0.9	0.95
8	0.7	0.95	0.97
16	0.7	0.97	0.99
3	0.8	0.92	0.96
6	0.8	0.96	0.98
18	0.8	0.99	0.99
3	0.9	0.96	0.98
6	0.9	0.98	0.99
18	0.9	0.99	~1

All numerical analysis begins with the construction of a data matrix of our informants (cases) and what they tell us or what we see (variables and their attributes or values). Numerical analysis consists of operations carried out on matrix rows, columns, or both. Different operations answer different questions, but all operations look for structure in what may constitute randomness.

For example, the following two matrices contain data from ten different informants (the rows) concerning ten different variables (the columns). One matrix consists of data coming from exploratory research on gender relations in the United States that looked at the question of how a woman should interact with a man she just met. We collected the data in Connecticut using the sampling frame in Table 10.3. We asked men and women aged 23–58, both Puerto Ricans and Connecticut Yankees, whether or not they found it acceptable for a woman who interacted with a man she just met to: (1) dress conservatively, (2) dress revealingly, (3) sit cross-legged, (4) reach out and touch, (5) laugh and smile a lot, (6) act relaxed, (7) be aggressive, (8) flirt, (9) be direct, and (10) kiss. The 1s and 0s in the matrix tell us whether a specific informant said one or another of these behaviors was acceptable (1) or not (0). The other matrix consists of a random scatter of responses.

Information collected on ten variables from just ten informants produces 100 codes, far too many to make sense of readily. If you study these matrices closely, you'll probably figure out which one consists of random digits. But you won't find it easy. Even then, you'll have to guess if our informants agreed about what was and wasn't acceptable behavior for women interacting with men they just met.

TABLE 10.3
Nested Sampling Frame

Gender	Men				Women			
Age	Young		Old		Young		Old	
Ethnicity	Y	PR	Y	PR	Y	PR	Y	PR

Key: Y=Yankee; PR=Puerto Rican

	1	2	3	4	5	6	7	8	9	0
	01	02	03	04	05	06	07	08	09	01
	-	-	-	-	-	-	-	-	-	-
1 R1	0	0	1	0	1	0	1	1	1	0
2 R2	1	0	1	1	0	1	1	1	1	1
3 R3	0	0	0	1	0	1	0	0	0	1
4 R4	0	0	0	1	0	0	0	0	0	0
5 R5	0	0	1	0	0	1	0	1	1	0
6 R6	0	1	1	1	0	1	0	0	1	1
7 R7	0	1	0	1	0	1	0	1	1	1
8 R8	1	0	0	1	1	1	0	0	1	1
9 R9	0	0	1	0	1	1	1	0	1	1
10 R10	1	1	0	1	1	1	0	1	1	0

	1	2	3	4	5	6	7	8	9	0
	01	02	03	04	05	06	07	08	09	01
	-	-	-	-	-	-	-	-	-	-
1 R1	1	0	1	1	1	1	1	0	0	0
2 R2	1	1	1	1	1	1	1	1	1	1
3 R3	0	0	1	1	1	1	1	1	0	0
4 R4	0	0	1	1	0	1	0	1	0	0
5 R5	1	1	1	1	1	1	1	1	0	0
6 R6	1	0	1	0	0	1	0	1	0	0
7 R7	1	1	1	1	1	1	0	1	0	0
8 R8	1	1	1	1	1	1	1	1	1	1
9 R9	1	0	1	1	1	1	1	1	1	1
10 R10	1	0	1	1	1	1	1	1	0	0

Consensus Analysis

To assess internal validity, consensus analysis (for example, Romney et al. 1986; Weller and Romney 1988; Borgatti 1992) tests for the existence of cultural consensus and the presence and basis of cultural differences. For any set of cultural data—drawn from text (field notes, transcribed interviews) or from structured interview formats like pile sorts, triads, ranking scales, or the agreement questions asked here—consensus analysis conducts a minimum residuals factor analysis of the similarities among what our informants told us, adjusted for random variation. The first factor consists of the additive combination of cases that explains the maximum amount of variability among our informants. That operation leaves unexplained some variability in what our informants told us. Subsequent factors consist of additive combinations of cases that account for variability left unexplained by successive factors. Consensus analysis asks if the responses of each informant constitute just one measurement of an unobserved consensus.

Factor Analysis

Factor analysis output includes correlations between each factor and your cases, called loadings. Each informant's loading on the first factor indicates how much he or she agrees with the consensus identified by the first factor. Their average is a measure of the reliablity and validity of the identified consensus (see Table 10.2). The square of a loading tells you how much variability in what a specific informant told you is explained by the consensus. The sum of squared loadings for a factor (its eigenvalue) tells you how much variability in what all of your informants reported is explained by the consensus. The consensus analysis procedure identifies the existence of significant agreement differences by the absence of a single major factor and either systematically low or negative factor loadings for some informants.

Matrices that contain real underlying structure exhibit a very sharp drop in the size of eigenvalues and a clearly identifiable point at which eigenvalues level off. A large proportion of the variance among informants explained by a single factor the eigenvalue of which is three or more times larger than the next largest warrants (subject to diagnostic analysis) inference of a cultural consensus.

Look at Random Variation

The following shows ANTHROPAC's consensus analysis output for the first matrix, which consists of randomly scattered 1s and 0s. The first factor accounts for less than half the variability in the matrix (46%). The procedure prints a warning that these data are not well explained by a single factor, since the eigenvalue of the first factor (2.252) is only about 1.7 times larger than the second (1.352).

EIGENVALUES

FACTOR	VALUE	PERCENT	CUM %	RATIO
1	2.252	46.2	46.2	1.665
2	1.352	27.8	74.0	1.068
3	1.266	26.0	100.0	

WARNING: Your data are not well explained by a single factor. This condition violates the One Culture assumption of the Consensus Model.

ANTHROPAC's consensus analysis procedure prints out factor loadings for each informant. If informants expressed an underlying agreement about what was and was not appropriate behavior for women interacting with men they just met, that agreement would constitute the knowledge that they share, and the factor loading would tell you the degree to which individual informants agreed with the aggregated consensus. The following loadings range from −.83 to .73 and exhibit an average amount of variability (.44) nearly three times the average level of agreement of .17.

Estimated Knowledge of Each Respondent
−0.83; 0.06; 0.73; 0.29; −0.10; 0.52; 0.61; 0.45; −0.21; 0.21
Average: 0.174; Std. Dev.: 0.442

The absence of structure in this matrix, which shows up in eigenvalues that exhibit no sharp drop and factor loadings that exhibit no pattern, also appears in the distribution of responses to each question, which in aggregate approximate a 50:50 split. See the following examples:

QUESTION 1: C1

Response	Frequency	Wtd. Freq.	Prob. Correct
0.0000	7	7.47	0.985
1.0000	3	2.53	0.015

QUESTION 2: C2

Response	Frequency	Wtd. Freq.	Prob. Correct
0.0000	7	5.33	0.660
1.0000	3	4.67	0.340

QUESTION 8: C8

Response	Frequency	Wtd. Freq.	Prob. Correct
0.0000	5	6.92	0.961
1.0000	5	3.08	0.039

QUESTION 9: C9

Response	Frequency	Wtd. Freq.	Prob. Correct
0.0000	2	3.55	0.101
1.0000	8	6.45	0.899

QUESTION 10: C10

Response	Frequency	Wtd. Freq.	Prob. Correct
0.0000	4	1.74	0.004
1.0000	6	8.26	0.996

The final portion of ANTHROPAC's consensus analysis output identifies the cultural consensus, had there been agreement among these hypothetical informants:

Estimated Correct Answers for Each Question

	1	2	3	4	5	6	7	8	9	0
	C1	C2	C3	C4	C5	C6	C7	C8	C9	C10
KEY	0	0	0	1	0	1	0	0	1	1

In this case, of course, the "answer key" means nothing.

Look at Structure

Compare the consensus analysis of randomness with the analysis of the second matrix. The first factor (4.483), 3.4 times larger than the second (1.330), accounts for 66.3% of the variability among informants.

With a few exceptions—you should always expect variation in points of view—the factor loadings are high (over .50) and exhibit an average level of variability (.19) less than one-third the average level of agreement (.64). These findings indicate that our informants told us that there exists a clear agreement about what constitutes acceptable and unacceptable behavior for women who interact with men they just met.

EIGENVALUES

FACTOR	VALUE	PERCENT	CUM %	RATIO
1:	4.483	66.3	66.3	3.371
2:	1.330	19.7	85.9	1.396
3:	0.952	14.1	100.0	

Estimated Knowledge of Each Respondent
0.76; 0.85; 0.59; 0.83; 0.49; 0.30; 0.86; 0.75; 0.61; 0.38
Average: 0.642; Std. Dev.: 0.191

Estimated Correct Answers for Each Question

	1	2	3	4	5	6	7	8	9	0
	C1	C2	C3	C4	C5	C6	C7	C8	C9	C10
KEY	1	0	1	1	1	1	0	0	0	1

The answer key tells us what the consensus is all about. (Answer keys for similarity data collected through triads tests or pile sorts, however, make sense only when you look at the multidimensional scaling maps they represent.) In this case, the following answer key tells us that people find it acceptable for a woman interacting with a man she just met to: (1) dress conservatively; (3) sit cross-legged; (4) reach out and touch; (5) laugh and smile a lot; (6) act relaxed; or (10) kiss. They find it unacceptable for her to: (2) dress revealingly; (7) be aggressive; (8) flirt; or (9) be direct.

Or do they? Look closely at the distribution of responses, particularly (2) dress revealingly, (8) flirt, and (10) kiss.

QUESTION 1: C1

Response	Frequency	Wtd. Freq.	Prob. Correct
0.0000	2	1.05	0.000
1.0000	8	8.95	1.000

QUESTION 2: C2

Response	Frequency	Wtd. Freq.	Prob. Correct
0.0000	6	5.26	0.590
1.0000	4	4.74	0.410

QUESTION 3: C3

Response	Frequency	Wtd. Freq.	Prob. Correct
0.0000	1	0.77	0.000
1.0000	9	9.23	1.000

QUESTION 4: C4

Response	Frequency	Wtd. Freq.	Prob. Correct
0.0000	1	0.95	0.000
1.0000	9	9.05	1.000

QUESTION 5: C5

Response	Frequency	Wtd. Freq.	Prob. Correct
0.0000	0	0.00	0.000
1.0000	10	10.00	1.000

QUESTION 6: C6

Response	Frequency	Wtd. Freq.	Prob. Correct
0.0000	1	0.47	0.000
1.0000	9	9.53	1.000

QUESTION 7: C7

Response	Frequency	Wtd. Freq.	Prob. Correct
0.0000	9	9.41	1.000
1.0000	1	0.59	0.000

QUESTION 8: C8

Response	Frequency	Wtd. Freq.	Prob. Correct
0.0000	6	6.42	0.998
1.0000	4	3.58	0.002

QUESTION 9: C9

Response	Frequency	Wtd. Freq.	Prob. Correct
0.0000	9	9.08	1.000
1.0000	1	0.92	0.000

QUESTION 10: C10

Response	Frequency	Wtd. Freq.	Prob. Correct
0.0000	4	4.54	0.206
1.0000	6	5.46	0.794

Close examination of the distribution of responses calls into question whether people find it acceptable for women to dress revealingly, be aggressive, or kiss men they've just met. Some people think so; others don't. A look at who thought what revealed Puerto Ricans and Yankees, men and women, and young and old are on both sides of these issues; they split their responses fairly evenly.

Look at a Strong Consensus About All Items

In short, the cultural consensus among these informants is about everything else. Reanalysis of the matrix, once we extract the data on dressing revealingly, being aggressive, and kissing, about which there exists significant variability in point of view, yields a first factor eigenvalue nearly ten times larger than the next, which accounts for over 90% of the variability in what our informants told us. The factor loadings rise, too, reflecting the strong cultural consensus about appropriate behavior for women interacting with men they just met.

EIGENVALUES

FACTOR	VALUE	PERCENT	CUM %	RATIO
1	6.796	90.6	90.6	9.649
2	0.704	9.4	100.0	

Estimated Knowledge of Each Respondent
1.00; 1.00; 0.68; 1.00; 0.68; 0.40; 1.00; 1.00; 0.68; 0.40
Average: 0.783; Std. Dev.: 0.238
Estimated Correct Answers for Each Question

	1	3	4	5	6	7	9
	C1	C3	C4	C5	C6	C7	C9
KEY	1	1	1	1	1	0	0

In short, it's acceptable for a woman interacting with a man she just met to: (1) dress conservatively, (3) sit cross-legged, (4) reach out and touch, (5) laugh and smile a lot, or (6) act relaxed. It's not acceptable for her to: (7) be aggressive, or

(9) be direct. There's no agreement over whether it's acceptable for women to: (2) dress revealingly, (8) flirt, or (10) kiss.

Generalizing Your Findings

Data collected to date reveal an agreement about how women ought or ought not to act with men they've just met that is both strong (the average level of agreement is nearly .80) and broad (it holds, irrespective of gender, age, or ethnicity)—with specific points of variability for which there exists no agreement. But analysis of data from just 10 informants doesn't warrant generalization.

Table 10.2 shows that average levels of agreement around .80 require at least three and preferably six interviews per sampling frame cell, 48 informants, to warrant generalization. If these findings hold up with further data collection, however, we could generalize with 96–98% certainty that, irrespective of gender, generation, or Yankee or Puerto Rican ethnicity, when interacting with a man she just meets, people in Connecticut find it acceptable for a woman to: dress conservatively, sit cross-legged, reach out and touch, laugh and smile a lot, or act relaxed; they find it unacceptable for a woman to be aggressive or direct; and they disagree about whether or not it is acceptable for a woman to dress revealingly, flirt, or kiss.

Generalization, however, remains contingent on identifying experiential variability that may influence the studied meanings. Earlier, I emphasized the importance of designing informal and semistructured interviews to elicit information on the adequacy of distinctions like age, gender, and ethnicity.

When you start research you always have to guess at the life experience markers that may influence how people come to look out at and respond to the world of experience. Achieving ethnography's goal of moving from a view that looks in from the outside to one that looks out from the inside requires you to actively search for sources of cultural difference and change how you select informants in ways to reflect knowledge you gain during the course of field research.

Evidence of Consensus and Disagreement

Sometimes you may encounter cultural differences unexpectedly. A consensus analysis will identify these differences by the presence of systematically low or negative factor loadings. The following factor loadings come from the addition of three new informants to the set of ten we just looked at.

Estimated Knowledge of Each Respondent
0.78; 0.83; 0.61; 0.83; 0.48; 0.31; 0.87; 0.74; 0.60; 0.39; −0.14; −0.14; 0.11
Average: 0.482; Std. Dev.: 0.340

These negative factor loadings signal the possible presence of a consensus directly opposite to the one we just looked at. A run of systematically low factor loadings warns you of significant cultural differences. In either case, findings like these tell you to return to your informants and search out the sources of difference. For the topic of gender relations, you might look for life experience differences that lead people to think of women as passive, inferior or vulnerable, subject to predation by men, or who think of sex as a subject far too serious for play or the subject of casual interaction.

In Short

First, explicitly identify the cultural phenomenon you want to study. That tells you whom to look to for cultural expertise. Second, explicitly identify a sampling frame that encompasses plausible influences on the historically and regionally situated social interaction through which those experts created their knowledge. Third, collect data. Start with small numbers of informants for each sampling frame cell. Apply consensus analysis and pertinent diagnostic tools to assess variability and consensus explicitly. Add informants as necessary. Change sampling criteria as appropriate to assess sources of cultural variability that you didn't think of before you started. Fourth, take your consensus analysis findings back to your informants, individually and in groups, to provide triangulation for finding validity. Fifth, continue steps 3 and 4 until you've exhausted yourself and your informants. Generalize your findings to all people participating in the historically and regionally situated social interaction through which the meaning you studied was created and may be changed, but limit your generalizations to people whose life experiences you explicitly identified.

QUESTIONS

1. Why do cultural data invalidate classical statistical tests?
2. Can you pick a topic for research and design and justify an appropriate fully nested sampling frame to guide your data collection?
3. What do consensus analysis factor loadings tell you? What is the significance of a pattern of high, positive loadings? What is the significance of a pattern of low or negative loadings?
4. What findings warrant a conclusion that your informants express a cultural consensus?
5. What are the limits to valid generalization of your findings?

Eleven

Consensus Analysis:
Do Scottish Business Advisers
Agree on Models of Success?

Background

Located between Edinburgh and Glasgow, central Scotland presents an industrial landscape that contrasts sharply with the tiny picturesque highland villages that delight tourists. However, the economy of the area is gradually being transformed from one dominated by coal mining and heavy industry to a more diversified economy of commerce, tourism, services, light manufacturing and, especially, computer and electronics manufacturing.

More than a decade ago I began my study of this economy by interviewing owner-managers of small, new, high technology firms. I wanted to discover how small firms contributed to regional development (Caulkins 1992).[1] I learned that all of these entrepreneurs received the support of a variety of business advisers early in the development of their firms. These business advisers represented different kinds of development agencies and different levels of government, but all aimed to help small businesses succeed and contribute to the economic growth of the region. However, about 20% of the entrepreneurs claimed that they received conflicting advice from different agencies, leaving them confused and, sometimes, resentful. From my own research, I knew that entrepreneurs, themselves, had very diverse experiences, goals, and values (Caulkins 1995a). I wondered whether the advisers had diverse goals and values as well. If so, the advisers' conflicting priorities might account for the confusion voiced by some entrepreneurs. Given the central role of business advisers in the small business sector in central Scotland, I thought it important to find out. Anything that threatens the development of the small business sector also threatens the economic revival of the region.

The Research Problem

I concentrated my study on a part of central Scotland that now calls itself "Braveheart Country," referring to Mel Gibson's 1996 Academy Award–winning film about the thirteenth-century Scottish martyr and national hero, William Wallace, who died resisting the domination of the English crown. Braveheart Country includes the affluent university town of Stirling, now an administrative and tourist center and the site of Wallace's greatest victory against the English in 1297. Near Stirling to the east, on the Firth of Forth, is the smaller working-class town of Alloa. Just a few miles to the south is Falkirk, the site of Wallace's greatest defeat, an industrial town with a comparatively high rate of unemployment.

Individuals starting up new businesses in Braveheart Country need to find suitable premises, get feedback on their business plans, learn about various government-funded business assistance schemes, and consult about commercial regulations. Business advisers can help with these problems. They are practical interpreters of new ideas in management, production, marketing, personnel, and sales. They dispense information about business problems and opportunities within the local area and can bring together the people and agencies with the expertise and resources to help make businesses succeed.

Business advisers are employed by the local and regional government, university business management departments, enterprise trusts, and by business development agencies financed by a combination of governmental and private funding. The advisers in each of these organizations have different educational backgrounds and different areas of expertise. Each organization has its own mission, although all of them have a stake in the economic development of Braveheart Country. A businessperson might interact with advisers from each of the organizations at different points in the launch of a new business.

A Composite Case Study

Consider the example of "Chris," a composite of several entrepreneurs, and her interaction with eight real business advisers in Braveheart Country. Chris, a recent graduate with a degree in studio art, took an enterprise workshop from Bob, a business trainer employed at the university. Bob is adept at showing liberal arts students how to think about going into business for themselves. With Bob's help, Chris developed a business plan for manufacturing original designs of "Chris's

Celtic Jewelry" for the tourist trade. Chris wanted to live in Stirling, a good place for tourist business, so she made an appointment to see Ronald, the director of STEP, the Stirling Enterprise Park, who manages a series of small business premises in a converted cigarette factory building. Chris learned about the business incubator units at the Park from Ronald and also spoke to Nigel, the business development officer of the Stirling District Council, the local government unit. Nigel is pleased at the prospect of another business starting up in town, and he tells Chris how local government can assist.

During the first year in the premises at STEP, Chris got frequent encouragement from Bob, her university mentor, and Ronald and his staff, whose offices were just a few doors away in STEP. Nigel was helpful as well, but she saw him less often since he was busy helping to put together funding packages to help attract several English firms to relocate in Braveheart Country. Chris didn't always take the advice of Bob, Ronald, and Nigel, but maintained her optimism while dealing with crisis after crisis during the first two years. Ronald disapproved of some of Chris's decisions but thought that she would learn quickly from her experience.

Surviving a couple of difficult years, Chris established herself in the market and wanted to expand her business and move out of her increasingly cramped premises in the Stirling Enterprise Park. With four new employees, she needed to reorganize her inefficient production process. She talked with Gordon, the industrial officer for the regional government, who suggested moving to Alloa, where Chris could lease a small disused factory. Gordon was preoccupied with the recent unexpected closing of an American computer manufacturer's branch plant in Stirling, throwing more than 100 people out of work. Some of those who lost their jobs lived in Alloa and might be retrained to work for Chris, he thought, although at a lower wage.

On Gordon's recommendation, Chris also visited ACE, the enterprise trust in Alloa, and talked with Richard, the director. Richard was in business for 30 years before taking the job at ACE and was now giving others the benefit of his vast experience. When Chris called, Richard had had a trying day, steering two unemployed men away from the unpromising idea of starting up yet another local taxi company. He was enthusiastic about Chris's plans to move to Alloa and develop a new line of "Braveheart sword" jewelry (tie pins, pendants, earrings, etc.) to take advantage of the continuing popularity of the film. Richard thought that this new line of jewelry might help Alloa, located near the William Wallace Monument, a tall Victorian tower erected to honor the Scottish hero and freedom fighter.

Up to this point, the larger towns have been the main beneficiaries of the Braveheart media tie-ins. Richard encouraged Chris to consider opening a retail shop in Alloa in addition to the manufacturing unit, but Chris was reluctant to plunge into retail. Richard also advised on acquiring capital—always a serious problem—for the expansion of her business. He phoned his friend John, director of the Falkirk Enterprise Action Trust (FEAT), another enterprise trust, to confer about some recent changes in government-subsidized training schemes for secondary school graduates. Richard thought that Chris might be able to take on a couple of trainees in the Alloa factory.

Meanwhile, Brenda, a new lecturer in business studies at the university, was teaching a workshop on enterprise for women, since women are underrepresented in business in Scotland. Brenda wanted women entrepreneurs to speak at her workshop, so called on Chris, who happily agreed because she wanted to inspire other women to follow her example. Brenda also recruited a recent graduate of her department, Jennifer, who had taken the job of assistant director of FEAT in Falkirk. Jennifer could talk about the kinds of problems and opportunities for women in business that she sees everyday on her job. Brenda was pleased that her first workshop would have two inspirational speakers: Chris, a successful entrepreneur, and Jennifer, a successful business adviser in Falkirk. Jennifer's boss, John, helped publicize the workshop and hoped that it would inspire a number of new entrepreneurs in Braveheart Country.

In this illustration of a fictional business and a composite entrepreneur (but real advisers), we can see that an entrepreneur is likely to encounter different advisers at different stages of the development of a business and for different problems. In that sense, advising organizations each have a different niche in the economy of regional development. The government-employed advisers are interested not just in the fate of individual firms, but also in the contribution of firms to the growth of jobs and the local economy. These officials help in coordinating economic development plans and encourage new firms to set up business in the area. Their academic degrees are more likely to be in public administration and planning than in business management. In contrast, the enterprise trust advisers are often pragmatic people with business experience, perhaps supplemented with some advanced education in management. The university lecturers/business trainers have graduate degrees in business management and are also driven by theoretical ideas rather than by pragmatic business or policy concerns.

I suspected that each organization had not only a different niche, but different priorities. From previous fieldwork I knew, for example, that some Scottish high technology entrepreneurs complained about conflicting recommendations from different advisers. Others resisted advice apparently based on goals or ideas of success that the entrepreneurs didn't share. In turn, some business advisers complained to me about the reluctance of businessmen and women to take useful and important advice.

The advising relationship, in short, was open to conflict and miscommunication, perhaps due to differences in the perspectives and assumptions of the participants. I knew that the entrepreneurs didn't all share the same views of success. Did advisers have different priorities, too? If so, that could account for the apparently conflicting advice. Given the central role of business advisers in the process of regional economic development, I thought it important to find out.

Shared Model of Success?

Consensus analysis is a good technique for assessing the amount of agreement among a group of people about some domain of cultural knowledge such as business success.[2] The technique requires a sample of knowledgeable individuals to make some kind of judgment (important/unimportant, good/better/best, right/wrong, etc.) about a series of concepts or things in a domain of culture. If we make a systematic record of those judgments we can then discover whether our sample agrees or disagrees on the answers. A high level of agreement indicates a shared understanding of that domain (Romney et al. 1986). If we think about a set of Scottish business advisers, employed by a variety of organizations, we can imagine at least the following four possible patterns of ideas of success:

> *High consensus*: Ideas of success shared by most business advisers, regardless of the kind of organization they work for. Constitutes a "business advising culture."
>
> *Subcultural*: Less tightly shared, with greatest agreement among advisers in similar institutions. Example: an "academic advising subculture" and a "governmental advising subculture," perhaps bridged by an "enterprise trust subculture" that has some similarities to both of the other subcultures.
>
> *Contested*: Sharply differing views of success, held by two or more groups, but lacking the overlap of the subcultural perspective. Example: "academic" versus "nonacademic" advising cultures.
>
> *Idiosyncratic*: No agreement on what constitutes business success. Every adviser has a different view.

These four possibilities are really competing hypotheses—they can't all be true. Guided by the comments of some business owners, I expected the subcultural or contested hypothesis to win out. Advising organizations with different missions might have different models of business success. This would account for the conflicting advice that some business persons reported to me. The least likely of the four, I thought, was the idiosyncratic hypothesis.

Determining Data Needs

As researchers we need to construct alternative hypotheses, as done above, to avoid becoming overly attached to one hypothesis and blind to others. We should be able to imagine or anticipate what kind of data would be needed to give each of the above hypotheses a fair chance to succeed or fail. Consider some alternatives. We could get a group of advisers together in the same room and ask them to discuss business success and see if they come to a consensus. This would violate one of the assumptions of consensus analysis, that the judgments of each individual in the sample are obtained independently. A better idea would be to interview advisers individually. But what kind of advisers? If they all come from the same kind of organization, such as local government, our results would be biased toward the consensus hypothesis and against the subcultural hypothesis. More importantly, a sample of advisers from one kind of organization would represent only one of the several types of advisers that a typical entrepreneur would encounter. So we need to select advisers from the major types of organizations, described above.

Next, we need to think about what information we want from each adviser. You or I could come up with a list of kinds of business success that we could ask the advisers to discuss. However, that would tell us more about our ideas than about theirs. A better approach is to ask the advisers, independently, to talk about their ideas of business success.

Freelisting Kinds of Success

Freelisting is described in greater detail in Chapter 4. In this research, I started collecting data from university business trainers whom I knew and then branched out to advisers in other organizations in Stirling, Alloa, and Falkirk. For almost a week I visited different business advice agencies, asking the question, "Apart from profitability, what kinds of small-business success are there?" I had discovered that "profitability" was a kind of self-evident threshold concept, universally considered a measure of success in business. We needed to go beyond the self-evident.

I tape recorded each interview, but also wrote copious notes. If you tempt fate and don't take notes during an interview, your tape recorder will fail. (Trust me.) After interviewing ten advisers, I wasn't getting any new items, so I stopped. With the help of some of my contacts, I consolidated the list of over 50 items and eliminated conceptual redundancies. In the end, I had 33 kinds of success (see Table 11.1). You need 20–40 items for stable results.

The advisers didn't confine their ideas to narrow technical measures of success. They mentioned not only the more conventional criteria, such as good customer relations, adequacy of financing, and increasing the profit margin, but also items related to the organization of the firms, such as "fully utilizing the skills of the employees." They also included social dimensions of business success, such as "having a good reputation in the community" or "having a business to pass on to the next generation." They listed items related to regional development, such as using local sources of goods and services and increasing the number of employees. These items contribute to the economic development of Braveheart Country but not necessarily to the success of individual firms. The domain of business success, then, included items relating to the firm, the business owner, the owner's family, the community, and the region.

As a validity check on the information from the advisers, I reviewed transcripts and field notes from previous research in the region (Caulkins 1995a) and found

TABLE 11.1
Kinds of Business Success,
Rank Ordered from Most to Least Important
(33 items, N = 8)

Rank	Consensus Score	Type of Success
1	1.72	Having a reputation for reliability
2	3.20	Enjoying running the business
3	3.34	Having adequate finances for the business
4	3.39	Customer satisfaction
5	3.91	Producing high quality goods/services
6	3.99	Learning from business mistakes and overcoming problems
7	4.38	Ability to appreciate the value of planning
8	4.67	Having a detailed knowledge of how the business is performing at all times
9	7.13	Increasing market demand
10	10.81	Increasing profit margin
11	11.23	Fully utilizing the skills of the management and employees
12	12.47	Having a sense of control over one's destiny
13	14.89	Satisfaction of having created or maintained a business
14	16.01	Taking calculated risks and surviving in business
15	17.01	Upgrading the skills of management and employees
16	18.09	Having a smooth-running organization
17	19.82	Increasing the number of employees in the firm
18	20.28	Involving the employees in running the business
19	20.34	Achieving a desired quality of life
20	20.41	Increased turnover
21	21.97	Introducing innovative products or services
22	22.36	Getting a living wage from the business
23	23.37	Acquiring personal wealth
24	23.47	Achieving a moderate level of profitability without creating a great deal of stress
25	24.52	Expanding premises
26	25.50	Establishing a business to be passed on to the next generation
27	26.00	Local sourcing of materials/services
28	26.33	Being able to run the business and still have adequate time for family, friends, and recreation
29	27.03	Having a public image as a successful business
30	28.53	Having the respect of the business community
31	29.76	Developing the business so that it can be sold at a substantial profit
32	32.19	Becoming a business leader
33	32.65	Having community approval and support

that most of the 33 forms of success were also mentioned by the business persons in my sample. But, of course, some forms of success are more important than others, and this brings us to the second phase of the research in which we learn how advisers prioritize different forms of success.

The Sample

Because I had learned how the advising system works, I picked the sample to represent theoretically important stages and functions in the advising process. To represent the different types of organizations, I selected the eight business advisers featured earlier in my case study of Chris's Celtic Jewelry: (1) business school lecturers and trainers (Bob and Brenda); (2) local and regional government administrators responsible for economic development (Gordon and Nigel); and (3) local business development organizations called enterprise trusts (Ronald in STEP, Richard in ACE, and John and Jennifer in FEAT) All eight advisers have frequent and widespread contacts with a variety of aspiring and current small-business owner-managers.

Prioritizing Types of Success

There were several possible alternative methods to determine the advisers' priorities. I decided on rank ordering, using a pile-sorting procedure (see Boster and J. Johnson [1989] or Weller and Romney [1988] for other examples).[3]

First, I typed each of the 33 kinds of success on the front of a separate 3 x 5 card (you can buy card stock to do this on a computer printer) and on the back of each card wrote an identification number, 1–33. Don't put numbers on the front of the card where they might distract your respondent or make her think that there is a "right" order of priority. Before each interview I shuffled the cards to eliminate the possibility of systematic **order bias** in which respondents treat the first cards differently from later cards (Borgatti 1993/94:266). By randomizing the order of presentation, the cards affected by "order bias" differ with each respondent, and the bias washes out.

Next, I asked each adviser to sort the cards into three piles, according his or her opinion of their priority: One pile was for highest importance, a second for medium importance, and a third for lowest importance. Then the adviser ranked the cards within each pile.

Finally, we combined the three piles—high, medium, and low—and checked through the complete deck to make certain that the adviser was satisfied with the order. Occasionally, someone would interchange a couple of cards, but in general, they found the task easy to do.[4]

I encouraged each adviser to give me a running commentary as they sorted the cards, giving me some insight into the meaning of their priorities. For example, one government adviser confessed that he didn't rank "local sourcing of goods and services" very highly, although it was government policy, because he felt that small businesses needed greater flexibility to develop their own network of suppliers.

Getting the respondents to talk about their sorting also alerts you to any misunderstandings or unusual interpretations of the cards. You need to take careful notes during these commentaries (tape record them if your respondent consents) because the notes will help you interpret your results. I found that the business advisers were very comfortable talking about business success. It is what they do much of the working day.

If, in contrast, your research involves a less central **cultural domain** or your respondents are less used to articulating their ideas about that domain, it may be easier for your respondents to do a **rating**, rather than a **ranking**, task. In a study in Wales, for example, we asked residents in two communities to rate the degree of "Welshness" of the actions in some brief stories on a scale of 1–5 (Caulkins and Trosset 1996). The rating procedure has the advantage of familiarity. As consumers, we are constantly bombarded with product ratings, for example, of four-star restaurants and three-star movies. The task of rating is also easier than ranking since it only requires the respondent to judge one item at a time against some standard. The ranking method, however, is excellent for studying individual differences among specialists, producing a great deal of information in a short time (Weller and Romney 1988:49), so it's a good technique to use with harried business advisers.

When the adviser finished the pile sort, I preserved the order of the cards by fastening the deck with a couple of good rubber bands until I had a chance to record the data (rubberbands can break; use two). If you are doing several interviews on the same day, I recommend having two or more sets of cards, plenty of rubber bands, and some blank cards on which you can write the name of the person who sorted the deck. After an interview, band the sorted cards together with an identifying name card. If you have time after an interview, quickly write down the order of the cards in your notebook before leaving the premises. This preserves a duplicate set of raw data in case something happens to the cards. It pays to be meticulously organized in this phase of the work, as I learned through experience.

Consensus Analysis

We can use consensus analysis to describe patterns of agreement among individuals about a domain or category of cultural knowledge, such as kinds of business success, cures for diseases, Scottish behavior patterns, or kinds of fish. If we think of culture as an information pool, consisting of many domains of knowledge, we can assume that no two individuals will have identical knowledge. Knowledge is distributed. William may know a great deal about business success, little about disease cures, practically nothing about Scottish behavior, and virtually everything about fish. Ian may be clueless about business, very knowledgeable about cures, insightful about Scottish behavior, and unable to distinguish a herring from a halibut. Consensus analysis is good for studying culture one domain at a time. You can't mix business success and romantic success—two different domains—at least not if you are doing consensus analysis. (Romney et al. 1986; Borgatti 1993/94).

Some cultural domains are high consensus domains, ones that are well known to a great many people. Virtually anyone could give us culturally correct answers about those domains. For the more specialized domains, such as business success, we need to ask the cultural specialists, such as our business advisers. Once again, we're trying to discover whether success is a high-consensus domain for our cultural specialists, is subcultural, is divided into contesting perspectives, or is simply chaotic, where everyone's view is different.

Borgatti's ANTHROPAC software provided a quick and convenient way of doing consensus analysis. Using the "Edit" module, I entered the raw data from the ranked cards into a file and created a data matrix of 8 rows, one for each adviser, by 33 columns, one for each form of success. Use the DATA—>IMPORT menu to get your raw data matrix into the program. Always check the accuracy of your data entry by using the DATA—> VIEW—> DISPLAY menu option to see your matrix. Next, I used the TOOLS—>CONSENSUS to start the analysis of my interval data (the other choices are "multiple choice" and "covariance").

The consensus analysis module in ANTHROPAC produces four kinds of information. First, it performs a **factor analysis** of the data set, which will reveal whether or not there's a single pattern of agreement among the advisers. Second, ANTHROPAC lists the scores for each of the respondents, showing their level of knowledge in this domain. Third, it lists the "culturally correct" answers to the question, in this case, of how the different types of success are prioritized by the sample. Fourth, it creates a person-by-person agreement matrix that can be displayed using **multidimensional scaling (MDS)**, **cluster analysis,** or both (Borgatti 1992:26–35). Let us consider these four program outputs in greater detail.

Factor Analysis of the Data Set

Factor analysis (see Bernard 1994:305) tells us whether or not there is a high or "cultural" level of agreement by our respondents about the domain of business success. If the analysis shows a single factor in the data, we can say that our sample of advisers share the same perspective on success. Frequently, however, analysis may reveal several factors in the data, their strength measured in **eigen values**. If one factor is dominant, with an eigen value at least three times larger than the second factor, we can still say that we have a **cultural level of agreement** (J. Johnson 1990:85). So the interpretative rule is: One factor means one culture. Alternatively, two factors, but one that has an eigen value at least three times larger than the other, still means one culture. ANTHROPAC reports the ratio between the first and second factors (if any). If the ratio in a data set is less than three, indicating two factors of roughly similar strength, subcultures rather than a single culture may be represented in the data.

My Scottish advisers were in strong agreement, well above the single cultural level of consensus. While there were two factors in the data, ANTHROPAC reported that the first was 5.1 times greater than the second, comfortably exceeding the threshold for a single culture. This result strongly supports the first hypothesis, that the advisers share a "business advisers' culture" with similar priorities for success. This, of course, was not the result I was expecting. I anticipated a "subcultural" or "contested" result. However, both of these hypotheses were thoroughly trashed because of the high level of agreement indicated by the factor analysis and, as we will see, the high scores for each of the advisers.

Cultural Knowledge Scores for Individuals

Next, ANTHROPAC displays **cultural knowledge scores**, normally ranging between 0 and 1, for each individual in the sample. A score of .5, for example, would indicate that an individual had the culturally correct answer 50% of the time. Anyone really knowledgeable about a culture should have a better score than that. The average score for the eight business advisers was .78, ranging between a high score of .83 for Gordon, the regional industrial development officer, and a low score of .66 for Nigel, the adviser from the local government. Although not everyone is equally knowledgeable, the range between highest and lowest scores (1.68) is narrow. Clearly this group of advisers is both well matched and very familiar with the shared business advisers' culture in Braveheart Country.

With a small sample of only eight persons, however, can we be confident of the results? Weller and Romney (1988:76–77) give tables for calculating confidence levels at various average levels of knowledge for different sample sizes.[5] Where there are high average levels of knowledge, as is the case with the Braveheart advisers, only a small sample is needed to establish the culturally correct view of a domain. As Weller and Romney (1988:77) assert, "Small samples can yield extremely reliable data."

Cultural Key: Ranked Types of Success

ANTHROPAC next displays the **cultural key**, the consensus ranking of the forms of success (see Table 11.1). This key answers the question, "What is the rank order of the forms of success in the business advisers' culture?" "Having a reputation for reliability" is the highest-ranked success item, and "Having community approval and support" is lowest ranked. As you can see, the advisers place greatest importance on types of success directly related to *business performance over which the entrepreneur has some control*, such as "a reputation for reliability" and "developing a customer base." The lower priority items in the model, such as having community approval, are secondary outcomes or results of the primary business activities.

Additional features of the cultural model of success can be inferred from the consensus rankings for the success items (see Table 11.1). These scores are simply the weighted average of the rankings by the eight advisers. Because they are weighted averages, they have the characteristics of an interval scale, not just an ordinal scale. The scores of the top 8 items have a narrow range, showing that they are relatively similar in importance. They are separated, however, from the next item by a big gap of 2.46. Similarly, the 9th item, "increasing market demand," is separated from the following item by another large interval in scores. Another interval occurs after item 12, then there is a relatively smooth sequence of decreasing scores until item 31. after which there is another large interval before the final two items. All these intervals are marked with solid lines in Table 11.1. Between these lines are bunches of items that have something in common.

The first eight items, with consensus scores ranging between 1.72 and 4.67, are all high-priority issues in the advisers' model of success: If the manager doesn't do these things, she or he is headed for serious trouble. If the firm is reliable, the owner enjoys the business, has adequate capital, satisfied customers, excellent goods and services, and the owner learns from mistakes, understands how to plan, and carefully monitors the business—then the business is performing as it should. In subsequent interviews with business advisers elsewhere I've heard the same points emphasized, so this hierarchy of success makes ethnographic sense. Note that the consensus scores for two, three, and four are almost ties or almost equally important to the business advisers.

The ninth item, "increasing market demand," is separated by large intervals from items above and below it. Here the business advisers' culture sends a message: if your business is in good shape (items one–eight), then start building up your business. Growth is good. At this point some of the high technology entrepreneurs that I studied earlier would become uncomfortable with this advice. For them, *some* growth is good, but not too much and not too fast. Success for them means staying small (Caulkins 1995b:23–24).

Items 10–12 deal with increasing management's control over the operation of the firm. This cluster of items represents fine-tuning of an already thriving business.

The largest grouping of items, 13–31, includes a series of optional successes that may be good for some businesses but not for others. It also includes items that I wrongly expected would be central priorities for some advising organizations. "Increasing the number of employees in the firm" and "local sourcing of materials and services," which I understood to be important concerns of local government, were only 17th and 27th. The academic advisers, I thought, would put a high priority on "upgrading the skills of management and employees," but it was only 15th. I had also assumed that "getting a living wage from the business" would be a high priority for the enterprise trusts, which deal so often with unemployed workers. That item was only 22nd, just above "acquiring personal wealth," which was a very high priority for some of the growth-oriented entrepreneurs that I knew. For other high tech firms, items such as "introducing innovative products and services," would have been near the top.

The last group of items, 32nd and 33rd, deal with business leadership and community approval. Those forms of success are perhaps personally gratifying and very important to some individuals, but not important in business advisers' culture. The potential sources of conflict in the advising situation are more clear, now that we can see that business persons may have very different priorities than the advisers.

While we have found a cultural level of agreement among all advisers, we also need to look carefully to see if advisers employed by the same or similar organization have greater levels of agreement than individuals working in different organizations. Within the one culture of business advisers, can we find subpatterns? To answer that question we need to compare the levels of agreement among all pairs of advisers.

Matrix of Agreement Among Respondents

The consensus analysis module in ANTHROPAC produces a square matrix showing the degree of agreement or similarity between all pairs of respondents in the data set. In our case, with eight respondents, the matrix is eight rows by eight columns. You can see the agreement matrix using the DATA>VIEW–>DISPLAY menu. Each cell of the matrix represents one pair of advisers and contains a coefficient of similarity, ranging between −1 and +1. If the coefficient of similarity between two advisers is +1, they gave identical answers; if the coefficient is −1, they gave no answers in common. This similarity matrix can be "mapped" in space using multidimensional scaling (MDS), or diagramed as a tree structure using hierarchical cluster analysis, both available in ANTHROPAC. Figure 11.1 shows the use of both MDS and, secondarily, cluster analysis (see chapters by Clark et al. and Roos, both this volume, for a detailed discussion of multidimensional scaling and cluster analysis). The MDS program plots each adviser in two-dimensional space. The greater the agreement between a pair of advisers, the closer they are in space. As you can see, Richard (ACE) and Gordon (RCIDO) are closer to each other, for example, than to Ronald (STEP).

Clusters, derived from the "average" method in ANTHROPAC's cluster analysis menu, are shown by ellipses. The innermost ellipses surround the two most similar individuals on the scatter plot, with outer rings enclosing successively less similar individuals. Jennifer (FEAT2) and Brenda (SUL2) form a cluster, joined by Bob (SUL1) at a lower threshold of similarity.

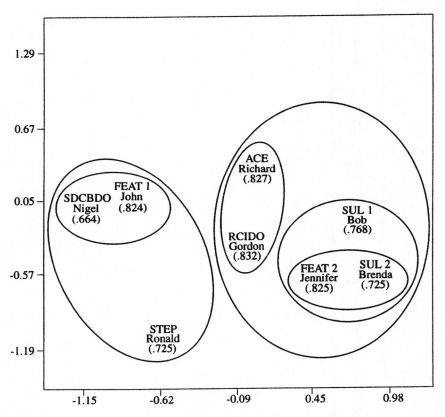

Figure 11.1. Success model: multidimensional scaling of agreement matrix of business advisers in central Scotland (cultural centrality score of each adviser in parentheses).

Stress = .067
Abbreviations:
  RCIDO = Regional council industrial development officer
  SDCBDO = Local government business development officer
  ACE, FEAT1, FEAT2, STEP = Entreprise Trust officers
  SUL1, SUL2 = University lecturers/trainers

We see that the three pairs of advisers with the highest agreement (Nigel/John, Richard/Gordon, Jennifer/Brenda) are not only in *different* organizations, but different *types* of organizations: government and enterprise trust pairings in the first two cases, and enterprise trust and university in the third. This evidence further undermines the subcultural hypothesis: Different kinds of advising organizations don't promote entirely different models of success. However, the diagram does show us some potential lines of interpersonal influence. The two university lecturers are in the same larger cluster, but one of the enterprise trust officers, Jennifer (FEAT2) and Brenda (SUL2) are even more similar in their views of success. Not coincidentally, Jennifer took courses at the university before getting her job with FEAT. Could it be that Jennifer was particularly influenced by Brenda? Or could it be that Jennifer's and Brenda's perspectives are similar because of their experiences as women? Over time, Jennifer's perspectives may come to resemble those of John, her boss, or their views may converge through mutual socialization. Further ethnographic interviewing could answer those questions. In any case, these questions illustrate the more general point that analysis always stimulates new questions for ethnographic investigation.

We have learned some new things about the data by using MDS, but should we trust the diagram? Is it a good picture, or does it distort the data? We can answer that question by considering the "stress" score (see the bottom left side of Figure 11.1), which tells how well the MDS solution represents the data in two-dimensional space. The lower the score the better the representation. A stress score below 0.2 indicates a satisfactory MDS solution (Borgatti 1993/94:269). With a stress score of 0.067, Figure 11.1 is an excellent representation of the data.

Conclusion

As we have seen in this case study, consensus analysis allows us to ask a series of questions about a domain of knowledge. First, does the knowledge held by a set of individuals constitute one culture, several subcultures, oppositional cultures, or idiosyncratic views? Second, if one culture is found, how knowledgeable about the domain are each of the individuals in the sample? Third, if again one culture is found, what is the "culturally correct" version of the structure and content of the domain? Fourth, how similar are the views of each of the individuals to all others in the sample?

Consensus analysis is an important tool for exploring cultural diversity and similarity (Romney et al. 1987). While this analytic technique is useful for identifying the "best" informant for in-depth interviewing on given topics (J. Johnson 1990), it has even more promise as a method for discovering how knowledge is distributed in a society. D'Andrade (1995:216) correctly notes that "The issue is not 'how culture is shared' but rather how to understand both distributed and high consensus aspects of cultural knowledge." I had expected to find diverse models of success with the Scottish business advisers, but found consensus instead. They spoke with one voice, although each didn't stress exactly the same points.

Having a favored hypothesis shattered is not an occasion for despair. On the contrary, it is a cause for elation because we have revised our provisional understanding, not simply confirmed what we thought we knew already. In retrospect, I know what originally persuaded me to favor the subcultural or contested models of success. I had listened too intently to those business owners who felt that they had been given contradictory advice, or perhaps just advice that contradicted their own priorities. Uncovering the consistency of the business advisers' model of success allows us to better understand all parties in the advising relationship and, ultimately, the trajectory of regional development.

QUESTIONS

1. In this case study what effort was made to assure that the sample, while small, would be diverse? Are there alternative possibilities? What are the advantages and disadvantages of each?
2. What kinds of questions work well as a rating task? As a ranking task?
3. If analysis showed that data were subcultural, why would you not use the "cultural key"?
4. If the data are subcultural, what further steps in analysis would you take?
5. Could you use consensus analysis to illuminate areas of agreement and disagreement among social groups in conflict?

NOTES

1. I am grateful to the people who participated in this study and to those who supported it. My thanks go especially to Michael Scott, Peter Rosa, and other staff at the University of Stirling, Scotland, to the Grinnell College Grant Board for funding, and to Hatfield College and the Anthropology Department of the University of Durham, England, where I was a Research Fellow in 1991.

2. Cognitive anthropologists have made systematic studies of the varieties of *social* success and failure in several cultures (Romney et al. 1979; Freeman et al. 1981). See also D'Andrade (1992) on goals and motivation.

3. By obtaining a complete rank ordering of the items, we avoid the "lumper-splitter" problem" encountered in using "free" pile sort data (Bernard 1994:249–250).

4. After you enter and import the raw data in ANTHROPAC, you need to transform the *individual-by-rank* matrix into a standard *individual-by-item* matrix. If you have ANTHROPAC 4.94 or higher, you can do this using the DATA>CONVERT>PERM–>RANK menu. In earlier versions of this program this routine produces a matrix in which the value in every cell is the correct number minus 1. In these earlier versions you can use the

following workaround to add 1 to each cell in the matrix RANKS (the output file name). Use the matrix algebra module in TOOLS to create a matrix of 1s that has the same dimensions as RANKS (in our case, 8 rows by 33 columns). Next, add the two matrices, calling the new matrix RANKS2, which can then be used in consensus analysis. These steps can be combined as one line in matrix algebra:

-->RANKS2 = ADD(RANKS MATRIX(1 8 33))

5. Weller and Romney (1988:76) note that the tables were prepared for dichotomous data rather than rank-ordered data used here. Nevertheless the tables give an approximation of the confidence levels that can be achieved for rank order data with small samples.

JAVIER GARCIA DE ALBA GARCIA ■
VICTOR DE MUNCK
ANA LETICIA SALCEDO ROCHA
GUADARRAMA L. A. VARGAS
TRINI GARRO

Twelve

Consensus Analysis: High Blood Pressure in a Mexican Barrio

In Mexico, cardiovascular diseases are the leading cause of illness and death (PAHO 1994). Hypertension, high blood pressure, is the least complex, most familiar, and most frequently measured index of cardiovascular diseases. If an effort is not made to understand the "local knowledge" Mexicans use to explain the causes of **high blood pressure**, then the frequency of cardiovascular health problems is likely to increase in the future (García de Alba García1989a, 1989b).

It's necessary to study the sociocultural as well as the biological and environmental conditions that are potential causes of high blood pressure. In this chapter, we examine and compare ideas about high blood pressure held by three different **age groups**. We have three goals: (1) to ascertain whether different cultural models of high blood pressure based on age exist; (2) to understand popular conceptions concerning both the causes and prevention of high blood pressure; and (3) to ultimately establish comprehensive, publicly accessible guidelines for the management and prevention of hypertension.

We intend to continue the pragmatic tradition of research in medical anthropology by using systematic data collection and analytic techniques to determine variability and consensus in conceptions about high blood pressure (Garro 1988; Dressler 1991, 1996). We hope that this study will contribute to the eventual implementation of educational public health programs addressing the prevention and treatment of high blood pressure among poor Mexicans, who are most susceptible to cardiovascular diseases.

Research on Hypertension and Cultural Change

In general, **medical anthropological** studies on diseases have been conducted with a focus on one cultural group. One of the first anthropological studies of arterial hypertension was conducted by Scotch (1961) among urban and rural Zulu populations. Scotch found statistically significant relationships between arterial hypertension and age, gender, obesity, menopause, and other variables. He argued that stress was a primary causal vector of hypertension and that stress measures varied with social context. Zulus in urban areas reported higher stress levels and had higher rates of hypertension than did Zulus in rural areas.

In the 1960s, the Ju'/Hoansi foragers of the Kalahari Desert were "famous" for their low cholesterol counts, blood pressures, and the near absence of heart disease (Lee 1993:156). In the 1980s, as a result of a shift from a primarily migratory to a primarily sedentary way of life, blood pressure rates were higher and cases of hypertension and heart diseases were recorded. Both Lee and Scotch noted that a shift from a migratory or rural way of life to a sedentary or urban way of life led to an increase in cardiovascular types of illnesses.

Dressler (1996) used consensus analysis to show that the percentage of locally rated "important" Western goods owned by people in the Brazilian city of Ribeirão Preto was positively associated with increased systolic blood pressure. He takes as axiomatic that "average blood pressure tends to increase as traditional societies move along a path of so-called Westernization or development" (p. 6). Along with Westernization and a shift from traditional to more sedentary, market-based life-styles comes increasing personal stress. Both the material adoption of new goods and lifestyles and the feeling of being culturally dislocated or disconnected from a cultural core contribute to an increase in hypertension among such populations.

Although we can identify most causes of hypertension, it's also important to understand local explanations for hypertension in order to develop locally effective treatment and preventive programs. Any study that seeks to investigate and reduce the causes of cardiovascular diseases in a population should look at **sociocultural variables** as well as biomedical variables (for example, age, sex).

Treating Hypertension and Local Knowledge

Sthal et al. (1975) argued that it's more difficult to alter perceptions than to manipulate behaviors. He proposed implementing treatment policies that manipulate sociocultural variables rather than seeking to alter beliefs about blood pressure through education. He argued for treatment policies that provided cash incentives for individuals to change from high cholesterol to low cholesterol foods.

However, it seems to us that such changes may provide short-term benefits but would be hard to maintain. For example, how long can cash incentives be provided and to how many people? Second, it would have to be determined how large the cash incentive should be to trigger a behavioral change (this may vary across individuals, families, and locales). Behaviorist models are difficult to transpose from the lab, where variables and choices are limited and controlled by the experimenter, to the field, where variables cannot be controlled. It may be more difficult to change perceptions in the field, but once changed, those changes are likely to be more enduring than behavioral changes affected through a stimulus-response model.

Blumhagen (1980) developed a **folk explanatory model** of hypertension that described the range of beliefs about the causes of hypertension among his informants. Blumhagen elicited informants' ideas about the reasons for hypertension (for example, diet, stress, pollution, obesity) and the direction of relationship between these reasons (for example, pollution causes stress, stress causes poor diets, poor diets lead to obesity, and obesity leads to hypertension). He drew egocentric (individual) network diagrams for each informant. These diagrams depicted the direction (or vector) of causal connections between conceptual nodes. Blumhagen aggregated these diagrams to produce a typical òr normative model with alternative models of relational networks also included. In this way, Blumhagen could present both general and idiosyncratic explanatory models of beliefs about hypertension.

Garro (1988) also investigated variations in beliefs about hypertension in her studies among the Ojibwa Indians in Canada. She found that different beliefs about the cause of hypertension tended to be the result of different experiences with hypertension by Ojibwa individuals. Garro noted that being diagnosed with high blood pressure often led individuals to question, and often reject, traditional beliefs. On the other hand, McMullin et al. (1996) observed that the rejection of local cultural disease models and the acceptance of dominant cultural models was often based on power relationships rather than experience. Western technological and political dominance might also be translated into cultural dominance. Our goal is to contribute to the growing ethnomedical literature on hypertension by examining age-group variations in knowledge and experience of hypertension.

The Place, the Sample, and the Research

This research was carried out in a *barrio* in the northern area of Guadalajara,[1] called Colonia Fábrica de Atemajac. It's a poor community; most of the adults were previously employed as unskilled laborers in the nearby textile factory that gave rise to the barrio. This textile factory, nicknamed "La Prosperidad" (the Prosperity), was one of the first textile factories established in the state of Jalisco, and it provided generations with employment until closing in 1992.

Thus, most adults work as seasonal and day laborers, and the local unemployment rate in 1992 ranged between 15% and 20%. The population is 5,941, with an average of 5.6 members per family. We estimated that 45% of the population had at least one former factory worker in their household, usually the eldest male. Houses are made of bricks and typically consist of two–three rooms including a kitchen. All houses have piped water, drainage, and electricity. Colonia was chosen because a previous epidemiologic study (García de Alba García 1989a, 1989b) was conducted on 374 factory workers aged 18–65. This study showed that 27% of them suffered from high blood pressure; 40% of those suffering from hypertension were over 40 years old. Since the factory was shut down in 1992, cardiovascular diseases have replaced infectious diseases as the leading cause of death in this area.

We conducted a population census to determine the structure of the sample. The sample size was calculated for each generational group of informants: Group one consisted of informants between 15 and 29 years of age; group two consisted of informants between 30 and 49 years of age; and group three consisted of all those who were 50 years old or older. We divided the barrio into sections of 13 blocks and chose an informant from each section, more or less at random, for a total of 35 informants. We began by simply walking down a block and then selected those individuals who agreed to participate in the study. To be selected, the informants had to have either been born in the barrio or to have lived there for more than 20 years and have no chronic disease, other than high blood pressure (to their knowledge). All the members of any one informant's household over 15 years of age were included in this study as informants.

In studying members of the same household but of different ages, we wanted to see whether ideas about blood pressure were shared across generations within a family. We wanted to minimize the effect of all other sociocultural variables except that of generational difference. We sought to understand the differential effect of age on evaluating the relative importance of those factors informants identified as causes of hypertension. We expected that there would be differences in relative rankings of variables across generations and that this would allow us to (eventually) develop educational and prevention programs that would be customized for or "speak to" a particular generation, as opposed to those that would target the population as a whole.

The youngest group consisted of 6 males and 5 females, with a mean age of 21.7. Their level of education ranged from the completion of junior high school to one college graduate. All were Catholic and had been born in Colonia. Only 1 of these informants suffered from hypertension. The second group consisted of 11 parents (7 women and 4 men) between the ages of 30 and 49 (an average of 41.2 years), all were Catholic and had been born in Colonia. The educational level for this group ranged from elementary school (7 informants) to high school (1 informant). All the women were housewives and all the men were former employees of the textile factory. One male was hypertensive. The third group consisted of 13 grandparents (10 women and 3 men) and ranged in age from 50–82, with an average of 71.2. Only 4 had been born in Colonia, all were Catholic, and none had completed elementary school. Six of the women and 3 of the men had been textile workers; the remaining 4 women were housewives. Ten (77%) members of this group suffered from hypertension.

The Structured Interviews

The researchers visited each of the homes and scheduled a date and time to interview the participants. In this first interview, we discussed the objectives of our research and obtained general information regarding education, age, health, and general life history. During the second interview, we asked informants to freelist as many of the causes of hypertension as they could think of (*"Dígame Usted todas las causas que conozca, o que le hayan dicho que producen la presión alta."*). We then selected for further study the 13 causes that everyone mentioned and that were mentioned at least twice. We wrote each cause (or item) on a separate 3 x 5 index card and then asked each informant to rank order the 13 index cards from the most significant cause for hypertension to the least important causal factor. This procedure allowed us to measure agreement between informants concerning the relative importance of each stated cause.

Our research objectives were: (1) to discover the perceived causes of hypertension in the community; and (2) to determine if there were intergenerational differences in the rankings of causal factors. We hypothesized that there would be greater consensus concerning the causes (or etiology) of hypertension within, rather than between, age groups.

Assumptions Behind Consensus Analysis

Following is a brief explanation of consensus analysis (see Handerwerker and Caulkins in this volume for more extended discussions). Romney (1994), Borgatti (1992), Weller and Romney (1988), and Romney et al. (1986) state that consensus analysis is predicated on three assumptions: (1) There is a unified cultural domain; (2) There is a single culturally shared and agreed-on answer to any given question about that domain; and (3) The questions (and answers) obtained and subsequently used for consensus analysis are independent of each other.

What Is a Domain?

The term **"domain"** implies that there are a finite number of items that are part of the domain and that the domain, as well as its most common items, are known by members of the culture. A domain has an internal structure in which items vary from well known to not well known. Well-known items of a domain are usually mentioned by all or most members of a culture and are also mentioned at the beginning of a list rather than at the end. For example, in the domain of colors, nearly all informants will name red and blue and mention them early in the list; few will say chartreuse, and those who do will likely mention it toward the end rather than the beginning of a freelist task.

What Is a "Culturally Unified Domain"?

An example of a unified cultural domain is a list of all the colors informants can think of. The domain is "cultural" in that it is learned; it's "unified" in that nearly all informants agree that a set of items are members of a specific domain rather than some other domain. For example, in the domain colors, most all English speakers would recognize that "cornflower blue" is a color while "cornflower" by itself is not, even though most English speakers would not be able to recognize the former color from, say, "robin's egg blue."

In a consensus analysis, the list of colors (or causes of hypertension) represents the cases, while the informants represent the variable: cultural knowledge or competence. To measure an individual's cultural competence in a particular domain means that all the items presented (for example, all the colors) must be members of the specified domain and not of another domain. Consensus analysis measures the degree to which all the items elicited constitute a culturally coherent domain and also measures the relative cultural competence (or knowledge) of each individual informant with respect to that domain (see Caulkins, this volume, for a discussion of how those measurements are made and evaluated).

A "single culturally shared and agreed-on answer" says that the list is not only unified, but that members of the culture agree with the organization of that list in terms of ranking and relative similarities in the meanings of terms in the domain. Doing fieldwork among the Aguaruna Jívaro tribal people of northern Peru, Boster (1985, 1986) grew a manioc garden and asked informants to name the various plants. He discovered that, in general, women knew more than men, and older women who were close kin "approached . . . [the] ideal of the omniscient informant . . ." (1985:194). Boster concluded that agreement had little to do with personal idiosyncrasies but with social variables (for example, age, gender, kinship).

The third assumption of independence means that, for example, the color blue doesn't imply or "cause" the color green. The list of things that constitute a cultural domain are united as members of the same category but are independent of each other. Another example is that giraffes and cats are both mammals, but the existence of giraffes doesn't cause the existence of cats or vice-versa. For our purposes, each elicited cause for hypertension must be thought by our informants to be an "independent" cause of hypertension. Thus, believing that pollution causes hypertension doesn't, by itself, imply that the person also believes diet causes hypertension.

A "competence" score indicates each individual's level of competence relative to the cumulative competence of the group. Romney (1994:271–272) notes that the idea of cultural competency is derived from the "item reliability theory" developed by Nunnally (1978) in which the main assumption is that "the correlation of knowledge between individual A and individual B is the product of the correlation of individual A with the 'truth' and of individual B with the 'truth'" (Romney and Weller 1988:61).

The idea is similar to that of a test. For example, to obtain a driver's license everyone must pass a written test that measures one's knowledge of the rules of the road in that particular society. If individual A gets 40% of the answer right and individual B 20%, the product of the correlation with the truth is .08, not very high. Therefore, we are left with three possible alternatives: the test is not good, both individuals are incompetent, there is no culturally unified set of driving rules. If both individuals score 90% then the product of their correlation with the truth is .81 and we can assume: (1) There is a unified cultural domain; (2) The test is a reliable and valid measure of that domain; and (3) These individuals are equally competent in that domain.

Data Analysis

We had first conducted a **freelist** exercise with each of our informants. As we were interested in a consensus both within and between age groups, we used only those terms that were cited two or more times. This limited us to 13 causes (see Table 12.1).

Definitions of Freelist Terms

The emotion "anger" (*corajes*) refers to a high level of frustration and suppressed rage generally attributed to economic conditions; "tensions" (*tensiones*) refers to general life stresses; "resentment" (*enojos*) is used as an expression of uneasiness caused by the behavior of people outside the immediate family; and "torment" (*mortificaciones*) refers to stresses caused by intimate relations. Suffering (*penas*) alludes to the feeling of sadness for the plight of the informants or those close to them and "fear" (*sustos*) to the dread of unexpected adverse events. Unanticipated joy (*alegrias*) was cited as a possible causal agent of hypertension as well as nervousness (*nervioso*) and feelings of anxiety.

TABLE 12.1
Frequency of Mention for Causes of Hypertension

Negative Emotions	
Anger	5
Tensions	9
Resentments	3
Mortifications	4
Suffering	5
Acute Emotions	
Fear	4
Positive Emotions	
Joy	2
Psychological conditions	
Nervousness	6
Habits	
Smoking	3
Poor Nutrition	3
Physiological conditions	
Obesity	4
Personal characteristics	
Aging	6
Environmental conditions	
Pollution	10

SOURCE: Freelist

Consensus Analysis

We used consensus analysis to compare inter- and intragroup rank-ordering of the list of causes of hypertension. Consensus is a particularly useful analytic procedure to measure intergroup variation and for working with small sample populations. Our three sample populations consisted of 11, 11, and 13 individuals respectively and the levels of "competence" (consensus) were .618, .682, and .538 (see Table 12.2).

In our study, the intragroup eigenvalues meet the "One Culture" assumption (see Table 12.3). The aggregate eigenvalue (3.630) also meets the "One Culture" assumption but the aggregate intergenerational eigenvalue is lower than the intragenerational eigenvalues. This suggests that there is one overall cultural model for the causes of hypertension but that there is greater inter- than intragenerational variation in the rankings of causal variables, as we had predicted.

Analysis of Rank-Order Data by Age Group

Negative habits cited included smoking, poor diet, and obesity. All three age groups rank two negative emotions—tension and resentment—as one of the five leading causes of hypertension (Tables 12.4, 12.5, and 12.6). Anger is a negative emotion that seems to increase in importance with age. Tension and resentment refer to relatively enduring (that is, chronic) negative emotions that our informants are, as a result of their poverty, powerless to "treat." Anger is a more transient, but immediate and explosive emotion (for example, Lakoff and Kovecses 1987) that may be perceived as more dangerous to health as one gets older.

TABLE 12.2
Estimated Agreement in Age Groups about Causes of Hypertension

Age group	Estimated agreement
15–29 years old	0.618
30–49 years old	0.682
>49 years old	0.538
Total	0.61

TABLE 12.3
Eigenvalues for Consensus about Causes of Hypertension

Group	Ratio of eigenvalues
15–29 years old	3.710
30–49 years old	6.247
>49 years old	3.796
Total	3.630

Smoking is cited as the leading cause of hypertension among the 30–49-year-old informants, perhaps because this group believes that it's more urgent for them to stop smoking before it is "too late." Among the members of the younger age group who smoke, smoking may still have positive connotations and have a negligible effect on day-to-day health.

Obesity is a causal agent that seems to decrease in importance with age. The younger group cited obesity as the leading cause of hypertension. This may also be a result of the younger age group being the most likely to be conscious of their weight as an index of their attractiveness.

Age, pollution, and joy are ranked in the bottom half of causes by all three age groups, with joy listed as last by all the groups. Age and pollution are also the only two variables on the list of causes that an individual has no direct control over. Joy is cited as a cause of hypertension by all members of both age groups, but appears

TABLE 12.4
Group 1 (Ages 15–29)

Informants	Negative emotions							Positive emotions	Bad habits	Eating habits			
	Sus	Nerv	Suff	Mort	Tens	Res	Ang	Joy	Smoking	Nutrition	Obesity	Aging	Pollution
1	12	8	10	9	4	11	6	13	3	5	1	2	7
2	7	9	5	3	2	8	4	6	12	10	1	13	11
3	8	12	9	6	1	13	7	10	5	3	2	4	11
4	6	5	8	3	7	7	4	12	1	9	10	13	11
5	5	1	4	10	9	2	3	7	13	12	8	6	11
6	9	1	4	12	8	2	3	7	5	13	6	12	13
7	4	5	12	10	1	8	2	11	6	7	9	3	11
8	10	4	8	2	1	7	11	13	9	6	3	5	12
9	8	7	11	5	2	9	4	12	6	3	1	13	13
10	7	10	11	12	5	9	8	13	3	1	2	4	10
11	10	4	11	7	1	9	3	13	5	6	2	8	6
11					9								12
Average	7.8	6.0	9.3	7.1	4.8	7.7	5.0	10.6	6.18	6.8	4.1	7.5	10.4
Rank	10	4	11	7	2	9	3	13	5	6	1	8	12

Key: Sus = *sustos* (fear); Nerv = *nervios* (nervousness); Suff = *penas* (suffering); Mort = *mortificaciones* (torment); Tens = *tensiones* (tension); Res = *enojos* (resentment); Ang = *corajes* (anger)

SOURCE: Freelist

TABLE 12.5
Group 2 (30–50 years old)

Informants	Negative emotions							Positive emotions	Bad habits	Eating habits	Obesity	Aging	Pollution
	Sus	Nerv	Suff	Mort	Tens	Res	Ang	Joy	Smoking	Nutrition			
1	5	8	4	7	1	6	2	13	3	10	9	11	12
2	11	7	5	6	3	8	4	12	2	9	1	10	13
3	3	11	5	7	6	2	4	12	8	1	13	10	9
4	10	6	11	8	2	4	5	13	1	7	3	9	12
5	10	6	13	3	2	7	9	12	4	8	5	11	
6	7	4	11	2	10	8	1	3	5	12	6	9	13
7	8	7	10	11	1	4	12	13	5	9	2	6	3
8	6	7	12	10	9	5	11	13	3	13	1	2	4
9	9	6	10	8	1	5	7	13	2	4	3	11	12
10	8	5	9	10	4	7	11	10	3	1	2	6	12
11	13	12	5	11	9	3	4	13	2	7	6	1	8
Average	8.2	7.2	8.6	7.5	4.3	5.3	6.3	11.5	3.4	7.3	8.7	7.8	9
Rank	9	5	10	7	2	3	4	13	1	6	11	8	12

Key: Sus = *sustos* (fear); Nerv = *nervios* (nervousness); Suff = *penas* (suffering); Mort = *mortificaciones* (torment); Tens = *tensiones* (tension); Res = *enojos* (resentment); Ang = *corajes* (anger)

SOURCE: Freelist

TABLE 12.6
Group 3 (50 Years and Older)

Informants	Negative emotions							Positive emotions	Bad habits	Eating habits	Obesity	Aging	Pollution
	Sus	Nerv	Suff	Mort	Tens	Res	Ang	Joy	Smoking	Nutrition			
1	9	3	6	12	7	1	8	5	2	13	11	10	4
2	1	10	9	11	8	3	7	13	2	12	4	6	5
3	2	6	8	7	1	3	4	13	12	10	5	11	9
4	11	13	12	5	1	9	3	10	4	8	6	7	2
5	3	1	4	2	10	5	7	13	6	9	12	11	3
6	10	6	5	1	2	7	8	12	3	11	4	9	13
7	5	3	8	6	7	9	2	12	13	4	1	11	10
8	8	6	8	9	3	4	5	11	1	12	2	10	13
9	8	8	9	7	2	1	3	13	4	12	6	8	10
10	4	7	10	2	11	1	9	12	3	6	13	8	5
11	9	6	10	11	8	1	5	5	3	8	7	2	1
12	9	12	1	4	8	2	7	5	13	8	11	6	3
13	6	11	4	9	2	10	7	5	13	8	3	1	12
Average	6.3	7.1	7.2	6.6	5.5	4.5	5.7	10.5	6.1	9.6	6.5	7.9	6.9
Rank	5	9	10	7	2	1	3	13	4	12	6	11	8

Key: Sus = *sustos* (fear); Nerv = *nervios* (nervousness); Suff = *penas* (suffering); Mort = *mortificaciones* (torment); Tens = *tensiones* (tension); Res = *enojos* (resentment); Ang = *corajes* (anger)

SOURCE: Freelist

to be an unimportant one. We suggest that it is cited because it refers, like anger, to a sudden arousal of emotional energy or intensity and implies that any intense emotion increases blood pressure. Unlike anger, which is ranked in the top five by the two older age groups, no age group perceives joy as "dangerous" relative to the other causes.

These rankings suggest that all three age groups agree that negative emotions and negative personal habits (that is, poor diet and smoking) are the primary causes of hypertension. Interage group variations in rank assignments seem to vary more as a result of age-specific concerns and experiences rather than age-based knowledge systems or theories of hypertension (this was also implied by intergroup eigenvalue). Therefore, we hypothesize that the younger age group informants will emulate the other two age group rankings as they get older; in other words, age-group rank differences are "fluid" rather than "hard."

Discussion

The consensus analysis indicates that there is no significant difference in knowledge concerning the causes of hypertension across age groups. However, this doesn't mean that public health agents should disregard age as a sociocultural variable in developing programs to educate populations about the causes of high blood pressure and how to prevent or manage hypertension.

Different age groups assign different weightings or saliencies to perceived causes, probably as a result of different interests and concerns associated with different age groups. Thus, older people perceive anger as a more important cause of hypertension than do young adults, who perceive obesity as the leading cause.

As Blumhagen (1980) noted, it's probably more difficult to alter these perceptions because they are wedded to larger age-group interests. From this perspective, policies could be implemented that are sensitive to and use these age-related concerns to promote good health practices. In addition, all age groups view negative emotions as leading causes of hypertension. For these reasons, economic policies that increase job opportunities and wages may have greater effects on decreasing negative emotions as a perceived and actual cause of hypertension than public health policies that ignore socioeconomic variables.

QUESTIONS

1. What are the three main assumptions of consensus analysis?
2. Did different age groups have different cultural models about the causes of hypertension in this study? What evidence can you cite to support your answer?
3. What were the primary differences in the way the different age groups understood the causes of hypertension?
4. What is rank-ordered data? Describe how you can collect it?

NOTE

1. Guadalajara has a population of over 3 million people and is the capital of the state of Jalisco, western Mexico.

JEFFREY C. JOHNSON
DAVID C. GRIFFITH

Thirteen

Visual Data: Collection, Analysis, and Representation

There are situations in which verbal stimuli are entirely inadequate to bring out data the researcher is trying to elicit. In such cases the interviewer may wish to develop projective devices. (Whyte, 1984:105)

Introduction

William Foote Whyte (1984), in his concern for the range of interviewing methods available to field workers, recognized the importance of **visual stimuli** in collecting data that may be difficult to obtain using standard verbal interviews. Visual cues enable interviews with nonliterate informants and promote comparisons and discussions about topics and domains often difficult to explore in purely verbal terms (see also Weller and Romney 1988). Additionally, cognitive anthropologists have used visual stimuli to systematically study domains that defy the use of written language, with informants who lack a written language, or with preliterate (for example, preschool children) or nonliterate informants. For example, J. Johnson et al. (1997) used photographs of children to interview three- and four-year-old preschoolers—a preliterate population not amenable to standard text-based approaches—about their play preferences.

Although it's certainly true that a "a picture is worth a thousand words," it's equally important, particularly with regard to ethnographic interviews, to know the content and nature of the "thousand words" associated with a given picture. In this chapter, we describe a variety of systematic data collection methods that involve the use of visual stimuli or methods for determining **visual saliency**, and give examples of analytical techniques particularly appropriate to analyze such data.

Background

Eliciting data through interviews is by no means simple. There is a large body of literature in the social sciences that discusses a wide variety of interviewing techniques and methods (see Bernard 1994). A primary concern has been how to get informants to "open-up" or how to prompt them in such a way that promotes discussions of rather complex issues or domains. Proper questioning and verbal prompting, text-oriented stimuli (Weller and Romney 1988), and focus groups, among others, have all been used to enhance an informant's ability to adequately express and articulate the knowledge they possess.

John Collier early on recognized the potential of projective materials in the interview process. In his original work, Collier (1967) discussed the advantages of using photographs in ethnographic research and provided an important comparison and contrast with other projective tools available at the time (for example, Rorschach tests and defined line drawings).

On the one hand, Collier outlined how photographic methods could be used to systematically collect ethnographic data that were amenable to quantitative analysis (for example, systematic comparisons of material culture). He also discussed the advantages of the photographic essay approach in both conducting interviews and for facilitating the systematic comparison of interviews. In this vein, the photographs of an individual's world could lead to more precise and detailed descriptions of community affairs or the place of individuals within the community, could help elicit more in-depth cultural explanations of phenomena of interest, and could facilitate the systematic comparison of interviews among members of the sample.

On the other hand, and in a more qualitative way, he found that these methods also triggered "emotional revelations" that may have been difficult to obtain otherwise or "can release psychological explosions and powerful statements of values" (Collier 1967:62). The most important contribution of this work, however, was the expansion of photography and similar visual tools beyond the realm of simple ethnographic description to the realm of native interpretation.

About the time Collier's book was published, Worth and Adair (1972) had been working on a visual project that involved an even more ambitious foray into the world of native visual interpretation. In contrast to letting natives interpret pictures taken by the anthropologist, Worth and Adair gave movie cameras to the natives, thus turning the entire enterprise of visual interpretation over to the natives themselves. This was important because it allowed the natives to take full charge of determining what was visually salient and allowed for pictures and themes to be subjectively related within some visual sequence.

In a series of two experiments, Ziller and Lewis (1981) used what they called "**auto-photography**" in studying the choice of photographic subject and its relation to social and self-perception in college undergraduates and young males in public and alternative schools for juvenile delinquents. Subjects were asked to take 12 pictures, either by themselves or by someone else, that best describes "who you are." They found a relationship between academic achievement and photographic subject matter in that better students tended to take pictures of books and plants while poorer students infrequently photographed such subject matter. This study is important in that it used native or auto-photography in a systematic attempt to understand how self-perception through photography relates to a variety of achievement and psychological factors.

Projective tools are not limited to photographs, line drawings, or movies. Anything tangible and visual is potentially useful in the interview process. Projective aids may also include cultural artifacts (for example, different kinds of fish hooks), plant and animal specimens (Boster 1987; Boster and D'Andrade 1989), people (J. Johnson et al. 1997), or various kinds of maps (J. Johnson 1990), to name a few.

Ericksen and Hodge (1991/92) provide a good example of using these techniques with nonliterate informants and a study domain that might be difficult to do research on with conventional interviewing methods. They examined occupational prestige and ritual in Egypt; traditionally, prestige had been studied with mostly literate populations and text-based stimuli. Ericksen and Hodge interviewed a mix of literate and nonliterate informants using artists' drawings of both occupations (for example, a Western-style physician) and rituals (for example, a physician performing a circumcision). Whether it is the analysis of native interpretations of projective aids or the comparative analysis of visual products (for example, photographs) produced by the natives under study, such approaches facilitate the collection and analysis of rather complex ethnographic data, both qualitative and quantitative.

The following examples show the range of visually oriented data collection techniques and methods of analysis. These examples are by no means exhaustive; projective materials can be used in ethnographic interviews to solve a wide range of problems in data collection. Many of these visual approaches involve using pile sorts, which have a long history of use in anthropology with a corresponding body of literature describing both the details of data collection and analysis (Weller and Romney 1988).

The first example by Boster and J. Johnson (1989) involves using artists' renderings and photographs in an ethnobiological study of variations in perception about common marine species of fish found in the southeastern United States. Boster and J. Johnson also discuss methods of data analysis that incorporate visual imagery to aid in revealing patterns in the data that may have been difficult to determine otherwise.

The second example provides a series of visually oriented data collection methods used in the ethnography of a small midwestern town. This example illustrates the flexibility of such methods in studying intracultural variation and social class (J. Johnson 1990).

The final example departs from the previous three in that the informants themselves produce the imagery in the form of photographs that are then interpreted and classified by the researcher instead of by the natives. Based on work by J. Johnson (1981) about a multiethnic fish camp in Alaska, this example illustrates the use of native photography or auto-photography, nonparametric statistical methods, and multivariate graphical techniques in studying the relationships among social organization, ethnicity, and visual saliency or photographic subject matter.

Ethnobiology and Visual Stimuli

In a series of studies by J. Johnson and Griffith (1985) and Griffith et al. (1989) both artists' renderings and photographs were used to understand and model recreational fishers' perceptions of common marine fish species found in the southeastern and northeastern regions of the United States. Additionally, Boster and J. Johnson (1989) engaged in a comparative study concerning intracultural variation in an attempt to unravel the underlying bases for informants' classifications of similarities among fish (that is, form versus function).

The use of visual stimuli in ethnobiological studies of this kind is certainly not new. Natural plants and stuffed animals are often used in **ethnobiology** (see Boster 1987). However, the fragile and often bulky nature of these more natural stimuli often makes their use unsuitable for certain field contexts (for example, isolated equatorial areas). Visual stimuli such as photographs, although less optimal because of their two-dimensional character, can be encased in plastic, making them exceptionally durable and portable in nearly all field settings.

Background and Problem

The study described here concerned the debate as to whether folk biological classifiers attend more to the morphological or utilitarian characteristics of fish (Boster and J. Johnson 1989). Do folk classifiers judge the similarities among fish more on the basis of what they look like (that is, morphology), or how much fun they are to catch, or how they behave, or other characteristics (such as utility)? A fundamental component of this study was the use of visual stimuli in determining folk classification.

Sample Selection

The study design was comparative in nature and involved the selection of informants for a treatment group of experts (that is, experienced recreational fishers) and a control group of novices (that is, individuals with little or no experience with recreational fishing). The expert group would have been exposed to both aspects of morphology and the utility of the fish, while novices would largely be limited to morphological information in the course of making their classifications. A comparison of the two groups would give some indication about the relative importance of morphology and utility in the folk classification of experts.

The expert sample consisted of four groups of recreational fishers chosen at random from sportfishing club rosters found in the states of North Carolina, Texas, and the west and east coasts of Florida. A total of 30 fishers from each of the areas was chosen randomly for face-to-face interviews. The novice group consisted of students from an introductory anthropology class at East Carolina University who had little or no experience with recreational fishing. Boster and J. Johnson administered a questionnaire to screen potential informants, and the pool of students with no fishing experience represented the universe from which novice group members were selected at random for interviews. The final set of comparative groups consisted of 15 informants from each of the four recreational fishing groups and 15 informants from the novice group.

Projective Devices and Analysis

The domain of study consisted of 43 marine species commonly found in the marine waters from Texas to North Carolina. Boster and J. Johnson elicited the possible range of common names used in the areas for the species in the domain in preliminary in-depth interviews with fishing experts. The visual stimuli consisted of artists' renderings of each of the 43 marine species with their common names placed on 3 x 5 cards and encased in plastic. Boster and J. Johnson placed the identification number of the fish on the back of each card to facilitate the recording of interview data.

Each informant was asked to perform a free pile sort of the fish. See Chapter 6 in this volume for an example of pile sorts using text-based stimuli. This unconstrained subjective pile sort task consisted of asking informants to place the fish into piles according to "how similar the fish were to one another." Informants could have as many piles (43) or as few piles (1) as they felt necessary. Determination of similarities and pile membership were left to the judgment of each informant. After each informant finished the task, they were asked to explain their reasons for grouping fish into each of the respective piles. Both pile membership and reasons were recorded in notebooks.

Pile sort data like these can be transformed into a similarity matrix using currently available software such as ANTHROPAC, a package particularly suited for solving many common problems in collection and analysis of anthropological data (Borgatti 1992). The raw pile sort data were transformed into matrix form by counting the number of times two fish showed up together in the same pile across all informants. This produces a species-by-species aggregated judged similarity matrix amenable to a number of factor analytic techniques such as multidimensional scaling (MDS) (Kruskal and Wish 1978). MDS facilitates understanding of the similarity structure in the data through its graphical representation in two- or three-dimensional Euclidean space, reflecting aspects of both the dimensionality of the data and the spatial proximities among domain items, in this case, fish.

Figures 13.1 and 13.2 are scalings of the aggregate similarity matrices for both the experts and the novices respectively. Items themselves are represented by the silhouettes of the fish to aid in understanding the role of morphology in folk classification. As discussed in more detail in Boster and J. Johnson (1989), the expert scaling appears to be influenced more by functional or utilitarian characteristics, while the novice scaling is organized more on the basis of morphological characteristics. Thus, these methods allow examination of the criteria that individuals use to classify items in a biological domain of interest.

In subsequent research Griffith et al. (1989) used photographs of marine fish commonly found in the northeastern waters of the United States. (Photographs had been obtained from a member of the American Fisheries Society for a small fee and

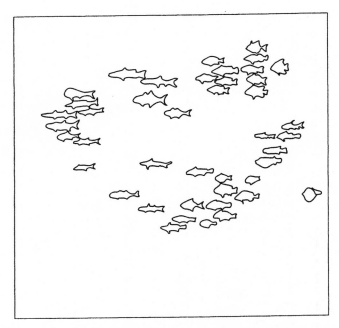

Figure 13.1. A multidimensional scaling of the similarities among the 43 marine fish for the North Carolina recreational sample (stress = .18).

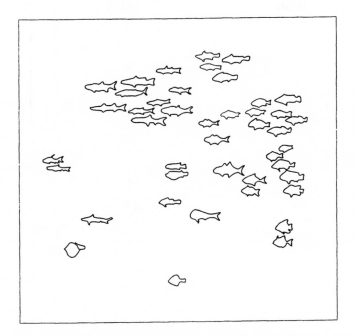

Figure 13.2. A mutidimensional scaling of the similarities among the
43 marine fish for the novice sample (stress = .10).

the use of these visual stimuli significantly increased the realism of the task.) New
developments in computer digitizing have enhanced researchers' ability to produce
and edit visual stimuli of various types and of better quality. The actual images
themselves can be brought into MDS configurations to further improve a
researcher's ability to interpret the data.

Meat, Housing, and Social Class

In a comprehensive study of food consumption in the United States, J. Johnson et
al. (1988) were interested in social, cultural, and economic factors that contributed
to variations in seafood consumption. A number of techniques that used **projective
devices** were incorporated into the study design. This section reports on the use of
projective devices for uncovering intracultural variation in people's perceptions of
various kinds of processed and fresh meats and for understanding the possible influences of social class in understanding variations in perceptions. The bulk of the

discussion comes from one of the ethnographic components of the study involving the study of food consumption and perceptions in a small midwestern community.

Background and Problem

The overall study involved two major components. The first of these components involved a large random sample of Americans focusing on factors that contributed to changes in dietary habits and social, cultural, and economic factors affecting consumption patterns. The second component was ethnographic in nature and involved in-depth interviews with "key kitchen" people (that is, either males or females in the household who were primarily responsible for cooking and shopping) and the ethnographic study of a small midwestern community. The primary purpose of the ethnographic component was to gain deeper understanding of the types of food consumption patterns revealed from the larger survey. In particular, J. Johnson et al. (1988) were interested in understanding the relationship between social class and both variations in the consumption and perceptions of various forms of meat found in the market (fresh beef, frozen fish, canned tuna, etc.).

Sample Selection

We report here on two of the samples in the overall study. J. Johnson et al. (1988) chose a small (N = 10) purposive sample of key kitchen people to elicit the most salient visual stimuli to use in the study. The key kitchen people were chosen according to expertise and demographic characteristics and came from households in one of the study regions that varied in size, composition, and social class.

A second sample consisted of a **snowball sample** of households in a small midwestern community (J. Johnson 1990). The sample involved the selection of two seed households, one from an upper-middle-class neighborhood and the other from a lower-middle-class neighborhood. Key kitchen actors in the seed households were interviewed and asked to name three other households they interact with on a regular basis. Then key kitchen actors in these households were interviewed and asked to name three households and so on, thus providing for a snowball sample through the community. The sampling was terminated once 15 households from each of the two original seeds was completed. Another sample of informants consisted of real estate and city code enforcement agents in the community.

Projective Devices and Analyses

J. Johnson et al. (1988) used two types of projective devices in the study. The first consisted of various types of meats and meat products typically found in grocery stores. The second device consisted of the pictures of the 30 informants' houses from the snowball sample. Each involved photography but differed in that the one set of stimuli involving groceries was carefully photographed in a laboratory setting while the pictures of houses was done while in the field.

Producing and eliciting the first set of stimuli, different types of meats and meat products, took several steps. The researchers conducted a survey in several grocery stores of the various types of meat and meat products available, including not only the type of meat and its particular form (for example, fresh fish, frozen chicken, canned tuna), but also any associated brand names (for example, Jimmy Dean Sausage). All possible meat types, forms, and brand names were compiled into a list by categories (for example, frozen products, fresh products, canned products, etc.).

This list was shown to the sample of ten key kitchen actors and they were asked to check the products in each category with which they were "most familiar." The products checked most frequently were then used as stimuli. Each of these "typical" products was purchased and brought to a laboratory for photographing. After the pictures were taken, the photographs were coded and encased in plastic. With the exception of the smoked salmon, which the authors consumed, the food was donated to the community homeless shelter. Table 13.1 lists the stimuli and also provides labels to be used in an example of the graphical analysis of the data.

The 30 informants from the snowball sample were each asked to perform an unconstrained judged similarity task as in the example above. Informants were asked to sort the pictures of meats into piles according to similarity. They could have as many or as few piles as they wished. After the informants completed the task, they were asked to explain their sorting behaviors. The explanations were taped and later transcribed. These taped interviews are important because they show the flexibility of this approach in terms of not only allowing for a quantitative analysis of the data, but also a qualitative one. Additionally, the qualitative component of the interviews helped in interpreting the quantitative analysis.

Before showing an example of the quantitative analysis of the pile sort data, it's instructive to examine some of the content of the qualitative interviews. As Collier (1967) noted, interviews involving pictures often have emotional content and allow for discussion of issues that may be too complex for semistructured questioning. The following is an example from an informant from the upper-middle-class seed of the snowball sample. This comment shows the importance of how a meat was processed. As she states:

> And these are all canned products and most of these would be fairly low-cal, well anyway salmon and tuna—oysters I guess aren't low-cal and sardines, but that was the reason for picking the canned seafood. And I put these two together because they were frozen fish products, and would be possibly a little healthier than the processed things and the red meat. And these are just fresh meat products—red meat, poultry, and fish.

This comment shows the informant's concern for health and the relationship between processing, meat type, and health.

In contrast, an interview with one of the lower-middle-class informants revealed a different logic in sorting the items. As she stated:

> I classified all of what I consider seafood items—the tuna, the medium shrimp, the oysters, pink salmon. I classified those because they all come from the water; they're all seafood. These three are poultry and I think the turkey would probably go with it. And these have chicken, and I classified those because they all have chicken ingredients. And the turkey is just turkey.

TABLE 13.1
Stimuli for Pile Sort Task

	Meat and Brand Name	Label for MDS
1.	"Carl Budding" turkey	CB Turkey
2.	"Jimmy Dean" Sausage	JD Sausage
3.	"Mrs. Paul's" Fishsticks	Mrs. Paul's
4.	"The Budget Gourmet" Seafood Newburg	TBG SNewburg
5.	"Lean Cuisine" Glazed Chicken	LC GChicken
6.	"Sizzlean" Pork Breakfast Strips	SIZPorkBS
7.	"Holly Farms" Whole Frying Chicken	HF WHChicken
8.	"Underwood" Deviled Ham	U DevHam
9.	"Oscar Mayer" Weiners	OM Weiners
10.	"Van de Kamp's" Ocean Perch	VdK OPerch
11.	"Booth" Cod Fillets	B CodFillet
12.	"Spirit of Norway" Sardines	SON Sardines
13.	"Orleans" Oysters	O Oysters
14.	"Libby's" Pink Salmon	L PinkSalmon
15.	"Armour" Vienna Sausage	A ViennsSaus
16.	"Hormel" Spam	H Spam
17.	Imitation crab meat (store packaged)	ImCrabTub
18.	Medium shrimp (store packaged)	Med Srimp
19.	Whole fresh flounder (store packaged)	WFreshFlound
20.	Ground beef (store packaged)	GrBeef
21.	Rib-eye steak (store packaged)	Rib-eye St
22.	Boneless pork chops (store packaged)	Bless PorkCh
23.	"DelicaSeas" Imitation Crab Meat	DImCrab
24.	"Banquet" Chicken Nuggets	BChNuggets
25.	"Weight Watchers'" Seafood Linguini	WWSeaLing
26.	"Gorton's" Crispy Batter-Dipped Flounder Fillets	GB-DipFlound
27.	"SeaPak" Shrimp 'n Batter Fantail Style	S BatShrimp
28.	"Starkist" Chunk Light Tuna (canned)	StarCanTuna
29.	"Virginia Capes" Smoked Salmon	VCSmSalmon
30.	"Stouffer's" Swedish Meatballs	StSwedMeatbl

The reasoning used by this informant is simple and is based almost entirely on the type of meat, independent of how it's been processed or its health benefits. In this case, the most salient determinant of pile membership was related purely to meat type. In total these interviews help in unraveling the underlying reasoning used by the informants to link the various stimuli together and, in and of themselves, provided important qualitative data. For example, J. Johnson et al. (1996) showed that the difference in approach to the pile sort task was based on social class as reflected in both the quantitative and qualitative analysis of the data.

Like the fish data above, the pile sort data here are amenable to multidimensional scaling. Figure 13.3 is a multidimensional scaling of the aggregated judged similarity matrix obtained from aggregating the pile sort data across all 30 informants. The matrix was produced using ANTHROPAC, while the MDS was produced with SYSTAT. The graph shows that there is a distinction between meats in the upper left that are fresh versus those in the lower right that are frozen. Another dimension of interest is largely a health dimension with seafood, no matter how processed, in the upper right of the graph, while processed meats, mostly sausages, in the lower left portion of the graph. It's important to note that two scalings, as in the example above, could have been produced from the data and then

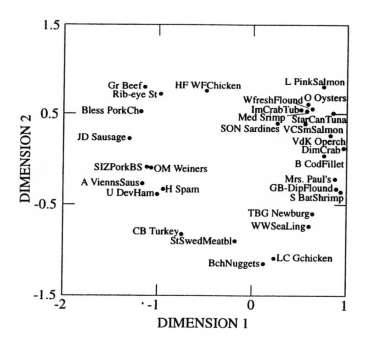

Figure 13.3. MDS of aggregated judged similarity of the pictures of 30 types and forms of meat (stress = 0.884).

compared, one from the upper-middle-class sample and one from the lower-middle-class sample. A comparison of scalings could inform us of differences, if they exist,between the two subsamples. This, combined with the qualitative explanations, could help in understanding how social class influences perceptions.

To learn more about the social class of the 30 informants, J. Johnson et al. (1988) used a projective device to elicit perceptions of experts. Pictures of all 30 informants' houses were taken and processed at an overnight photo processing store. A local photocopy business encased the 30 pictures in plastic. As in the other examples, each picture was encoded with a number and then encased in plastic. The researchers sought experts who would know something about the houses and their corresponding neighborhoods. Those most familiar with housing included real estate agents and code enforcement agents from city government. One real estate agent was interviewed from each of the four major real estate agencies in town, while the two code enforcement agents represented the whole of their department.

Informants were handed the cards and told to sort them into piles according to similarity in a manner similar to that described above. They were asked to explain their sorting behavior and their explanations were recorded. Real estate agents and code enforcement people use a great deal of photography in their work (see J. Johnson 1990), so this task came naturally to this sample of informants.

The naturalness of this task enabled the informants to talk a lot about their neighborhoods, real estate values, poverty, wealth, and social problems in a manner that would have been difficult to achieve using standard interviewing techniques. Similar to the examples above, the data can also be graphically represented in a MDS and clusters of houses can be determined using hierarchical clustering (S. Johnson 1967). For a more detailed discussion of the use of this combination of methods in this case, see J. Johnson (1990).

Ethnicity, Kinship, and Visual Saliency

This example is different than the others because in this case the visual data were produced by the informants and interpreted and systematically compared by the researcher. In an ethnographic study of an Alaskan fish camp, J. Johnson (1981) gave cameras to key informants so that he could document, through their eyes, activities on the water and around the fish camp and compare picture themes among and between the two primary ethnic groups. The fish camp wasn't far from the village of Naknek in the Bristol Bay region of western Alaska. Owned by Peter Pan Seafood, Inc., commercial fishers from Alaska and the "Lower 48" (for example, California and Washington) came to the camp to drift gillnet for sockeye salmon primarily during June, July, and August. A more detailed ethnographic description of the setting can be found in J. Johnson (1981) and Miller and J. Johnson (1981).

Background and Problem

A primary feature of the fish camp was the multiethnic character of the fishers. Of the 65 boat captains, 29% were Italian, 1.5% Finnish, 4.6% Norwegian, 4.6% Serbo-Croatian, 16.9% Eskimo/Aleut, and 43.4% white (native English speakers with no strong ethnic identity).

The Italians had mostly come to the United States from Sicily in the 1960s and dominated two of the five bunkhouses. A particularly important feature of the social organization of the camp concerned the density of the kinship relations within each of the ethnic groups. As reported in J. Johnson (1981), the Italians had a very dense kinship network, while the largest group, the white fishers, had very few kinship links. In addition, the Italians were very social, displaying a high degree of group cohesiveness and engaged, to a large degree, in group behaviors (for example, cookouts, parties in the Italian bunkhouse) as opposed to individual behaviors (for example, playing cards in their room with other crew). In contrast, the other groups of fishers were much more atomistic in their social behavior, tending to interact mostly with other members of their boat and to a limited degree other members of their bunkhouse.

An interesting question relates to how variation in degrees of sociality or group versus individual behavior affects visual saliency in the taking of photographs. In other words, do one's social linkages and social behaviors influence the thematic content of an individual's photographs? In this task, the informants are unconstrained in taking pictures rather then being unconstrained in judging similarities among pictures as, for instance, in the previous examples.

In this setting, everyone has opportunities to take pictures of a similar nature. Some of the themes may include sunsets, local animals, tundra landscapes, bunkhouse life, and work life including fishing (see Miller and J. Johnson [1981] and Van Maanen et al. [1982] for a discussion of the importance of work among commercial fishers). It was hypothesized that aspects of an informant's social world would be reflected in the thematic nature of their pictures. Thus, Italian informants would be expected to take pictures that reflected more the group character of their social world (for example, pictures of people, particularly in groups), while white fishers (referred to henceforth as Lower 48ers) would be expected to take pictures that, although possibly of a social nature, were less group oriented (for example, pictures of animals, sunsets, and landscapes), reflecting more the atomistic character of their social world.

Sample Selection

Informants were selected from the two largest ethnic groups. Five Kodak Instamatic cameras were used, each with two rolls of film. These cameras were the least expensive on the market at the time and were relatively easy to use, even for someone not familiar with photography. Given the nature of relatively inexpensive photographic technology today (for example, throw-away cameras), approaches of this kind are even more feasible and can be applied to a wider range of problems. Although the small sample of five individuals certainly limits the ability to capture the range of variation in the two groups, informants were selected so as to reflect the character of the age structure of the two ethnic groups as much as possible. In addition, informants were selected who were willing to participate, an extremely important criterion in such a task.

Each informant was allowed to keep the camera and the pictures under the proviso that copies of the pictures could be made and kept by the researcher and that all development costs would be paid for by the researcher. The informants chosen included: an older Italian (in his mid-40s) who was a native speaker of Italian and had moved to the United States from Sicily in the mid-'60s; a younger Italian (in his 20s) who had been raised primarily in the United States and was a competent speaker in either Italian or English; and three fishers from the Lower 48 who ranged in age from the 30s–50s (see J. Johnson [1990] for a discussion of selection issues of this kind).

Projective Device and Analysis

In contrast to Ziller and Lewis (1981) who constrained subjects' picture taking to subject matter that best described who the subjects were, informants in this study were instructed to take pictures of whatever they wanted, keeping in mind at all times that the camera and the pictures were theirs to keep. Although copies of the pictures were to be given to the researcher, it was stressed to the informants that they had total control. There is some question about whether the informants felt constrained in any way by the task such that it could have influenced the nature of pictures taken. However, with careful selection of informants and proper development of trust and rapport, potential biases can be significantly reduced.

The cameras were given to informants at the beginning of the season and the two exposed rolls of film were collected just before they left Bristol Bay. Given the isolation of the fish camp, the pictures had to be developed in the Lower 48 and then sent to each of the informants. With today's easy access to rather quick photographic development and processing (for example, 30-minute technology), even in areas outside the United States, this type of project is even more feasible now.

After the pictures were developed, the total group of pictures was given to other researchers not originally affiliated with the project for determination of thematic categories. These independent observers were asked to determine categories of themes most commonly found in the pictures.

Based on this process of categorization, four primary themes were identified. The first category concerned group photographs in which the picture consisted of two or more people who were "asked" to pose for the camera. The second category was of pictures of individuals who, like the previous category, were asked to pose. The third category contained pictures that dealt with work or daily living themes. Although this category may have included pictures containing people, either individually or in groups, the difference here concerned the "natural" state of people in the picture and often the distance from which the picture was taken. In this case, most of the people found in the pictures were unaware their picture was being taken. This is an important distinction in that the pictures in the first two categories were more often "orchestrated" while those in the third category were more "natural." The final category included pictures of an aesthetic nature involving sunsets, landscapes, local animals, and nature themes.

Table 13.2 shows the distribution of pictures across categories for each of the five informants. It should be noted that although all informants received two rolls of film, not all were equally proficient at taking pictures, so there was some variation in the total number of usable pictures per informant. It appears from the table that there is a difference between members of the two ethnic groups with respect to the thematic content of their photographs. The Italians have the vast majority of pictures showing group scenes or scenes of everyday work and life. On the other hand, although the Lower 48ers also have group photos, their single largest category is aesthetic themes. But is there really a difference and, if so, to what extent?

Statistical analysis of data of this type can be problematic. The sample of informants wasn't chosen at random and the number of informants is quite small. These types of problems are typical in anthropology and can present problems in terms of the proper statistical analysis of data. However, there are a variety of nonparametric permutational and randomization statistical procedures currently available that can aid anthropologists in dealing with theses types of problems (see J. Johnson and Murray [1997] for a more detailed discussion). Although not the total solution to problems of small samples, nonrandom samples, and other distributional concerns, these methods do hold promise.

In this case, the row and column independence was tested using StatXact 3 statistical software for exact nonparametric inference. For example, some of the cells in Table 13.2 are less than five, creating potential problems with the assessment of p in a given Chi-square test. This sparseness is not a problem for permutational methods and p will remain valid no matter the sparseness of the data (Mehta and Patel 1995). Based on the **Fisher Exact Test**, rows and columns aren't independent, informing us of differences in the distribution of informants' categories. The exact p-value was determined using a Monte Carlo technique and the 99% confidence interval for p is given at the bottom of the table and is valid independent of the sparseness of the data. Although there is a difference in informant's thematic content, is it in the expected direction?

TABLE 13.2
Table of Informants by Distribution of Picture Themes

	Groups	Single	Work	Aesthetic
Older Italian	11	5	7	0
Young Italian	11	2	14	7
Lower48–1	2	12	11	14
Lower48–2	8	7	9	15
Lower48–3	9	6	6	12

Fisher Statistic = 36.47; Monte Carlo estimate of p-value: 99% confidence interval (0.0000, 0.0006).

The exact test informs us that differences do exist between informants, but it doesn't inform us as to the nature of these differences. In tables larger than two rows and two columns, it becomes increasingly difficult to interpret and visualize the nature of the relationships among the row and column variables. **Correspondence analysis** is a multivariate graphical technique particularly well suited for such a problem (Greenacre 1984). This method allows for the graphical examination of relationships among and between both row and column variables of a contingency table in the same low-dimensional space. Thus, one can visualize, for example, what row variables are associated with what column variables without the arduous task of interpreting such relationships through an examinations of the numbers alone.

Figure 13.4 is a correspondence analysis of the data in Table 13.2. Lines between informants and thematic categories illustrate the first (solid) and second (dashed) most frequent thematic categories for each of the five informants. As expected, the theme reflecting the highest degree of sociality, group photos, is associated with the Italians, particularly the older Italian, while the theme reflecting the lowest degree of sociality, aesthetic photos, is associated with the Lower 48ers. It's also interesting that pictures of work and life in the camp was the most common theme shared by both groups, supporting the central role of work in the lives of fishers independent of their ethnic identity (Van Maanen et al. 1982). Although this information could have been gleaned from Table 13.2, the graph in Figure 13.4 is intuitively more appealing and more informative of the nature of relationships among and between all the variables.

This example has provided a set of tools for the collection and analysis of projective data. In this case, informants' photographs were systematically compared and analyzed in an attempt to understand how features of an informant's social world influences visual saliency. As mentioned above, given the availability of relatively inexpensive photographic technology and the availability of rapid film processing, such methods can be used in exploring a wide range of problems.

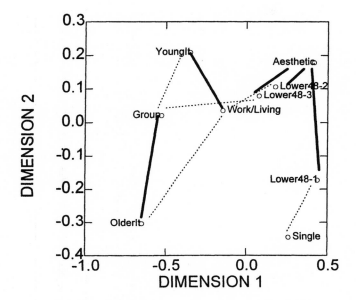

Figure 13.4. Correspondence analysis of picture themes by informants from Table 13.2. Solid line denotes category with highest frequency and dashed line denotes category with second-highest frequency.

The advent of rapid film processing will make it easier to add an additional step in the data collection process in that informants can be asked to describe their reasoning behind the photographs taken. This may lead to richer and deeper qualitative understandings reminiscent of Collier's (1967) discussion of how the use of photographs in interviews often leads to "emotional revelations." Furthermore, recent developments in digital technology may have an impact on the future of approaches of this kind in that digital pictures can be taken and both viewed and printed with current computer technology, putting the enterprise totally in the control of the researcher. Finally, there are a variety of analytic tools appropriate for the analysis of such data, even in cases where there are a small number of informants or, even with more informants, a large number of categories with less concern than has traditionally been the case for the validity of the analysis.

Summary

We have presented a range of examples that have shown the utility of visual and projective devices for collecting both quantitative and qualitative data. Methods that help informants express themselves, particularly with regard to complex domains or issues and with special populations (for example, preliterate), are clearly an important component of any ethnographers' methodological toolkit. It's also valuable to be able to systematically compare responses across informants or across groups of informants, and the methods described here are well suited for such comparisons. With the advent of innovations in photographic and visual computer technology, the application of visual and projective devices in solving a variety of data collection problems is virtually unlimited. Currently, the limits on the use of these methods is almost purely a matter of the creative limits of researchers themselves.

QUESTIONS

1. In what ways might visual stimuli or projective devices be useful in understanding how different ethnic groups or social classes perceive themselves and their surroundings?
2. What are some of the advantages of using visual stimuli produced by natives versus visual stimuli produced by researchers?
3   How might graphic representations of visual stimuli support the interpretation of research results?
4. What are the advantages and disadvantages of having informants sort and discuss pictures they themselves have taken?
5. Using current computer technology, how might photographic representations of automobiles be used in the study of Americans' perceptions of automobiles available on the U.S. market?

LAUREN CLARK ■
CAROL VOJIR
NANCY O. HESTER
ROXIE FOSTER
KAREN L. MILLER

Fourteen

MDS and QAP: How Do Children Rate Painful Experiences?

Introduction

We all have ideas about pain. In fact, it would be difficult to find someone without an opinion about the degree of pain related to an illness or operation. If someone were to ask you, "What do you think is more painful, a broken bone or a case of pneumonia?," you would probably have no trouble discussing your own past experiences with broken bones and pneumonia, friends or family who had suffered with either of these problems, and differences in the kinds of pain you might expect from each. Answering the question in each of these ways demonstrates your cultural knowledge about pain and your individual experience with different kinds of pain. Cultural knowledge is general, typological, and impersonal. Children whose experiences with pain don't fit standard cultural models may not be noticed by health care providers who rely solely on cultural knowledge to assess pain.

Of course, nurses and physicians have cultural knowledge about pain, too. Part of health care providers' cultural knowledge about pain comes from their educational preparation (which is an enculturation process), but part of their working knowledge may have its origins in popular models of pain that professionals share with laypersons. Professionals assemble general ideas about pain from their own experience and from observing ill and injured people. Like you and me, they can answer the question, "What is more painful, a broken bone or pneumonia?" based on cultural models of pain. They may or may not ask their patients how much pain they are in, because they think they have a pretty good idea of how painful a broken bone or pneumonia is likely to be. But how good are our impressions of pain? Do we share cultural knowledge about pain, and how does that cultural knowledge compare to real pain?

What Do We Know About Hospitalized Children's Pain?

If you are hospitalized for a broken bone or pneumonia, you may find yourself in pain. Unfortunately, you could suffer alone and unnoticed by the nurses and doctors assigned to care for you. For children, hospitalizations frequently involve undetected and untreated pain. Less than 6% of children from a sample of 169 reported being pain-free for a day in the hospital. Nearly half of the same children rated their pain as either moderate or severe at least once during the day (Hester et al. 1989).

This lack of pain assessment and treatment could be related to at least two causes. First, nurses and physicians share cultural knowledge about what is supposed to hurt and how much. Second, nurses and physicians bring with them their own past experiences with pain. An individual's past experiences are far from typological and impersonal; in fact, any person's experience of pain is highly unique, symbolic, and personal.

Once a person's unique pain experience is stored in memory, it can become distorted or embellished, making the remembered experience even more idiosyncratic than the lived one. Based on her own remembered past experience with a broken bone, a nurse may feel heightened empathy for a child with a similar problem. The other possibility is that a nurse's past experience breeds intolerance for "whiners" and an unwillingness to be drawn into their "supposed pain" and its treatment.

The most promising antidote to undiagnosed and untreated pain is asking children about their pain while they're in the hospital. In one study, none of the nurses who worked in a large urban children's hospital used any standardized pain assessment measurements with children in their care (Foster 1990).

Standardized assessment measures are a way for nurses to measure the amount of pain reported by a child. One way of doing this is to ask a child, "On a scale from zero to ten, where zero means no pain at all and ten means the most possible pain, how much pain are you in right now?" Another way of assessing pain is to use four poker chips to represent "pieces of hurt" (Hester 1976, 1979). One then says, "This (first chip) is a little bit of hurt and this (fourth chip) is the most hurt you could ever have. How many pieces of hurt do you have right now?"

Determining which assessment method is most appropriate for a given child is a matter of clinical judgment based on the child's developmental level and other considerations. But instead of using either of these two methods to find out from children how much pain they have, nurses generally rely on nonspecific and unreliable indicators of pain—like fussing or crying and elevated pulse or blood pressure (Hester et al. 1992). Although adequate protocols for assessing and managing the pain of hospitalized children have been developed, professional practice standards and institutional policies don't enforce their use. Even so, the situation of hospitalized children is improved in comparison to conditions 60 years ago when experts told us "Children don't feel pain" and recommended surgery without anesthesia for babies.

Using Existing Data to Answer New Questions

Given an existing data set containing information about hospitalized children and their pain, this secondary analysis will reexamine the existing data using new methods to answer new questions. This process, known as **secondary analysis**, saves time and money for students (and other enterprising individuals) by eliminating the necessity of instrument development and data collection. Sometimes data sets in the public domain are collected by governmental agencies studying health and nutrition, disability, morbidity, or illness risk factors. Smaller data sets are available from researchers who often find they have collected more data than they can possibly use in the course of answering their research questions. Graduate students are another source for data sets. For theses and dissertations, graduate students often conclude their project and realize there are more ways to analyze the data, but cannot bear to look at the data one more time. Whatever the source, data sets abound in the public domain and in hands of professors and fellow students.

In this particular case, a secondary analysis was conducted using data from the Child Pain Study (funded by the National Institutes of Health [NIH]). The purpose of the study was to determine the effectiveness of a program to improve the way nurses and physicians assess and treat children's pain. While the principal investigators on the Child Pain Study answered their research questions about changing nursing and medical practice, the data collectors on the project asked questions of their own about the data.

The composition of the data set will be described in detail in the methods section. Using the Child Pain Study data set, the data collectors asked three new research questions.

1. What does the empirical model of children's pain look like for nine diagnostic categories?
2. What does the proxy model (based on parents' perceptions of children's pain) look like for these same nine diagnostic categories?
3. How does the proxy model of child pain (based on parents' perceptions of pain) compare to the empirical model (based on children's own pain ratings)?

To be clear, the **empirical model** is considered the representation of degree of pain experienced by a child in response to the question, "How many pieces of hurt do you have now?" The child then chooses the number of poker chips, or pieces of hurt, that correspond to his or her pain at that moment. The range of responses are from zero (meaning the child has no hurt or pain at all) to four (meaning the worst pain a child could have).

One assumption we made in analyzing the child's answer to the pain question was that the children understood the relationship of poker chips ("pieces of hurt") to pain and could use the measurement system in a valid and reliable way. Justification for this assumption came from prior research designed to assess the developmental appropriateness of poker chips to measure pain among children considered developmentally "preoperational" (Hester 1976, 1979). Preoperational children are usually about four–seven years old and have mastered the idea of 1:1 correspondence and are still relatively concrete in their thinking. Hester's research found preoperational children were developmentally capable of using poker chips to describe their pain.

Another assumption we made about children's reported pain levels was that all the pain they reported was related directly to their primary diagnosis. In other words, we assumed that a child who had just undergone an appendectomy and reported a "three" for his or her pain rating was referring to the surgical site as the source of the pain, as opposed to a sore toe or a headache as the cause.

These assumptions still allow for the relativity of pain ratings between different children. This means that the pain experienced by one child and rated a "four" could be very much like the pain experienced by another child and rated only a "two." Differences in cultural values, socialization, and the child's range of prior life experiences with pain can all contribute to the relative differences in pain ratings ascribed by any two children.

A **proxy model** is not based on the child's pain perception, but on a parent's perception of the degree of pain experienced by the child. Before we asked the child about pain, we asked the parents "How many pieces of hurt does your child have now?" Parents circled a number (0–4) as opposed to saying the number out loud in an attempt to maintain independent reports of pain from the parent and child.

One assumption we made in analyzing parents' data on children's pain was that parents know their children well enough to make good guesses about child pain. A second assumption about parents' reports of their children's pain was that no parent knows absolutely and perfectly how much pain another person is experiencing, so some degree of error in a parental guess is to be expected.

The amount of error in a parental report is hard to judge, but some experts believe any deviation between parent and child scores is completely attributable to parental error, since the child is considered the infallible expert about his or her own pain. Part of the error in a parental guess can be attributed to a parent's cultural model about how painful the child's primary diagnosis *should* be. So a parent's proxy report of child pain is similar to a child's self-report and also similar to a general, widely shared cultural model of pain. In this research, we want to find out if the amount of error in a parental guess of child pain is insignificant or if it is sufficient to make parent and child models incomparable. We will do this by comparing child and parent models.

To answer the three new questions, the data collectors began to look at the existing data set in a new way. In the following section we will describe the existing data set we started with and what we did to modify it, how we imported the data and completed preliminary data reductions, and finally we will describe the multidimensional scaling (MDS) and quadratic assignment procedures (QAP) we used to look at child and parental models of pain.

Methods

To answer the research questions, we formulated several steps. First, we constructed a data set that contained all the information on the children's diagnosis and pain rating scores. Second, we imported the data set into ANTHROPAC (Borgatti 1992) and produced a similarity (or correlation) **matrix**. Third, we used MDS to look for underlying relationships among the variables (diagnoses) based on their attributes (pain ratings). Finally, QAP compared the MDS models to determine the degree of fit between the empirical (child) and proxy (parent) pain models.

Constructing a Selective Data Set

The Child Pain Study began collecting data on children in 1993 and finished in 1995. During that time, 6 hospitals participated by allowing data collectors to enroll hospitalized children and talk with nurses about pain management. To protect study participants, the Combined Institutional Review Board reviewed and approved the process used to gain consent for parents and children to participate in the study. To follow human subject protection standards for minors, at least one parent for each child who participated signed an informed consent for participation.

In the phase of the study reported here, a total of 395 children were enrolled in the experimental group and 398 children were enrolled in the control group. Only experimental group children had the data needed for these analyses, so data submitted by the control group participants were excluded from this paper. Nurses (n = 223) also participated in the study, but are not included either. The mean age of the children in the entire study was 6.3 years, ±6.1 years.

For the purposes of this paper, we needed to sift through the data for the 395 experimental group children and create a new data set suited for this particular secondary analysis. The new data set would eliminate information irrelevant to the new research questions. First, we eliminated data on child pain from nurses' notes on patient records. We only needed data from children and parents. Second, we eliminated from the sample of children all nonspeaking infants and toddlers, since we needed data to form the empirical model based on children's self-reported pain ratings. Third, we eliminated children from the sample if their parents didn't give pain ratings. Sometimes a parent would consent for the child to be in the study, but then the parent would leave the hospital for the day. We eliminated those cases because we needed matched parent-child data to construct the empirical and proxy models of pain and compare them.

The fourth step in paring down the data set was a review of the reasons for hospitalization among the children. The reason for each child's hospitalization was reviewed and assigned a diagnostic code. A diagnostic code takes a particular health problem and places it in a category of similar problems. For example, if one patient had her arm broken at a softball game and another patient had his leg broken in a fall from a horse, both children would be placed in the orthopedic diagnostic category. Similarly, meningitis and seizures would be placed in the neurologic diagnostic category.

In reviewing the entire data set, outlier diagnoses were eliminated, meaning we removed children who had diagnoses that differed from typical medical and surgical diagnoses for children, and we eliminated diagnoses with only one or two cases. Outlier diagnoses included anorexia nervosa and genetic syndromes, among others. Nine diagnostic codes remained. Finally, we eliminated children from the data set who left the hospital before providing enough pain ratings. We tried to have children rate their pain four times during the measurement period, but some children were discharged after only a few hours, so we set a limit of three out of four possible ratings as the criterion for inclusion. When each of these steps was completed, we had pain ratings on 143 children and 143 parents for three–four points during a day in the hospital.

Importing the Data and Running the
Similarity Matrix

Once we had 143 matched parent-child pairs, we edited the data file from the large project and made two new files. The first file, called Kid-Dat, looked like this:

Subject ID	Diagnostic Code	Pain1	Pain2	Pain3	Pain4
1	Respiratory	2	1	0	0
2	Neurologic	1	0	0	0
3	Endocrine	0	0	1	0
4	Respiratory	2	2	1	2
...					
143	Orthopedic	3	2	3	3

The Subject ID column is used to identify each of the 143 children with a unique number. The first child entered is listed as "1" in the subject identification column. This child was hospitalized with a respiratory problem of some sort. It could have been croup, asthma, or pneumonia. The numbers in the Kid-Dat data set under the headings of Pain1, Pain2, Pain3, and Pain4 refer to the answer the child gave at four points during the day when asked, "How many pieces of hurt do you have now?" This means the first time the Research Nurse asked the child about his or her pain, the child said he or she had two pieces of hurt. An hour later, the child reported one piece of hurt. Later in the day, the child twice reported no pain at all. The three dots (...) in Kid-Dat in the Subject ID column indicate a gap in the table. Subjects 5–142 were deleted from the printed table to save space.

The Kid-Dat data set is a compilation of the data used to address the question about an empirical model of children's' pain, but we needed another data set using parents' information for the proxy model. Because the parents rated child pain at the same time the children gave a self-rating, the parental data set looked like Kid-Dat, except the numbers in the columns for pain ratings were given by parents.

For each set of data (child and parent), we selected subjects in each diagnostic code and computed mean pain ratings. In other words, every child in the Kid-Dat data set listed with a Respiratory diagnosis was selected and a mean pain rating for Pain1 was calculated, followed by a mean pain rating for the Respiratory group for Pain2, Pain3, and Pain4. We then used the same procedure for calculating mean pain ratings and selected all the children in each of the other diagnostic code groups.

Altogether, there were nine diagnostic codes: respiratory (RESP), cardiovascular (CV), neurologic (NEURO), orthopedic (ORTHO), genitourinary (GU), gastrointestinal (GI, ear/ eye/ nose/ throat (EENT), endocrine (ENDO), and skin (SKIN). The new mean score data sets, shown in Tables 14.1 and 14.2, are calculations reflecting the mean pain score of all the children in each diagnostic category. This procedure condensed the data from a table showing individual scores to a table showing the mean score for groups of children based on their diagnostic category (Table 14.1). A table organized with a systematic display of data in rows and columns is also called a matrix. This table shows each of the nine diagnostic codes as rows, and each of the mean pain ratings as columns, forming a 9 x 4 matrix.

Comparing the child mean scores to the parent mean scores shows differences in both the amount of pain reported by parents and children in each diagnostic code and also differences in the pattern of pain reports over time. We'll learn more about the similarities and differences in the models of pain when we perform the QAP procedure.

The mean score matrices were imported into ANTHROPAC software. Once the mean score matrices were imported into ANTHROPAC, the next step was computation of similarity (or correlation) matrices for each. A **similarity matrix** or **correlation matrix** displays systematic relationships between two variables. In

TABLE 14.1

Children' Mean Pain Scores by Diagnostic Code

IMPORT>DL

Input dataset:	AVCPXDX.DAT
Output datatype:	REAL
Output dataset:	AVCPXDX

		1 CPCT1	2 CPCT2	3 CPCT3	4 CPCT4
		----	----	----	----
1	RESP	0.70	0.60	0.60	0.50
2	CV	2.00	2.00	2.00	2.00
3	NEURO	1.60	1.60	1.00	1.10
4	ORTHO	1.30	1.40	1.70	1.70
5	GU	1.40	1.70	1.60	1.80
6	GI	1.80	2.00	1.90	1.80
7	EENT	2.10	2.00	1.70	2.00
8	ENDO	0.90	0.50	0.50	0.70
9	SKIN	1.40	0.80	0.20	0.20

Elapsed time: 2 seconds. 11/24/1997 1:54 PM.

ANTHROPAC (Borgatti 1992).

TABLE 14.2

Parents' Mean Pain Scores by Diagnostic Code

IMPORT>DL

Input dataset:	AVPPXDX.DAT
Output datatype:	REAL
Output dataset:	AVPPXDX

		1 PPCT1	2 PPCT2	3 PPCT3	4 PPCT4
		----	----	----	----
1	RESP	0.90	0.90	0.70	0.40
2	CV	2.00	1.00	1.00	1.00
3	NEURO	0.90	1.00	0.40	0.60
4	ORTHO	1.70	1.20	1.50	1.30
5	GU	1.50	1.50	1.20	1.80
6	GI	2.00	1.90	1.60	1.60
7	EENT	2.10	1.40	1.50	1.10
8	ENDO	0.90	0.70	1.00	0.20
9	SKIN	0.80	0.80	2.30	0.00

Elapsed time: 3 seconds. 11/26/1997 3:11 PM.

ANTHROPAC (Borgatti 1992).

this case, the similarities calculated are those between pairs of diagnostic categories across pain measurements. Using the utility in the ANTHROPAC program under the menu selection of Tools>Similarities, the similarity matrices for children and parents compared pairs of diagnostic categories across pain measurements. Table 14.3 shows the child similarity matrix.

Because the matrix is a similarity matrix, higher numbers between two diagnostic categories represent high similarities. For example, Table 14.3 shows that respiratory and neurologic diagnoses share a moderately high correlation of 0.64, whereas respiratory and orthopedic diagnoses are strongly negatively correlated at −.79. In this instance, respiratory and neurologic diagnoses are more similar in terms of mean pain ratings across time than are respiratory and orthopedic diagnoses.

Finally, we learn that the diagnostic codes were not equally painful over time, as we might have suspected. If the pain ratings were perfectly valid and reliable, and if pain were equal across hospitalized children regardless of their diagnosis, we would have seen a perfect correlation of 1.00 in each cell of the similarity matrix. The variation in mean pain ratings by diagnostic group shows us that pain variation over time follows different patterns within and between diagnostic categories.

The similarity matrix computed from parent data (not shown) contained the same information, except from the parent's perspective. After both similarity matrices had been computed, the next step was to use the similarity matrices (one for parents and one for children) as the input data sets for the multidimensional scaling of the pain models.

The MDS Output: Models of Pain
for Children and Parents

The multidimensional scaling (MDS) procedure is found within the ANTHROPAC program under Tools>Scaling>MDS. The purpose of MDS is to transform the similarities (which are relationships) into coordinates in a multidimensional space. The more similar the diagnostic categories on pain, the closer together they are located in two-dimensional space, where the two dimensions represent objective and subjective perceptions used by parents or children to rate their pain. The pain scale, ranging from 0–4, met the requirements for metric MDS, having a true zero point and approximately equal distances between each pain level. The MDS calculation and display produced numerical and visual representations of the pattern of similarities among each set of diagnostic codes across pain ratings. In the numerical display, the nine diagnostic codes are rows (Figure 14.1). The numbers next to each diagnostic code indicate the coordinates of each diagnostic code in the two-dimensional space.

The visual MDS display shows in two-dimensional space which diagnoses were perceived to be similar in pain (as shown by close proximity in space) and which

TABLE 14.3
*Similarity Matrix of Diagnostic Categories Across
Child Pain Measurements*

```
SIMILARITIES

  Measure:            CORRELATION
  Variables are:      ROWS
  Input dataset:      AVCPXDX
  Similarity matrix:  CORRELATION
```

	1 RESP	2 CV	3 NEURO	4 ORTHO	5 GU	6 GI	7 EENT	8 ENDO	9 SKIN
1 RESP	1.00	0.00	0.64	-0.79	-0.96	0.00	0.24	0.43	0.85
2 CV	0.00	1.00	0.00	0.00	0.00	0.00	0.00	0.00	0.00
3 NEURO	0.64	0.00	1.00	-0.97	-0.44	0.24	0.75	0.35	0.90
4 ORTHO	-0.79	0.00	-0.97	1.00	0.64	-0.13	-0.70	-0.46	-0.97
5 GU	-0.96	0.00	-0.44	0.64	1.00	0.25	-0.17	-0.56	-0.76
6 GI	0.00	0.00	0.24	-0.13	0.25	1.00	-0.30	-0.82	-0.09
7 EENT	0.24	0.00	0.75	-0.70	-0.17	-0.30	1.00	0.70	0.70
8 ENDO	0.43	0.00	0.35	-0.46	-0.56	-0.82	0.70	1.00	0.64
9 SKIN	0.85	0.00	0.90	-0.97	-0.76	-0.09	0.70	0.64	1.00

```
Similarity matrix saved as dataset CORRELATIONC
Elapsed time:  1 second.  11/26/1997 3:21 PM.
```

ANTHROPAC (Borgatti 1992).

```
METRIC MULTIDIMENSIONAL SCALING

        Starting config:    GOWER'S PRINCIPAL COORDINATES
        Type of Data:       Similarities
        Input dataset:      CORRELATIONC

        Initial Stress = 0.183
        Final Stress = 0.134 after 6 iterations.

                              1        2
                            ----     ----
        1   RESP           -0.53     0.19
        2   CV              0.19    -0.39
        3   NEURO          -0.29     0.15
        4   ORTHO           0.73    -0.22
        5   GU              0.61     0.08
        6   GI              0.22     0.43
        7   EENT           -0.30    -0.22
        8   ENDO           -0.41    -0.41
        9   SKIN           -0.47    -0.02

        Coordinates saved as dataset COORDC
```

Figure 14.1. Multidimensional scale of diagnostic codes based on child pain ratings.

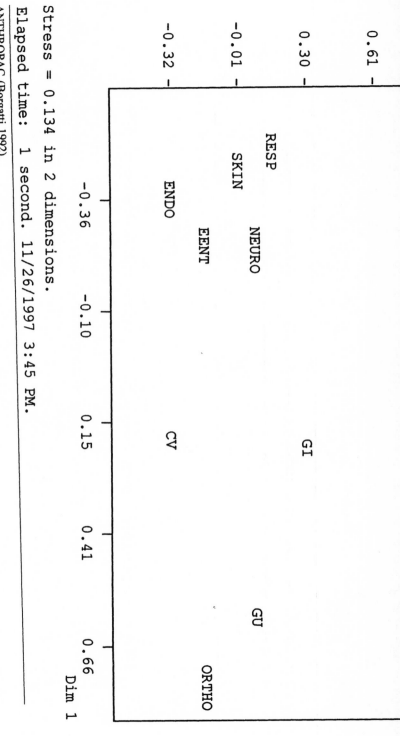

Stress = 0.134 in 2 dimensions.

Elapsed time: 1 second. 11/26/1997 3:45 PM.

ANTHROPAC (Borgatti 1992).

were perceived to be different (as shown by large distances between them). The stress of the solution for two dimensions was 0.134 after six iterations, which indicates some level of distortion in the pictoral representation given the input data.

Stress, as used in MDS, refers to the amount of distortion between the actual numerical values in a similarity matrix and the closest representation of those values in space, given the number of dimensions specified. Possible reasons for distortion in an MDS display (as indicated by stress level) are that a two-dimensional solution is insufficient to fit the model or random measurement error distorted the model (Kruskal and Wish 1978).

Ideally, zero stress would show a perfect fit of the data with the number of dimensions selected. Since the stress was above zero, it would be possible to rerun the MDS with more dimensions specified in an effort to approximate zero or at least reduce the stress in the model below 0.10. Because a two-dimensional model is easier to understand and picture mentally, we discarded the idea of searching for better-fitting, higher-dimensionality models.

What might be the two dimensions of orientation for this MDS display? There is no predetermined answer to this question, and each MDS can be interpreted differently based on what logical axes can be inferred from the positions of the data in space. Look at the horizontal, or x-axis (Figure 14.1) in this study. On the left side of the MDS display is a cluster containing respiratory, neuro, skin, endocrine, and EENT diagnoses, and on the far right orthopedic and genitourinary diagnoses. That horizontal dimension appears to separate medical from surgical diagnoses, with medical diagnoses on the left and surgical diagnoses on the far right.

Medical diagnoses usually require a treatment such as antibiotics or oxygen or insulin, as opposed to surgical diagnoses, which require anesthesia, incisions, and suturing. But does a dimension of medical/ surgical difference in diagnostic category appear to completely explain the clustering of diagnoses? Not really. Ear, eye, nose, and throat diagnoses often require surgical correction, and the EENT category is on the left, near the more medically oriented diagnoses. On the right side of the display are orthopedic, genitourinary, and cardiovascular diagnoses, all of which often require surgery, but the typically medical gastrointestinal diagnosis is not far away. So the medical/surgical differences may indicate one dimension with some distortion. The vertical or y-axis dimension may represent a relative level of pain in the raw data, though this, too, is distorted.

When analyzing the MDS graphic display, it's important to remember that the plotted location of each diagnosis is based on the vector of mean pain rating scores at times 1–4. The graphic display doesn't directly indicate which diagnostic codes are more painful or less painful, it only shows us which mean ratings for Pain1, Pain2, Pain3, and Pain4 (taken together as a vector) for each diagnostic code were similar to and different from vectors for other diagnostic codes. Spatial arrangement of diagnostic codes could be explained, in part, by increasing or decreasing mean pain scores over time as well as by the magnitude of pain scores.

Referring back to the mean pain rating scores (Table 14.1) we can see that the most painful diagnostic code using child data was cardiovascular, with stable ratings of 2.00 at each point. The EENT diagnostic code had the next highest pain ratings, followed by genitourinary pain ratings. Each diagnostic code exhibited a pattern of pain ratings, with some holding constant over time (CV), others declining (respiratory, neuro, and skin), some increasing (GU), and a few with variable ups and downs (GI, EENT). Analyzing the raw data and looking for patterns in the vectors help us solve the mystery of the dimensions in the MDS by suggesting a clustering of RESP, SKIN, and NEURO based on their shared declining pain ratings over time.

The MDS graphic output for parental pain ratings (Figure 14.2) shows a very different clustering of diagnostic codes. The dissimilarities between the child and parent MDS displays are more notable than the similarities. Interestingly, the stress in the parental model (0.07) is significantly less than the stress in the child model, meaning the model fit for parents contains less distortion.

Using QAP to Compare Empirical and Proxy Models of Child Pain

By inspecting the visual MDS displays of mean pain ratings by diagnostic codes for parents and children, we can see striking differences. But using visual assessment alone we cannot determine whether a proxy model of child pain is similar to or different from an empirical model because we have no way of judging what counts as "similar" or "different." We need to find a numerical way of matching the two MDS displays to establish their similarity or difference. QAP is a procedure that will answer our question about comparability of child and parent models by correlating the two data matrices (parent and child) cell by cell and computing a permutation test (see Borgatti 1992 [Reference Manual]:85–89). The procedure was accomplished in ANTHROPAC by selecting Tools>QAP>correlation, then selecting the child correlation matrix as the structure matrix and the parent correlation matrix as the observed matrix. The program permuted the rows and columns of the parent matrix 500 times and left the child matrix alone (see Table 14.4).

The results of the QAP tell us that the parent model doesn't approximate the child model of pain. The proportion (.108) of correlations as large as the average correlation between parent and child data sets (.226) is above a 0.05 level of significance. According to the QAP printout, about 10.8% of randomly generated data sets would have correlations as large as the correlation between the child MDS and the parent MDS. For us to determine in a probabilistic sense that the empirical and proxy models were actually based on a shared cultural model of pain, we would need the "proportion of correlations as large" to be less than 0.05. In this case, a

```
METRIC MULTIDIMENSIONAL SCALING

     Starting config:    GOWER'S PRINCIPAL COORDINATES
     Type of Data:       Similarities
     Input dataset:      CORRELATIONP

     Initial Stress = 0.126
     Final Stress = 0.070 after 6 iterations.

                         1         2
                        ----      ----
           1  RESP      -0.11     -0.32
           2  CV         0.10      0.15
           3  NEURO      0.35     -0.32
           4  ORTHO     -0.18      0.28
           5  GU         0.77      0.14
           6  GI         0.16     -0.21
           7  EENT      -0.10      0.02
           8  ENDO      -0.39     -0.14
           9  SKIN      -0.64     -0.03

     Coordinates saved as dataset COORDP
```

Figure 14.2. Multidimensional scale of diagnostic codes based on parent pain ratings.

Dim 2

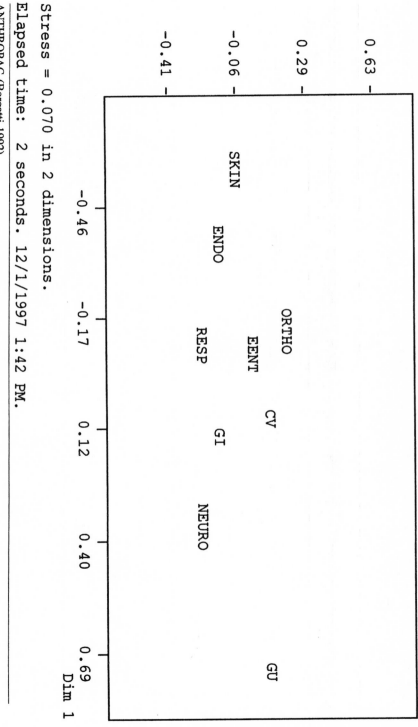

0.63 –

0.29 –

-0.06 –

-0.41 –

SKIN

ENDO

ORTHO

EENT

RESP

CV

GI

NEURO

GU

-0.46   -0.17   0.12   0.40   0.69
                                                 Dim 1

Stress = 0.070 in 2 dimensions.

Elapsed time: 2 seconds. 12/1/1997 1:42 PM.

ANTHROPAC (Borgatti 1992).

TABLE 14.4
Multidimensional Scale of Diagnostic Codes
Based on Parent Pain Ratings

QAP MATRIX CORRELATION

Observed matrix:	CORRELATIONP
Structure matrix:	CORRELATIONC
# of Permutations:	500
Random seed:	534

Univariate statistics on CORRELATIONP

		1

1	Mean	0.27
2	Std Dev	0.51
3	Sum	19.60
4	Variance	0.26
5	Euc Norm	4.89
6	Minimum	-0.98
7	Maximum	0.91
8	N of Obs	72.00

Univariate statistics on CORRELATIONC

		1

1	Mean	-0.02
2	Std Dev	0.55
3	Sum	-1.59
4	Variance	0.30
5	Euc Norm	4.66
6	Minimum	-0.97
7	Maximum	0.90
8	N of Obs	72.00

	CORRELATION	MATCHES
Observed value:	0.226	0.028
Average:	-0.018	0.006
Standard deviation:	0.177	0.011
Proportion as large:	0.108	0.206
Proportion as small:	0.892	1.000

Hubert's gamma: 4.108

Elapsed time: 3 seconds. 11/26/1997 3:37 PM.

ANTHROPAC (Borgatti 1992).

visual scan of the two MDS displays suggested the models were different, and QAP confirmed this by determining that the differences between the models failed to meet the criterion for statistical significance based on similarity of the two models.

Discussion

In reviewing the methods used and the research questions asked, we are now able to display an empirical model of children's pain for nine diagnostic categories based on 143 hospitalized children's responses to a pain question, "How many pieces of hurt do you have now?" asked four times during one day during their hospitalization. The empirical model produced through MDS suggests that dimensions in pain ratings reflect both trends and intensity of pain over time. We can also examine the proxy model of children's pain based on parental assessments of children's pain. Although the parental MDS model of children's pain looks different from the children's model of pain, similarities between the models could only be ruled out as statistically nonsignificant through QAP.

For parents and clinicians, these results suggest child and parent pain models are related, but not identical. Empirical measures of pain elicited from children themselves would be preferable to a parental proxy measure of pain whenever possible. As a general rule, parents' pain ratings for their children serve as only fair proxies for their children's own assessment of their pain. The results also highlight the possibility of wide variability in models of pain and its intensity. If parents' models of pain correlate imperfectly with children's models—and parents supposedly know their children and can interpret their emotions and discomforts with skills honed throughout the child's lifetime—then it seems unlikely that someone even further removed from the child's experience, like a nurse or physician, would appraise child pain more accurately. Models of pain for particular diagnoses don't appear to be widely shared even among children, since MDS stress was moderately high in the child model, indicating difficulty fitting the data to a two-dimensional solution.

For students, the results of this paper illustrate the process of conducting a secondary analysis of an existing data set. Determining research questions, adapting the data set, and analyzing the data were reviewed. MDS and QAP procedures were employed, and the interpretation of the data was discussed, with implications for the clinical assessment of children's pain in hospitals.

QUESTIONS

1. What is a secondary analysis? What are the advantages and disadvantages of performing a secondary analysis?
2. The MDS of children's pain was accomplished in two dimensions and yielded a stress of .134. What are two possible explanations for this moderate level of stress in the MDS solution?
3. What is the optimal level of stress for MDS and the cutoff for a tolerable level of stress? Are there reasons for terminating additional MDS solutions before reaching a tolerable stress level?
4. In this study, QAP was selected to compare the empirical and proxy models of pain. What did the analysis reveal about the comparability of the two models? If QAP reached the opposite conclusion about the comparability of the two models, what would the printout show?
5. One of the most important parts of answering a research question with a new method is disseminating information about the results to appropriate audiences. How would you explain the techniques and results of this study to a parent of a currently hospitalized child and a nurse working on the pediatric unit where the study was conducted?

STEPHEN P. BORGATTI ∎

Afterword

The Methods

I first learned about the *kinds of methods* found in this book in the late '70s, when I was a graduate student at UC-Irvine. At the time, everything was done on mainframes using a collection of heavy duty FORTRAN programs from Bell Labs, together with a number of small utility programs written locally that would reformat data, do needed transformations, and generally fill the gaps between the big programs. They were pretty painful to work with, but we graduate students became quite adept. Many of us even learned to program a bit (this sort of thing was encouraged at Irvine), creating tools of our own. I remember, for example, that Kim Romney asked me (as his R.A.) to write a program for creating the expected values for a quasi-symmetry model, which was to be used to analyze endogamy data.

Then, in 1980, I left to go to work in the private sector, ending up at a consulting firm, Management Decision Systems (MDS), which, it turned out, used many of *these methods* to understand consumers' belief systems. One of the principals of MDS, Glen Urban, was the co-author of the seminal book *Design and Marketing of New Products* (1980), which featured *these methods* heavily.

When I finally returned to UC-Irvine in the mid '80s (still working part-time for MDS), I found a revolution in progress: The faculty had gone PC (no, not politically correct—that came later). Everybody had acquired personal computers and were using them to type their own manuscripts (in WordStar, and later, MultiMate) and even to do some statistical analyses (Systat was a favorite; you could also get BMDP compiled for the PC). But most of the software tools for *the methods* were still on the mainframe. I bought myself an IBM PC (black-and-white screen, 1 megabyte of RAM, 20 megabytes of hard-disk space, $5,000) and taught myself Pascal using Borland's $49.95 Turbo-Pascal.

Pretty soon, I had programmed many of the tools, creating a program for IBM PCs called AL ("Analytic Language"). In addition to *the methods*, AL contained routines for social network analysis, in imitation of Lin Freeman's UCI-NET suite of programs. Eventually, AL was split in two, with one half (the one with *the methods*) becoming ANTHROPAC, and the other half (the one with network analysis) becoming UCINET Version 4. The menu-driven ANTHROPAC was much easier to use than the mainframe tools and made it a lot more fun to analyze data. It is now sold to researchers in several disciplines worldwide, and earlier versions are available for free on the web (www.analytictech.com). Increasingly, I have observed that ANTHROPAC is also being used in undergraduate research methods classes. (Not my own, though: I teach at a campus where everyone uses Macintosh computers!)

It is interesting and surprising to see the present surge of interest in *the methods*. After all, they are ancient: most were developed by psychometricians in the '60s, building on work that goes back to the '30s. They were brought over and extended in anthropology by Kim Romney, Roy D'Andrade, Jack Roberts, and many other cognitive anthropologists and ethnoscientists. The methods are essentially the methods of cognitive anthropology. Yet cognitive anthropology, as a field, has quite a bit less presence today than it did back then.[1] Why the current interest in its methods?

It is especially puzzling when one considers that anthropology has, for some time now, been dominated by such a different epistemological paradigm. Implicit in *the methods* is a simple faith in empiricism—that is, the belief that we can learn something about the world (the social world, for us social scientists) by asking questions, by observation, by measuring things. (See, for example, the introduction to Penn Handwerker's chapter in this volume.) Yet the dominant paradigm has been one that sees all reality (especially the scientist's!) as socially constructed, where there can be no discovery, only invention. Measurement can only reveal what we already believe: a case of the right brain playing a trick on the left.

Also implicit in *the methods* (particularly in the systematic data collection tasks and in the use of simple statistics to check hypotheses) is the notion that bias is bad and that positive steps should be taken to reduce it. (See, for example, Doug Caulkins's paper in this volume, where he randomizes the order in which cards are presented to each respondent.) Yet, until now, the dominant paradigm has seen bias as something that can't be reduced, only exposed, if not, perversely, celebrated. Bias is not in the methods, it is in us—our culture, our gender, our history. We do not reduce bias, we use it as a catalyst for personal transformation, for overcoming original sin.

Similarly, *the methods* implicitly separate inquiry from advocacy. For example, an applied anthropologist wants to change a behavioral practice. The anthropologist's working model is that to effect change, one must first understand the causes of the behavior—the factors that support that behavior. *The methods* are applied to understand the belief systems. Once these are understood, an appropriate intervention is designed and implemented. *The methods* play no part in this second step. Yet the dominant paradigm has been one that believes that values cannot and must not be separated from inquiry; it is an action-oriented paradigm in which questions are asked not to reveal beliefs but to expose them, not to document but to liberate.

Why are *the methods* so acceptable? Maybe the dominant paradigm has run its course—the cultural pendulum is beginning the big swing back. Or maybe most of the interest is coming from people who are peripheral to mainstream anthropology. They certainly are not a general cross-section of anthropologists: purchasers of ANTHROPAC are, as far as I can tell, disproportionately applied anthropologists, medical anthropologists, and non-American anthropologists. Or perhaps the dominant paradigm has room in it for a few techniques which, while inconsistent with some planks of the dominant paradigm, are—surprisingly—in complete harmony with others. Let me count the ways.

First, the espoused goal of most dominant paradigm work is emic in character. That is, the objective is to understand the world from the natives' point of view. Instead of imposing the researchers' categories, we seek to uncover the natives' own categories, and let those structure our understanding and our reporting. This is exactly the goal of *the methods*. In studying beliefs about illnesses, we focus on the illnesses provided by the informants (for example, via a freelist task), not the ones recognized by the American Medical Association. In categorizing illnesses, we use the taxonomic structure revealed by informants, not the one we researchers feel is right.

Second, the dominant paradigm favors qualitative data analysis. Now, conventional wisdom assumes that "qualitative" modifies both "data" and "analysis." But *the methods* make it obvious that the qualitative/quantitative distinction can be applied to either data or analysis, independently. Regardless of whether we collect qualitative or quantitative data, we can analyze them via qualitative or quantitative methods. For example, suppose we collect text data by transcribing tape-recorded interviews with informants. Then we pore over the texts, writing notes on the margins, and developing a theory about what's going on. This is qualitative analysis of qualitative data. But if we use those texts to count words of a certain type (for example, relationship-oriented words) in each interview to test a hypothesis (using a chi-square test) that females use more relationship words than males, we are doing a quantitative analysis of qualitative data. (Note that the paper by Ryan and Weisner in this volume is very much like this.) Table 1 gives examples of the other two combinations: qualitative analysis of quantitative data, and quantitative analysis of quantitative data.

TABLE 1

Examples of Different Combinations
of Qualitative and Quantitative
Data Collection and Analysis Methods

		Data Analysis	
		Qualitative	Quantitative
Data Collection	Qualitative	1. Grounded theory analysis of interview notes 2. Intuitive interpretation of a ritual	1. Content analysis of interview text: correlating codes 2. QAP comparison of pile sort data from different groups
	Quantitative	1. Looking for patterns in maps where the size of circles representing towns indicates the number of cases of a new disease 2. Using MDS plots to interpret correlations among variables	1. Regression analysis of demographic variables to predict income 2. Factor analysis of attitudinal variables

So where do *the methods* fit in? Well, many of them involve data collection techniques that are technically qualitative, but are so structured and systematic as to have a quantitative spirit. Many of them also involve data analysis techniques that use binary computers to generate qualitative displays, like pictures. In short, *the methods* are a deliciously postmodern blend of qualitative and quantitative. Consider, for example, the paper by Johnson and Griffith. This paper reports the results of several different studies. One of the studies—on food consumption—consists of a pile sort data collection task (qualitative, though structured), followed by counting the number of people placing each pair of items in a pile together to create a similarity metric (quantitative), followed by a multidimensional scaling (quantitative) to produce a cognitive map (qualitative), which was then interpreted directly (qualitative).

Finally, I'd like to point out that *the methods* assume, along with the dominant paradigm, that people do see the world differently. Whereas one group will see shrubs as different from trees, another group will make no such distinction. *The methods* provide a way to document both the unity and the diversity of human thought.

I congratulate Victor DeMunck, E.J. Sobo, and all the authors of the many chapters, on a really fine book. I am heartened both by the methodological interest that it reflects, and by the usage that I know it will spur.

NOTE

1. For example, I don't see job ads requesting cognitive anthropologists, nor is there a AAA section for cognitive anthropology.

Appendix

The history of social scientific methods is complex, as well as on-going, and cannot be treated in this book. However, a small amount of background information on anthropological methods will be helpful. The British Association for the Advancement of Science (B.A.A.S.), founded in 1883, published the first anthropological literature to deal specifically with methods: a series of documents titled *Notes and Queries*.

First written by Edward B. Tylor and subsequently by other anthropologists, *Notes and Queries* served as a professional guidebook for how to do anthropology (Stocking 1990).

In the first *Notes and Queries*, Tylor advocated that the anthropologist live in the community under study, observe customs and behaviors first-hand, and be fluent enough to speak the local language to ask questions and understand answers. In the 1912 edition of *Notes and Queries*, W. H. Rivers laid down what has become the canon of anthropological fieldwork: "The anthropologist should live for a year or more among a community of perhaps four or five hundred people and study every detail of their life and culture; in which he comes to know every member of the community personally; in which he is not content with generalized information, but studies every feature of life and custom in concrete detail by means of the vernacular language" (p. 7, quoted in Stocking 1990:36).

From about that time on, anthropologists (ideally) lived in the communities they studied and learned the language there spoken. Because they (ideally) participated in activities they studied as well as observing them, the primary ethnographic technique was termed "participant observation."

With the exception of *Notes and Queries*, not much on methods was published until the 1970s (see Trotter 1991:181). The seminal volume published in this period was Pertti Pelto's (1970) *Anthropological Research: the Structure of Inquiry*. New methods were added to the anthropological tool kit: Decision making, frame elicitations, the semantic differential test (Osgood et al. 1957), cultural domains (Spradley 1979), taxonomic and paradigmatic analyses of categories, Goffman's (1959) metaphor of stage led to actors' and role analysis, and game theory approaches (for example, Bailey 1969) extended the stage metaphor to view individuals as actors manipulating cultural norms for their own ends.

The early 1980s saw the publication of several important "how-to" ethnographic manuals, most of which relate to particular techniques that can be practiced in the context of participant observation or ethnographic interviews and other larger research efforts. Some examples of these are: Michael Agar's *The Professional Stranger* (1980) and James Spradley's back-to-back contributions, *The Ethnographic Interview* (1979) and *Participant Observation* (1980). Sage Publications began publishing a series of research methods papers (for example, Weller and Romney 1988). More recently, H. Russell Bernard published what has become the 1990s classic, *Research Methods in Anthropology: Qualitative and Quantitative Approaches* (1994).

The burgeoning of methods literature was spurred in part by the emergence of methodology as a subdisciplinary specialization and also by the evolving needs of anthropologists working in interdisciplinary settings or on contemporary problems at home rather than in classic field sites abroad. The needs of modern medical anthropologists have particularly helped underwrite the new wave of methodological inquiry (Trotter 1991:183). The availability of computers, cheap and easy-to-learn, menu-driven software programs, multimedia packages, and the Internet are all reshaping how social science is done. This book is part of that revolution, for it is unlikely that most of the participants in this volume would have used these methods 20 or even 10 years ago when neither classes in these methods nor software was readily available or affordable.[1]

NOTE

1. We recommend reading Weitzman and Miles (1995) sourcebook on "computer programs for qualitative data analysis" for brief commentaries and evaluations of software programs. The journal *Cultural Anthropology Methods* (*CAM*) is also very useful for checking out reviews of various programs.

Glossary

age group: A sample population in which the sample is selected on the basis of age parameters. An entire population can be divided into age groups in order to make internal comparisons.

ANTHROPAC: A computer program capable of performing numerous procedures on data including the making of questionnaires, editing, importing, and statistical analysis.

ASCII: Acronym for American Standard Code for Information Interchange, an information-coding scheme. **ASCII file**: American Standard Code for Information Exchange format file, which can be accessed by a wide range of programs.

attrition: The rate at which a sample of informants becomes smaller over time. If you begin with a sample of 100 and five years later you go back to find the sample and can only find 92 people, then the rate of attrition is 8%.

auto-photography: Informants take the pictures.

average: Mean, a measure of central tendency, the sum of the scores or values of a variable divided by the total number of cases.

backstage: From the theater; refers to informal behaviors that occur hidden from public view.

bias: Internalized cultural "filters" or "lenses" that systematically distort how people—scientists included—interpret signals or data. Biases are usually tacit and systematically applied.

causal relationship: Correlation in which one variable causes the other to exist as it does in relation to the former.

closed-ended questions. Questions constructed for an interview schedule or questionnaire that demand that the respondent answer within the options provided to the questions. Options are given with each question.

cluster analysis: A method of graphically representing similarities or distances between a set of objects, showing objects which are most similar to each other as starting points for increasingly comprehensive clusters of objects.

code: A symbol that refers to a larger and significant unit of information (for example, the code "COOP" for any expression of cooperation between individuals).

codebook: A systematic collection of codes and meanings for them.

coefficient of reproducibility (CR): A measure of the proportion of errors to correct responses in a Guttman scale analysis. CR = 1−(#error/# total responses). A CR of greater than 0.90 is considered significant.

common word list: A list of frequently occurring words in languages that have little meaning when read alone. Articles such as "a," "the," and prepositions like "to" and "with" can often be dropped from a content analysis of words because they add little to the analysis.

complete triad design: A design for a set of triad questionnaires that has each item appearing with each other item in every possible triad position.

consensus analysis: Both a theory of culture as shared knowledge and a method for discovering (1) the degree to which cultural knowledge is shared; (2) the key, or "culturally correct" information about that domain; and (3) the degree of knowledge about that domain expressed by each respondent.

correlation: The simple co-occurrence of two variables; variables can move in the same direction (in a positive relationship, both going up or down together) or in the opposite directions (in a negative or inverse relationship; as one goes up, the other goes down); see also **causal relationship** and **direction**.

correspondence analysis: A multivariate statistical test and graphical technique for comparing two nominal variables. Correspondence analysis allows one to visually associate rows and columns.

criterion: A standard on which a judgment or decision is based.

cultural domain. All things that are recognized to be members of a cultural category. For example, "chairs" and "tables" are members of the cultural category "furniture."

cultural key: The "answers" or knowledge about a cultural domain when there is a cultural level of agreement among respondents. These answers are revealed by the analysis and are not necessarily known to the analyst in advance.

cultural knowledge score: Sometimes call cultural competence score. Some individuals will know more about the cultural domain than others and individual scores can be calculated from the degree to which their answers correspond to the "cultural key."

cultural level of agreement: A high level of agreement among individuals reflects their shared knowledge about a cultural domain. Operationally, when a factor analysis reveals only one major factor in the data.

cultural model: A representation of a body of knowledge (for example, regarding marriage) or of experiences (for example, dating) that is shared by members of a culture.

culture: The learned, shared knowledge and practices of a group of people.

decision criteria. The reasons respondents make decisions. Factors that influence people's actions or nonactions with regard to solving a specific problem.

decision rules. The constraints and conditions placed on specific behavioral responses to a problem or situation.

decision tree model. A model of the set of alternative rules people use in making a decision, with the choices or rules organized sequentially and hierarchically (as a tree).

domain (category): A set of related items.

eigenvalue: In factor analysis, a measure of variance accounted for by a dimension or factor. For a single culture solution in consensus analysis, the eigenvalue for the first factor should be substantially larger than that of a second factor, if any.

emic: Concepts, categories, and distinctions that are meaningful to members of the cultural group in question.

epistemology: The study of how we know what we know.

error of commission: A case where a response is present that should be absent.

error of omission. A case where a response is absent that should be present.

ethnobiology: Folk biology; emic biological understandings.

ethnography: A description of a culture or a part of a culture; collecting data needed for such a description.

etic: Using concepts, categories, and distinctions that are universally applicable but that may not have local meaning (except within the scientific community).

explanatory models. Models of belief and behavior that include the following components: (1) believed-in causes of illness; (2) perceived symptoms; (3) perceived options for treatment; (4) treatment responses; and (5) evaluation of outcome of treatment. Most explanatory models are constructed through using data collected in illness narratives. They are constructed for individuals and composites are built for groups.

factor analysis: A statistical method for discovering whether or not a set of observed variables are highly intercorrelated and can be reduced to a smaller set of underlying dimensions or factors. The one-culture model in consensus analysis is satisfied if there is one major factor in the data.

Fisher's Exact Test: A nonparametric statistical test for comparing two nominal variables.

folk explanatory model: A culturally common explanation for a specific culturally recognized condition or event.

formal ethnographic methods: Explicit, systematic procedures used to collect cultural data.

freelisting: A procedure where informants are asked to name all the items in a specific cultural domain.

frequency: The number of times an attribute is observed expressed as proportion of 100.

frontstage: How people behave when an audience is watching; usually such behavior follows a culturally known script, as raising a hand to ask a question in class.

gatekeepers: Individuals who control access to outside resources for insiders and control access to inside resources (for example, votes) by outsiders.

generalize: To assume that what applies in one case applies to another, similar case.

grama sevaka: A Sri Lankan civil servant who serves as the government representative or factotum in a community.

grounded theory: Theory revised during the data collection phase of a research project in which theory and method exist in an interactive feedback loop rather than a unilateral relationship in which one determines the other.

Guttman scale: A form of data analysis intended to demonstrate that a single dimension underlies a particular distribution of data.

hierarchical clustering: See cluster analysis.

hypothesis: A proposition asserting a relationship between two or more phenomena that is derived from a **theory** and phrased as a verifiable or falsifiable statement.

hypothetical questions. If/Then questions designed to ascertain decision criteria.

illiterate: A person who cannot read or write, although living in a society with a writing system: A nonliterate society is one in which there is not a writing system.

independent data collection: One informant provides answers without knowing the answers of any other informant. For example, mothers and fathers did not copy each other's answers.

independent variables: Factors that influence, shape, or determine a specific outcome.

informant: An individual who shares his or her cultural knowledge with an ethnographer. Nowadays, often referred to as "participant."

investigator bias: When investigators look at data and insert their own interpretations, categories, or themes rather than those of the informants.

key informants: Local people who become friends of the researcher and who are knowledgeable about what people in the community know and are willing and even eager to be the researcher's confidant. Key informants often have the same ascriptive and personality characteristics as the researcher.

lambda-2 design: A balanced incomplete block design for triad questionnaires that pairs every item twice with each of the other items.

life experience markers: Measurements of life experiences that may influence how individuals now interpret and respond to the world of experience. Examples include age, gender, class, and ethnicity.

macro: A feature found in most word processors that allows the computer to remember and replay a particular set of keystrokes. A macro is like a tape recorder of computer steps. Once you record the steps, you can play them back automatically. Macros are especially useful for long repetitive tasks. Look under Help on your computer to learn how to create and play macros.

matrix: A table of data characterized by rows and columns, where the rows signify individual cases and the columns signify attributes.

mean: Average, a measure of central tendency, the sum of the scores or values of a variable divided by the total number of cases.

medical anthropology: The study of the sociocultural understanding of diseases and illnesses.

methods: Procedures for procuring, organizing, analyzing, and interpreting information.

multidimensional scaling (MDS): A method of spatially representing the pattern of similarities among a set of objects. Often used in conjunction with cluster analysis.

nominal data: Mutually exclusive names or things that can be listed but not compared directly using math as they are qualitative caregories.

open-ended questions. Questions constructed for an interview guide or questionnaire that allow respondents to answer in their own words, rather than being given choices.

operationalize: To explicitly determine how to measure a variable or the relationship between two or more of them.

order bias: Responses to first items in a series can affect responses to later items.

outcome (dependent) variables: Measurable factors that depend on or are affected by and correlate with independent variables.

outlier: A case or data point where an error is so unusual it is clearly exceptional and may reasonably be said not to belong to the domain being scaled.

pair comparison method: A method that has informants rate the similarity or the dissimilarity of pairs in a set, or to rank order the two items of pairs.

participant observation: Fieldwork in which the researcher obtains data through a long-term (for example, one or more years) period of participating in the lives of the people he or she is studying and observing their behavior. The researcher relinquishes experimental control over the flow of data.

particularists: Scholars interested in holistic, richly detailed accounts of social life.

pile sort method: A task in which informants are instructed to sort cards into piles that contain items more similar to each other than to those in other piles that they are sorting.

pretest: Asking informants to review questions to see if they make sense to them and to make sure they are valid.

projective devices: Visual objects that help prompt informants in the interview process.

proxy model: A representation of one group's perceptions created through research carried out with another group; for example, a model of children's beliefs based on parents' reports of same.

qualitative data: Nonnumerical data; often, narrative data.

quality of life: The material and social conditions of living for a particular group of people.

quantitative data: Numerical data.

ranking: The complete ordering of a set of elements according to the degree of some quality or characteristic each possesses (for example, class rank based on grade point average).

rank order data: Data sorted by rank (first, second, third, etc.). Rank data make no inferences about the size of the difference between ranks other than that one is bigger than the other. For example, the difference between the first and second items might be very small or very large. We cannot tell with rank order data.

rating: Assigning a score to an item according to a set of standard criteria (for example, letter grades are a rating system for student performance).

reactivity: The effect that the researcher has on participants and the context in which work is carried out.

reflexivity: The researcher's introspective awareness of his or her own internal biases as they influence his or her research.

reliability: The extent to which a measurement tool that works once will work the same way if applied again, barring any change in the participant or his or her environment.

replicability: When an experiment or project carried out by one person can be carried out again by another person.

sample: A microcosm of the larger population in terms of the relevant characteristics of that population that the researcher is interested in; an **ethnographic sample** is a nonrandom sample that establishes the range of cultural phenomena but not the frequency distribution of those phenomena.

sampling frame: Any means of systematically selecting informants based on an explicit set of life experience markers.

scalable: A distribution of data that fits the requirements of a particular form of scale analysis such as Guttman scaling.

secondary analysis: Given an existing data set compiled for a particular purpose, a secondary analysis reexamines the data to answer new questions, possibly using new methods

similarity data: The measure of likeness of items using a consistent criterion.

similarity matrix or correlation matrix: A table displaying the systematic relationships between two variables. Each cell displays the same degree of of similarity between two cases.

snowball sample: A sampling technique that asks informants to suggest other informants who suggest other informants and so on.

sociocultural variables: Social rather than biological or individual (idiosyncratic) factors that produce different measures and can have biological consequences. For example, dietary practices are sociocultural variables that affect rates of hypertension in a population.

standardize: To make two measures equivalent so they can be compared. For example, if in a poll of 50 men, 25 say they like chocolate and in a poll of 100 women, 25 say they like chocolate, the data need to be standardized before comparing men and women's preference for chocolate. In this case, standardize the data by calculating the percent of men (25/50 = 50%) and women (25/100 = 25%) who like chocolate. The two polls suggest that men like chocolate more.

stress: In multidimensional scaling, the amount of distortion between the actual numerical values in a similarity matrix and the closest representation of those values in space, given the number of dimensions specified.

structured interviews. Interview schedule or questionnaire comprised of structured questions as opposed to unstructured interviews that are principally conversations. Structured interviews structure the respondents' answers.

systematic data collection: Formal methods of collecting data that consist of explicit, consistent procedures.

theory: A statement that stipulates the goals we hope to achieve through the application of methods by shaping the research questions we ask in the first place.

thick description: Describing behaviors, intentions, situations, and events as they are understood by one's informants, in as much detail as possible.

transactional theory of conflict: Individuals compete with each other to gain culturally defined "prizes" (for example, wealth, grants, prestige, political power, mates).

triad method: A task that has informants select similarities or rank order items of a domain that are arranged in sets of three.

triangulation: The collection of data through multiple methods so that data collected with one specific method can be compared with data collected with other methods.

type-token rate, or **concentration rate**: The average rate at which words in a text are used multiple times. The rate is calculated with the formula: 1−(total unique words/total words).

unique words forms: The list of all the words that appear in a text regardless of how often they occur. For example, the words "Sam," "ran," and "and" are the only three unique word forms in the sentence "Sam ran and ran and ran."

validity: When a test actually measures what it is supposed to be measuring.

verifiability: A concept or measurement is verifiable when it can be found to be true or false. Verifiability demands the use of empirical, repeatable methods of measurement. For example, estimates used to rank order individuals by height can be verified with a tape measure.

visual saliency: The most frequent themes or subject matter in auto-photography.

visual stimuli: Similar to a projective device in that its purpose is to get informants to open up and discuss complex issues.

References

Agar, Michael. 1980. *The Professional Stranger: An Informal Introduction to Fieldwork.* New York: Academic Press.

Anthropology Newsletter. 1996. Annual Meeting Edition.

Bailey, Frederik G. 1969. *Stratagems and Spoils.* New York: Schocken.

Barlett, Peggy. 1977. The Structure of Decision Making in Paso. *American Ethnologist* 4(2):285–307.

Beals, Alan R., and Bernard Siegel. 1966. *Divisiveness and Social Conflict.* Stanford: Stanford University Press.

Becker, Howard S. 1986. *Writing for Social Scientists: How to Start and Finish Your Thesis, Book or Article.* Chicago: University of Chicago Press.

Becker, Howard S., B. Geer, E. C. Hughes, and A. Strauss. 1961. *Boys in White: Student Culture in Medical School.* Chicago: University of Chicago Press.

Bernard, H. Russell, Pertti J. Pelto, Oswald Werner, James Boster, A. Kimball Romney, Allen Johnson, Carol R. Ember, Alice Kasakoff. 1986. The Construction of Primary Data in Cultural Anthropology. *Current Anthropology* 27:382–396.

Bernard, H. Russell. 1994. *Research Methods in Anthropology: Qualitative and Quantitative Approaches,* 2d ed. Thousand Oaks, CA: Sage Publications.

Bernard, H. Russell. 1995. Review of *Words 2.0. Cultural Anthropology Methods Journal* 7(3):11–12.

Bernard, H. Russell, and Gery R. Ryan. 1998. Qualitative and Quantitative Methods of Text Analysis. In *Handbook of Research Methods in Cultural Anthropology.* H. Russell Bernard, ed. Walnut Creek, CA: AltaMira Press. In press.

Best, Deborah L., Amy S. House, Anne E. Barnard, and Brenda S. Spicker. 1994. Parent-Child Interactions in France, Germany, and Italy: The Effects of Gender and Culture. *Journal of Cross-Cultural Psychology* 25(2):181–193.

Bluhagen, D. 1980. Hyper-Tension: A Folk Disease with a Medical Name. *Culture Medicine and Psychiatry* 4:197–227.

Bogdan, Robert C., and Sari Knopp Bilken. 1992. *Qualitative Research for Education: An Introduction to Theory and Methods*, 2d ed. Boston: Allyn and Bacon.

Bordo, Susan 1993. *Unbearable Weight: Feminism, Western Culture, and the Body*. Berkeley: University of California Press.

Borgatti, Stephen P. 1992. ANTHROPAC. Columbia, SC: Analytic Industries.

Borgatti, Stephen P. 1993/94. Cultural Domain Analysis. *Journal of Quantitative Anthropology* 4(4):261–278.

Boster, James S. 1985. "Requiem for the Omniscient Informant": There's Life in the Old Girl Yet. In *Directions in Cognitive Anthropology*. J.W.D. Dougherty, ed. Pp. 177–198. Urbana: University of Illinois Press.

Boster, James S. 1986. Exchange of Varieties and Information Between Aguaruna Manioc Cultivators. *American Anthropologist* 88:569'-583.

Boster, James S. 1987. Agreement Between Biological Classification Systems Is Not Dependent on Cultural Transmission. *American Anthropologist* 89(4):914–920.

Boster, James S., and Roy D'Andrade. 1989. Natural and Human Sources of Cross-Cultural Agreement in Ornithological Classification. *American Anthropologist* 91(1): 132–142.

Boster, James S., and Jeffrey C. Johnson. 1989. Form or Function: A Comparison of Expert and Novice Judgments of Similarity among Fish. *American Anthropologist* 91:866–889.

Bourdieu, Pierre. 1984 *Distinction: A Social Critique of the Judgement of Taste*. Cambridge: Harvard University Press.

Boyd, R., and P. J. Richerson. 1985. *Culture and the Evolutionary Process*. Chicago: University of Chicago Press.

Brazill, Timothy J., A. Kimball Romney, and William H. Batchelder. 1995. A Comparison of Methods for Collecting Judged Similarities Among Items in a Semantic Domain. *Journal of Quantitative Anthropology* 5:359–374.

Brown, Cecil H. 1984. *Language and Living Things: Uniformities in Folk Classification and Naming*. New Brunswick: Rutgers University Press.

Burton, Michael L., and Sara B. Nerlove. 1976. Balanced Designs for Triads Tests: Two Examples from English. *Social Science Research* 5:247–267.

Butler et al. v. Reno et al. 1984. CIV. ACTION 84–2604–TPJ.

Caulkins, Douglas. 1992. The Unexpected Entrepreneurs: Small High Technology Firms and Regional Development in Wales and Northeast England. In *Anthropology and the Global Factory: Studies in the New Industrialization of the Late Twentieth Century*. Frances Abrahamer Rothstein and Michael Blim, eds. Pp. 119–135. New York: Bergin & Garvey.

Caulkins, Douglas. 1995a. High Technology Entrepreneurs in the Peripheral Regions of the United Kingdom. In *Economic Futures on the North Atlantic Margin: Selected Contributions to the Twelfth International Seminar on Marginal Regions*. Reginald Byron, ed. Pp. 287–299. Aldershot (Hants.): Avebury Press.

Caulkins, Douglas. 1995b. Stumbling into Applied Anthropology: Collaborative Roles of Academic Researchers. *Practicing Anthropology 17*(1–2):21–24.

Caulkins, Douglas, and Carol Trosset. 1996. The Ethnography of Contemporary Welsh and Welsh-American Identity and Values. *Proceedings of the First North American Conference on Welsh Studies*. Pp. 9–16. Rio Grande University, Rio Grande, OH, June 1995.

Clifford, James 1986. On Ethnographic Allegory. In *Writing Culture: The Poetics and Politics of Ethnography*. James Clifford and George Marcus, eds. Pp. 98–121. Berkeley: University of California Press.

Collier, John. 1967. *Visual Anthropology: Photography as a Research Method*. New York: Holt, Rinehart and Winston.

Conklin, Harold C. 1954. The Relation of Hanunóo Culture to the Plant World. Ph.D. diss., New Haven: Yale University.

Counihan, Carole, and Penny Van Esterik, eds. 1997. *Food and Culture: A Reader*. New York: Routledge.

Crispell, Diane. 1994. Pet Projections. *American Demographics 16*(9):59.

Coyne, Amanda. 1997. The Long Good-Bye: Mother's Day in Federal Prison. *Harper's Magazine* (May):70–74.

D'Andrade, Roy. 1992. Schemas and Motivation. In *Human Motives and Cultural Models*. Roy D'Andrade and Claudia Strauss, eds. Pp. 23–44. Cambridge: University of Cambridge Press.

D'Andrade, Roy. 1995. *The Development of Cognitive Anthropology*. Cambridge: Cambridge University Press.

Denzin, Norman K., and Yvonna S. Lincoln, eds. 1994. *Handbook of Qualitative Research*. Thousand Oaks, CA: Sage Publications.

di Leonardo, Micaela. 1997. It's the Discourse, Stupid! *The Nation*, March 17:35–37.

Doerfel Marya L., and George A. Barnett. 1996. Developing Categories from Interview Data: Text Analysis and Multidimensional Scaling. Part I. *Cultural Anthropology Methods Journal 8*(2):15–16.

Dressler, William W. 1991. Culture, Stress and Disease. In *Medical Anthropology: A Handbook of Theory and Method*. T. M. Johnson and C. F. Sargent, eds. Pp. 248–267. New York: Greenwood Press.

Dressler, William W. 1996. Culture and Blood Pressure: Using Consensus Analysis to Create a Measurement. *Cultural Anthropology Methods Journal 8*(3):6–8.

Dreyfus, Hubert L. 1984. What Expert Systems Can't Do (Artificial Intelligence). *Raritan 3*(4):22–36.

Dreyfus, Hubert L. 1987. From Socrates to Expert Systems: The Limits of Calculative Rationality. *Bulletin of the American Academy of Arts and Sciences 40*(4):15–31.

Eiduson, Bernice T., and Thomas S. Weisner. 1978. Alternative Family Styles: Effects on Young Children. In *Mother/Child Father/Child Relationships*. Joseph H. Stevens, Jr. and Marilyn Mathews, eds. Pp. 197–221. Washington, DC: National Association for the Education of Young Children.

Ericksen, Karen P., and Robert W. Hodge. 1991/92. Occupations and Ritual in Contemporary Egypt. *Journal of Quantitative Anthropology* 3(3):207–228.

Federal Bureau of Prisons. 1997. Characteristics of Federal Inmates Incarcerated in Federal Bureau of Prisons Facilities Only. Washington, DC: U.S. Department of Justice, Federal Bureau of Prisons.

Fennell, Valerie. 1994. Meanings of Aging in a Southern Town. In *Many Mirrors: Body Images and Social Relations*. Nicole Sault, ed. Pp. 155–174. New Brunswick, NJ: Rutgers University Press.

Fiddes, Nick. 1991. *Meat: A Natural Symbol*. London: Routledge.

Fieldhouse, Paul. 1995. *Food and Nutrition: Customs and Culture*, 2d ed. London: Chapman & Hall.

Fine, Gary A., and Kent L. Sandstrom. 1988. *Knowing Children: Participant Observation with Minors. Qualitative Research Methods*, Vol. 15. Newbury Park, CA: Sage Publications.

Fleisher, Mark S. 1989. *Warehousing Violence*. Newbury Park, CA: Sage Publications.

Fleisher, Mark S. 1996. Management Assessment and Policy Dissemination in Federal Prisons. *The Prison Journal* 76(1):81–91.

Foster, Roxie 1990. A Multimethod Approach to the Description of Factors Influencing Nurses' Pharmacologic Management of Children's Pain. Ph.D. diss., Denver: University of Colorado Health Sciences Center.

Frake, Charles O. 1964. A Structural Description of Subanum Religious Behavior. In *Explorations in Cultural Anthropology*. W. Goodenough, ed. Pp. 111–130. New York: McGraw-Hill.

Freeman, Derek. 1983. *Margaret Mead and Samoa: The Making and Unmaking of an Anthropological Myth*. Cambridge: Harvard University Press.

Freeman, Howard E., A. Kimball Romney, Joao Ferreira-Pinto, Robert E. Klein, and Tom Smith. 1981. Guatemalan and U.S. Concepts of Success and Failure. *Human Organization* 40(2):140–145.

Fry, Christine, ed. 1980. *Aging in Culture and Society: Comparative Viewpoints and Strategies*. Brooklyn: Bergin.

Fry, Christine, ed. 1981. *Dimensions: Aging, Culture and Health*. Brooklyn: Bergin.

Gans, Herbert. 1976. On the Methods Used in This Study. In *The Research Experience*. P. Golden, ed. Pp. 49–59. Itasca, IL: F. E. Peacock.

García de Alba García, Javier E. 1989a. Evolución del concepto salud-enfermedad. *Cirugia y Cirujanos 56*(1):113–132.

García de Alba García, Javier E. 1989b. Un ensayo clinico en una fábrica: La presión alta en obreros textiles. *Revista de la Asociación Médica de Jalisco 7*: 8–12.

Garro, Linda. 1982. The Ethnography of Health Care Decisions. *Social Science and Medicine 16*:1451–1452.

Garro, Linda. 1986. Decision-Making Models of Treatment Choice in Illness Behavior. In *Illness Behavior: A Multidisciplinary Model*. Sean McHugh and T. Michael Vallis, eds. Pp. 173–188. New York: Plenum Press.

Garro, Linda. 1988. Explaining High Blood Pressure: Variation in Knowledge about Illness. *American Anthropologist 15*:98–119.

Geertz, Clifford. 1973. *The Interpretation of Cultures*. New York: Basic Books.

Gladwin, Christina H. 1976. A View of the Plan Puebla: An Application of Hierarchical Decision Models. *American Journal of Agricultural Economics 58*(5):881–887.

Gladwin, Christina H. 1983. Contributions of Decision Tree Methodology to a Farming Systems Program. *Human Organization 42*(2):146–157.

Gladwin, Christina H. 1989. *Ethnographic Decision Tree Modeling*. Newbury Park, CA: Sage Publications.

Gladwin, Christina H., and Judith Garis. 1996. Decision Theory. In *Encyclopedia of Cultural Anthropology*. David Levinson and Melvin Ember, eds. Pp. 316–319. New York: Henry Holt.

Glaser, Barney G., and Anselm Strauss. 1967. *The Discovery of Grounded Theory: Strategies for Qualitative Research*. New York: Aldine de Gruyter.

Goffman, E. 1959. *The Presentation of Self in Everyday Life*. Garden City, NY: Doubleday.

Golden, Patricia M. 1976. *The Research Experience*. Itasca, IL: F. E. Peacock Publishers.

Goode, Judith G. 1989. Cultural Patterning and Group-Shared Rules in the Study of Food Intake. In *Research Methods in Nutritional Anthropology*. Gretel H. Pelto, Pertti J. Pelto, and Ellen Messer, eds. Pp. 126–161. Hong Kong: The United Nations University.

Grady, Katheleen E., and Barbara S. Wallston. 1988. *Research in Health Care Settings*. Newbury Park, CA: Sage Publications.

Greenacre, Michael J. 1984. *Theory and Applications of Correspondence Analysis*. New York: Academic Press.

Griffith, David C., Jeffrey C. Johnson, James S. Boster, Michael Voiland, and James D. Murray. 1989. Increasing the Use of Underutilized Species Among Marine Recreational Fishermen in the Northeast and Mid-Atlantic Regions. A Report to the Sea Grant Marine Services of the Northeast and Mid-Atlantic Regions.

Handwerker, W. Penn, Jeanne Hatcherson, and Julie Herbert. 1997. Sampling Guidelines for Cultural Data. *Cultural Anthropology Methods Journal 8*:7–9.

Handwerker, W. Penn, and Danielle F. Wozniak. 1997. Sampling Strategies for Cultural Data: An Extension of Boas's Answer to Galton's Problem. *Current Anthropology 8*:869–875.

Harman, Robert C. 1996. Intergenerational Relations Among Maya in Los Angeles. In *Selected Papers on Refugee Issues*, Vol. 4. Ann M. Rynearson and James Phillips, eds. Pp. 156–173. Arlington: American Anthropological Association.

Harman, Robert C., and Nancy E. Briggs. 1991. Sietar Survey: Perceived Contributions of the Social Sciences to Intercultural Communication. *International Journal of Intercultural Relations 15*:19–28.

Harris, Robert. 1996. Variation among Style Checkers in Sentence Measurement, Text Technology. *Journal of Computer Text Processing* 6(2):80–90.

Heider, Karl. 1988. The Rashomon Effect: When Ethnographers Disagree. *American Anthropologist 90*:73–81.

Hester, Nancy O. 1976. The Preoperational Child's Reaction to Immunization. Master's thesis, Kansas City: University of Kansas.

Hester, Nancy O. 1979. The Preoperational Child's Reaction to Immunizations. *Nursing Research 28*(4):250–255.

Hester, Nancy O., Roxie Foster, and Judith Beyer. 1992. Clinical Judgment in Assessment of Children's Pain. In *Pain Management for Nurses*. J. Watt-Watson and M. Donovan, eds. Pp. 236–294. Philadelphia: B. C. Decker.

Hester, Nancy O., Roxie Foster, Karen Kristensen, and Linda Bergstrom. 1989. Measurement of Children's Pain by Children, Parents, and Nurses: Psychometric and Clinical Issues Related to the Poker Child Tool and the Pain Ladder. Final report for study titled Generalizability of Procedures Assessing Pain in Children. Research funded by National Institutes of Health Research, Grant Number R23NR01382.

Hill, Carole E. 1985. Local Health Knowledge and Universal Primary Health Care: A Behavioral Case from Costa Rica. *Medical Anthropology 9*(1):11–24.

Holaday, Bonnie, and Anne Turner-Henson. 1989. Response Effects in Surveys with School-Age Children. *Nursing Research 38*:248–250.

Holland, Dorothy. 1992. How Cultural Systems Become Desire. In *Human Motives and Cultural Models*. Roy D'Andrade and Claudia Strauss, eds. Pp. 61–89. Cambridge: Cambridge University Press.

Jang, H-Y., and George Barnett. 1994. Cultural Differences in Organizational Communication: A Semantic Network Analysis. *Bulletin de Méthodologie Sociologique 44*(September):31–59.

Jehn, Karen A., and Lorna Doucet. 1996. Developing Categories from Interview Data: Text Analysis and Multidimensional Scaling. Part I. *Cultural Anthropology Methods Journal 8* (2):15–16.

Jehn, Karen A., and Lorna Doucet. 1997. Developing Categories for Interview Data: Consequences of Different Coding and Analysis Strategies in Understanding Text. Part 2. *Cultural Anthropology Methods Journal 9*(1):1–7.

Johnson, Allen. 1975. Time Allocation in a Machiguenga Community. *Ethnology 14*: 310–321.

Johnson, Allen, and Orna Johnson. 1988. *Time Allocation among the Machiguenga of Shimaa. Cross Cultural Studies in Time Allocation*, Vol. 1. New Haven: Human Relations Area Files.

Johnson, Eric. 1995. Counting Words and Computing Word Frequency Project Report: WORDS. *TEXT Technology 5*(1):8–17.

Johnson, Jeffrey C. 1981. Cultural Evolution and the Organization of Work: Scarcity and Resource Management in an Alaskan Fishery. Ph.D. diss., Irvine: University of California.

Johnson, Jeffrey C. 1990. *Selecting Ethnographic Informants. Qualitative Research Methods*, Vol. 22. Newbury Park, CA: Sage Publications.

Johnson, Jeffrey C., and David C. Griffith. 1985. Perceptions and Preferences for Marine Fish: A Study of Recreational Fishermen in the Southeast Region. UNC–SG–85–01. Raleigh: University of North Carolina Sea Grant.

Johnson, Jeffrey C., David C. Griffith, and James S. Boster. 1996. Intercultural Variation and Network Position: The Place of Meat in Everyday Life. Paper presented at the 95th Annual Meeting of the American Anthropological Association. San Francisco, November 20–24.

Johnson, Jeffrey C., David C. Griffith, and J. D. Murray. 1988. Grant funded by Sea Grant/National Oceanic and Atmospheric Administration titled Social and Cultural Dimensions Among Seafood Consumers: Implications for Consumer Education.

Johnson, Jeffrey C., M. Ironsmith, A. L. Whitcher, G. M. Poteat, and C. W. Snow. 1997. The Development of Social Networks in Preschool Children. *Early Education and Development* 8(4):389–406.

Johnson, Jeffrey C., and J. D. Murray. 1997. Evaluating FAD Effectiveness in Development Projects: Theory and Praxis. In *Fish Aggregation Devices in Developing Fisheries: Potential and Pitfalls*. R. Pollnac and J. Poggie, eds. Pp. 143–158. ICMRD: Kingston.

Johnson, Stephen C. 1967. Hierarchical Clustering Schemes. *Psychometricka* 32:241–254.

Kania, Richard R. E. 1983. Joining Anthropology and Law Enforcement. *Journal of Criminal Justice* 11:495–504.

Kaufman, Sharon R. 1986 The Ageless Self: Sources of Meaning in Late Life. Madison: The University of Wisconsin Press.

Kirk, Jerome, and Marc L. Miller. 1986. *Reliability and Validity in Qualitative Research*. Newbury Park, CA: Sage Publications.

Kleinman, Arthur. 1978. Concepts and a Model for the Comparison of Medical Systems as Cultural Systems. *Social Science and Medicine* 12B:85–93.

Krippendorff, Klaus. 1980. *Content Analysis: An Introduction to Its Methodology*. Beverly Hills, CA: Sage Publications.

Kronenfeld, David B. 1996. *Plastic Glasses and Church Fathers*. New York: Oxford University Press.

Kruskall, Joseph B., and Myron Wish. 1978. *Multidimensional Scaling. Quantitative Applications in the Social Sciences*, Vol. 11. Newbury Park, CA: Sage Publications.

Kuhn, Thomas. 1970. *The Structure of Scientific Revolution*, 2d ed. Chicago: University of Chicago Press.

Lakoff, George, and Zoltan Kovecses. 1987. The Cognitive Model of Anger Inherent in American English. In *Cultural Models in Language and Thought*. Dorothy Holland and Naomi Quinn, eds. Pp. 195–221. Cambridge: Cambridge University Press.

Lee Richard 1993. *The Dobe Ju/'hoansi*. New York: Harcourt Brace.

Lupton, Deborah. 1996. *Food, the Body and the Self*. London: Sage Publications.

Martin, Joanne 1982. A Garbage Can Model of the Research Process. In *Judgments Calls in Research*. Joseph E. McGrath, Joanne Martin, and Richard A. Kulka, eds. Beverly Hills, CA: Sage Publications.

Mathews, Holly. 1982. Illness Classification and Treatment Choice: Decision Making in the Medical Domain. *Reviews in Anthropology 9*:170–186.

Mathews, Holly. 1987. Predicting Decision Outcomes: Have We Put the Cart Before the Horse in Anthropological Studies of Decision Making? *Human Organization 46*(1):54–61.

Mathews, Holly, and Carole E. Hill. 1990. Applying Cognitive Decision Theory to the Study of Regional Patterns of Illness Treatment Choice. *American Anthropologist 92*(1):155–170.

Maxwell, Joseph A. 1996. *Qualitative Research Design: An Interactive Approach*. Thousand Oaks, CA: Sage Publications.

McIver, John P., and Edward G. Carmines. 1981. *Unidimensional Scaling*. Sage University Papers Series on *Quantitative Applications in the Social Sciences*. Beverly Hills, CA: Sage Publications.

McMullin, J. M., L. R. Chavez, and F. A. Hubbell 1996. Knowledge, Power and Experience: Variation in Physicians' Perceptions of Breast Cancer Risk Factors. *Medical Anthropology 16*(4):295–317.

Mead, Margaret. 1928. *Coming of Age in Samoa*. New York: William Morrow.

Mehta, Cyrus R., and Nitin R. Patel. 1995. *StatXact 3 User Manual*. Cambridge: Cytel Software Corporation.

Messer, Ellen. 1989. Methods for Studying Determinants of Food Intake. In *Research Methods in Nutritional Anthropology*. Gretel H. Pelto, Pertti J. Pelto, and Ellen Messer, eds. Pp. 1–33. Hong Kong: The United Nations University.

Michela, John L., and Isobel R. Contento. 1984. Spontaneous Classifications of Foods by Elementary School-Aged Children. *Health Education Quarterly 11*:57–76.

Miles, Matthew B., and Michael A. Huberman. 1984. *Qualitative Data Analysis: A Sourcebook of New Methods*. Newbury Park, CA: Sage Publications.

Miles, Matthew B., and Michael A. Huberman. 1994. *Qualitative Data Analysis: An Expanded Sourcebook*, 2d ed. Newbury Park, CA: Sage Publications.

Miller, Mark L., and Jeffrey C. Johnson. 1981. Hard Work and Competition in the Bristol Bay Salmon Fishery. *Human Organization 40*(2):131–139.

Mingers, John. 1989a. An Empirical Comparison of Selection Measures for Decision-Tree Induction. *Machine Learning 3*:319–342.

Mingers, John. 1989b. An Empirical Comparison of Pruning Methods for Decision Tree Induction. *Machine Learning 4*:227–243.

Nardi, Bonnie. 1983. Goals in Reproductive Decision Making. *American Ethnologist 10*(4):697–714.

Nunnally, Jim C. (1978). *Psychometric Theory*. New York: McGraw-Hill.

Obeyesekere, Gananath. 1981. *Medusa's Hair*. Chicago: University of Chicago Press.

Orans, Martin. 1995. *Not Even Wrong*. San Francisco: Chandler and Sharp.

Osgood, Charles E., George J. Suci, and Percy H. Tannenbaum. 1957. *The Measurement of Meaning.* Urbana: University of Illinois Press.

Oths, Kathryn S. 1994. Health Care Decisions of Households in Economic Crisis: An Example from the Peruvian Highlands. *Human Organization* 53(3):245–254.

PAHO (Pan-American Health Organization). 1994. *Las condiciones de salud en las Américas. Publicación Científica*, No. 549. Washington, DC: Pan American Health Oreganization.

Peacock, James. 1978. *The Anthropological Lens.* New York: Wiley.

Pelto, Pertti. 1970. *Anthropological Research: The Structure of Inquiry.* New York: Harper and Row.

Pelto, Pertti, and Gretel Pelto. 1978. *Anthropological Research: The Structure of Inquiry.* New York: Cambridge University Press.

Peshkin, Alan. 1991. *The Color of Strangers, the Color of Friends: The Play of Ethnicity in School and Community.* Chicago: University of Chicago Press.

Phillips, Denis C. 1990. Subjectivity and Objectivity: An Objective Inquiry. In *Qualitative Inquiry in Education: The Continuing Debate.* Elliot W. Eisner and Alan Peshkin, eds. Pp. 19–37. New York: Teachers College Press.

Phothiart, Pravit. 1989. Karen: When the Wind Blows. In *Hill Tribes Today: Problems in Change.* John McKinnon and Bernard Vienne, eds. Pp. 369–392. Bangkok: White Lotus Co.

Quinn, Naomi. 1975. Decision Models of Social Structure. *American Ethnologist* 2:19–45.

Quinn, Naomi. 1978. Do Mfantse Fish Sellers Estimate Probabilities in Their Heads? *American Ethnologist* 5:206–226.

Rabinow, Paul. 1977. *Reflections on Fieldwork in Morocco.* Berkeley: University of California Press.

Raghavan, Chemba. 1993. Parental Cultural Models of Female Gender Role Identity: Beliefs of Asian Indian and Euro-American Mothers. Ph.D. diss., Philadelphia: Pennsylvania State University.

Raybeck, Douglas. 1992. Getting Below the Surface. In *The Naked Anthropologist.* P. de Vita, ed. Pp.3–15. New York: Wadsworth.

Renard, Ronald D. 1980. Karieng: History of Karen-T'ai Relations from the Beginnings to 1923. Ph.D. diss. Honolulu: University of Hawaii.

Richardson, Miles. 1975. Anthropologist: The Myth-Teller. *American Ethnologist* 2(3): 517–533.

Roberts, Carl W. 1997. "A Theoretical Map for Selecting among Text Analysis Methods." In *Text Analysis for the Social Sciences: Methods for Drawing Statistical Inferences from Text and Transcripts.* Carl W. Roberts, ed. Pp. 275–283. Mahwah, NJ: Lawrence Erlbaum Associates.

Robson, Charles. 1993. *Real World Research: A Resource for Social Scientists and Practitioner-Researchers.* London: Blackwells.

Romney, A. Kimball. 1994. Cultural Knowledge and Cognitive Structure. In *The Making of Psychological Anthropology*, Vol. 2. G.M.M. Suárez-Orozco, ed. Pp. 254–283. New York: Harcourt Brace.

Romney, A. Kimball, William H. Batchelder, and Susan C. Weller. 1987. Recent Applications of Cultural Consensus Theory. *American Behavioral Scientist 31*(2):163–177.

Romney, A. Kimball, Tom Smith, Howard E. Freeman, Jerome Kagan, and Robert E. Klein. 1979. Concepts of Success and Failure. *Social Science Research* 8:302–326.

Romney, A. Kimball, Susan C. Weller, and William H. Batchelder. 1986. Culture as Consensus: A Theory of Cultural and Informant Accuracy. *American Anthropologist* 88:313–338.

Romney, A. Kimball, and Susan C. Weller. 1988. Predicting Informant Accuracy from Patterns of Recall among Individuals. *Social Networks* 4:59–77.

Roos, Gun. 1995a. Cultural Analysis of Children, Food and Gender in the United States. Ph.D. diss., Lexington: University of Kentucky.

Roos, Gun. 1995b. Relationship Between Food and Gender among Fourth-Grade Children. *Crosscurrents* 7:97–108.

Rossi, Peter H., and R. A. Berk. 1991. A Guide to Evaluation Research Theory and Practice. In *Evaluation and Effective Risk Communication: Workshop Proceedings*. A. Fisher, M. Pavlova, and V. Covello, eds. Pp. 201–254. Washington, DC: Interagency Task Force on Environmental Cancer and Heart and Lung Disease. London: Blackwell.

Ryan, Gery. 1991. Can Expert Systems Really Help Us Model Decisions in the Field? *Cultural Anthropology Methods Newsletter* 3(1):5–7.

Ryan, Gery, and Homero Martínez. 1996. Can We Predict What Mothers Do? Modeling Childhood Diarrhea in Rural Mexico. *Human Organization* 55(1):47–57.

Schnegg, Michael, and H. Russell Bernard. 1996. Words as Actors: A Method for Doing Semantic Network Analysis. *Cultural Anthropology Methods Journal* 8 (2):7–10.

Scotch, Norman A. 1961. Sociocultural Factors in the Epidemiology of Zulu Hypertension. *American Journal of Public Health* 53:1205–213.

Stahl, Sidney M., Clarence E. Grim, Cathy Donald, and Helen Jo Neikirk. 1975. A Model for the Social Sciences and Medicine: The Case of Hypertension. *Social Science and Medicine* 9:31–38.

Sobo, Elisa J. 1995. *Choosing Unsafe Sex: Aids-Risk Denial among Disadvantaged Women*. Philadelphia: University of Pennsylvania Press.

Spradley, James. 1979. *The Ethnographic Interview*. New York: Holt, Rinehart and Winston.

Spradley, James. 1980. *Participant Observation*. New York: Holt, Rinehart and Winston.

Stocking, George W., Jr. 1990. *The Ethnographer's Magic*. Madison: University of Wisconsin Press.

Stoner, Bradley P. 1985. Formal Modeling of Health Care Decisions: Some Applications and Limitations. *Medical Anthropology Quarterly 16*(2):41–46.

Strauss, Anselm, and Juliet Corbin. 1990. *Basics of Qualitative Research: Grounded Theory Procedures and Techniques*. Newbury Park, CA: Sage Publications.

Super, Charles, and Sara Harkness. 1986. The Developmental Niche: A Conceptualization at the Interface of Child and Culture. *International Journal of Behavioral Development* 9(4):545–569.

Tesch, Renata. 1990. *Qualitative Research: Analysis Types and Software Tools*. New York: Falmar Press.

Thompson, Frances E., and Tim Byers. 1994. Dietary Assessment Resource Manual. *Journal of Nutrition 124*:2245S–2317S.

Trotter, Robert T., III. 1991. Ethnographic Research Methods for Applied Medical Anthropology. In *Training Manual in Applied Medical Anthropology*, Professional Series Special Publication 27. Carole E. Hill, ed. Pp. 180–212. Washington DC: American Anthropological Association.

Tylor, Edward B. 1889. On a Method of Investigating the Development of Institutions; Applied to Laws of Marriage and Descent. *Journal of the Royal Anthropological Institution of Great Britain and Ireland 18*:245–272.

Van Maanen, John, Mark L. Miller, and Jeffrey C. Johnson. 1982. An Occupation in Transition: Traditional and Modern Forms of Commercial Fishing. *Work and Occupations 9*(2):193–215.

Weber, Linda R., Andrew Miracle, and Tom Skehan. 1994. Interviewing Early Adolescents: Some Methodological Considerations. *Human Organization 53*:42–47.

Weber, Robert Philip. 1990. *Basic Content Analysis*, 2d ed. Newbury Park, CA: Sage Publications.

Weisner, Thomas S. 1986. Implementing New Relationship Styles in Conventional and Nonconventional American Families. In *Relationships and Development*. Willard Hartup and Zick Rubin, eds. Pp. 185–206. Hillsdale, NJ: LEA Press.

Weisner, Thomas S., and H. Garnier. 1992. Nonconventional Family Lifestyles and School Achievement: A 12-Year Longitudinal Study. *American Educational Research Journal 29* (3):605–632.

Weisner, Thomas S., H. Garnier, and J. Loucky. 1994. Domestic Tasks, Gender Egalitarian Values and Children's Gender Typing in Conventional and Nonconventional Families. *Sex Roles 30* (1, 2):23–54.

Weiss, R. S. 1994. *Learning from Strangers: The Art and Method of Qualitative Interviewing*. New York: Free Press.

Weitzman, E. A., and M. B. Miles. 1995. *Computer Programs for Qualitative Data Analysis: A Software Sourcebook*. Thousand Oaks, CA: Sage Publications.

Weller, Susan C. 1987. Shared Knowledge, Intracultural Variation, and Knowledge Aggregation. *American Behavioral Scientist 31*:178–193.

Weller, Susan C., and A. Kimball Romney. 1988. *Systematic Data Collection. Qualitative Research Methods*, Vol. 10. Newbury Park, CA: Sage Publications.

Weller, Susan C., Trenton R. Ruebush, II, and Robert E. Klein. 1997. Predicting Treatment-Seeking Behavior in Guatemala: A Comparison of the Health Services Research and Decision-Theoretic Approaches. *Medical Anthropological Quarterly 11*:224–245.

Wellman, Barry, and Susan Sim. 1990. Integrating Textual and Statistical Methods in the Social Sciences. *Cultural Anthropology Methods Newsletter 2*(1):1–3, 10–11.

Werner, Oswald. 1989a. Short Takes: Keeping Track of Your Interviews I. *Cultural Anthropology Methods Newsletter 1*(1):6–7.

Werner, Oswald 1989b. Short Takes: Keeping Track of Your Interviews II. *Cultural Anthropology Methods Newsletter 1*(2):8.

Werner, Oswald, and H. Russell Bernard. 1994. Ethnographic Sampling. *Cultural Anthropology Methods Journal 6*(2):7–9.

Werner, Oswald, and Mark G. Schoepfle. 1987. *Systematic Fieldwork.* Vol. 1: *Foundations of Ethnography and Interviewing.* Newbury Park, CA: Sage Publications.

Whyte, William F. 1984. *Learning from the Field: A Guide from Experience.* Newbury Park, CA: Sage Publications.

Wolcott, Harry F. 1990. On Seeking—and Rejecting—Validity in Qualitative Research. In *Qualitative Inquiry in Education: The Continuing Debate.* W. Eisner and A. Peshkin, eds. Pp. 121–152. New York: Teachers College Press.

Worth, Sol, and John Adair. 1972. *Through Navajo Eyes.* Bloomington: Indiana University Press.

Young, James C. 1980. A Model of Illness Treatment Decisions in a Tarascan Town. *American Ethnologist 7*(1):106–131.

Young, James C., and Linda Garro. 1981. *Medical Choice in a Mexican Village.* Prospects Heights, IL: Waveland Press.

Young, James C., and Linda Garro. 1982. Variation in the Choice of Treatment in Two Mexican Communities. *Social Science and Medicine 16*:1453–1465.

Ziller, Robert C., and Doublas Lewis. 1981. Orientations: Self, Social and Environmental Percepts Through Auto-Photography. *Personality and Social Psychology Bulletin 7*(2):338–343.

About the Authors

DOUGLAS CAULKINS is professor of anthropology at Grinnell College, where he has taught since 1970. He has published articles and book chapters on Chippewa cultural diversity, Norwegian organizations and social networks, Welsh and Welsh-American ethnic identity, careers and values of British high technology entrepreneurs, and roles in applied anthropology.

LAUREN CLARK joined the faculty of the University of Colorado School of Nursing after completing her doctorate at the University of Arizona in 1992. Her education has concentrated on nursing, anthropology, and the intersection of culture and health care. She currently teaches community health nursing and culture and health courses. After working on the child pain project described in this volume, Dr. Clark shifted her research focus to child health in the Latino community of northwest Denver. She is currently examining the cultural context of children's health from birth through infancy and childhood.

VICTOR C. DE MUNCK is an assistant professor of anthropology at SUNY-New Paltz. He conducted research in Sri Lanka on local patterns of conflict and cooperation in the context of nationalization and modernization. He is a cognitive/political anthropologist and has published articles on Sufism, orthodox Islamic movements in Sri Lanka, mate selection, romantic love, household disputes, exorcism, gender, conceptions of the self, cross-sibling relations, and the effect of national development projects on local practices and perceptions of self, village and nation. He has just edited a volume called *Romantic Love and Sexual Practices: Perspectives from the Social Sciences* (Greenwood, 1998) and is currently working on a cross-cultural study of the relationship between the public and intimate arenas of social life.

MARK S. FLEISHER is a cultural anthropologist and an associate professor of criminal justice sciences at Illinois State University. He does research on youth gangs and on management in federal prisons. He is the author of *Warehousing Violence* (Sage, 1989), *Beggars and Thieves: Lives of Urban Street Criminals* (University of Wisconsin Press, 1995), and *Dead End: Gang Girls and The Boys They Know* (University of Wisconsin Press, 1998).

ROXIE FOSTER is assistant professor at the University of Colorado Health Sciences Center and co-director of the Pain Consultation Service at The Children's Hospital in Denver. She has done research related to children's pain and has examined the utility of research findings for the clinical practice of pain management specialists.

JAVIER E. GARCIA DE ALBA GARCIA is head of the Social, Epidemiological, and Health Services Research Unit of the Social Security [National Health Service] in Guadalajara, Jalisco, Mexico. He received his MD at the University of Guadalajara and his MPH at the Public School of Mexico. García de Alba García also has a Ph.D. in anthropology from the Universidad National Autonóma of Mexico.

TRINI GARRO is managing editor of *Reviews in Anthropology* and has worked on numerous anthropology projects as editor and research assistant.

DAVID C. GRIFFITH is a senior scientist at the Institute for Coastal and Marine Resources and an associate professor in the Department of Anthropology, East Carolina University. He has written about low-wage workers, immigrants, ethnicity, and the anthropology of work, in addition to his work on fishing families, publishing in journals such as *American Ethnologist, American Anthropologist, Human Organization,* and *International Labor Review.* His books include *Jones's Minimal: Low Wage Labor in the United States* (1993, State University of New York Press), *Working Poor: Farmworkers in the United States* (1995, Temple University Press, with Ed Kissam), and *Any Way They Cut It: Meat Packing and Small Town America* (1995, University Press of Kansas, with Don Stull and Michael Broadway). He has two book manuscripts currently under review by university presses: The Estuary's Gift: An Atlantic Coast Cultural Biography and Fishers at Work, Workers at Sea: Domestic Production and Wage Labor in the Fisheries of Puerto Rico. He is currently at work on a book of essays about changing ethnic relations in the U.S. South.

JENNIFER A. HARRINGTON has an masters degree in criminal justice sciences from Illinois State University. She has conducted research at the Federal Prison Camp and the Federal Correctional Institution, Pekin, Illinois, and is now a researcher in the Gang Crime Prevention Center, Office of the Illinois Attorney General.

NANCY O. HESTER is professor at the University of Colorado Health Sciences Center. She has focused her research on issues pertaining to children's health. Her primary area of research is pain in children; in 1975 she developed the Poker Chip Tool to measure children's pain. Hester is currently examining the effects of a multidimensional program on children's pain and satisfaction with pain management, health care provider attitudes toward pain, and behaviors such as documentation of pain and patient and organizational costs. Unique to this study is the examination of this intervention within the organizational context.

CAROLE E. HILL, professor of anthropology, Georgia State University, Atlanta, has conducted applied research in Costa Rica and the American South for the past 30 years. She is currently studying the fit between rural health policy and local cultural practice. She is working with the Southeast Rural Mental Health Research Center (University of Virginia) on local cultural knowledge of mental disorders in rural Virginia, and with Morehouse Medical School to design breast cancer intervention strategies for rural African American women. Publications include *Community Health Systems in the Rural South* and two edited volumes: *The Global Practice of Anthropology* (edited with Marietta Baba) and *Cultural Diversity in the American South* (edited with Patricia Beaver).

JEFFREY C. JOHNSON is a senior scientist at the Institute for Coastal and marine Resources, and professor in the Department of Sociology, Department of Anthropology, and Department of Biostatistics, East Carolina University. He received his Ph.D. from the University of California, Irvine, and is currently working on a long-term research project comparing group dynamics of the winter-over crews at the American South Pole Station with those at the Polish, Russian, Chinese, and Indian Antarctic Stations. He has published extensively in anthropological, sociological, and marine journals and was the former editor-in-chief of the *Journal of Quantitative Anthropology*.

KAREN L. MILLER is dean and professor at the School of Nursing and interim dean of the School of Allied Health at the University of Kansas. Before becoming dean, Miller was vice-president at The Children's Hospital, Denver, and associate professor, College of Nursing, University of Colorado Health Sciences Center (UCHSC). Miller was appointed to the National Institutes of Health, National Institute of Nursing Research Advisory Council in 1995. She is a member of the editorial board for *IMAGE: Journal of Nursing Scholarship*. In 1995, Miller was named a fellow of the American Academy of Nursing.

ANA LETICIA SALCEDO ROCHA is professor of social sciences in the MPH program of the University of Guadalajara and an associate researcher in the Social, Epidemiological, and Health Services Research unit of the Social Security [National Health Service] in Guadalajara, Jalisco, Mexico. She received her MD and MPH at the University of Guadalajara and her Ph.D. in sociology through the University of Guadalajara's CIESAS.

GUN ROOS is a researcher in the Health Education Unit in the Department of Epidemiology and Health Promotion at the Finnish National Public Health Institute. She is interested mainly in the social and cultural factors that affect food habits. Her current research includes qualitative exploration of health behavior and lifestyle among various occupational groups and a review of socioeconomic differences in food habits in Europe. Dr. Roos started her studies in nutritional sciences and received her Ph.D. in anthropology from the University of Kentucky in 1995 for an interdisciplinary cultural analysis of children, food, and gender.

GERY RYAN is an assistant professor of anthropology at the University of Missouri, Columbia. He is a co-editor of *Cultural Anthropology Methods Journal (CAM)* and has written and lectured on qualitative data collection and analysis techniques, ethnographic decision modeling, and response biases in the field. For two years, he was associate director of the Fieldwork and Qualitative Data Laboratory at the UCLA Medical School, where he consulted and trained researchers in text analysis. His substantive interests in medical anthropology focus on how laypeople select among treatment alternatives across illnesses and cultures. He has conducted fieldwork in Mexico and Cameroon and has published in *Social Science & Medicine*, *Human Organization*, and *Archives of Medical Research*.

ELISA J. SOBO (Cancer Prevention and Control Program at the University of California in San Diego) is a medical anthropologist active in applied research. Sobo is involved in numerous multisite projects on topics such as: identity and HIV seropositive status, breast cancer and binge eating, celibacy, and snack food consumption patterns. Some of her publications are: *One Blood: The Jamaican Body* (SUNY, 1993), *Choosing Unsafe Sex: AIDS Risk Denial and Disadvantaged Women* (University of Pennsylvania Press, 1995), and a co-authored textbook, *The Cultural Context of Health, Illness, and Medicine* (Bergin & Garvey, 1997, with M. Loustaunau).

GUADARRAMA L. A. VARGAS is the dean of the Anthropological Research Institute of the National University Autonóma of Mexico. Vargas, a medical doctor, received his masters in anthropology at Mexico's National School of Anthropology and his Ph.D. at the University of Paris.

CAROL P. VOJIR, Ph.D., is an associate research professor in the University of Colorado Health Sciences Center (UCHSC) School of Nursing; she assists the associate dean for research with the school's research mission activities. Dr. Vojir is also project evaluator for the Colorado AHEC Program at UCHSC, helping to determine the effect of the AHEC's programs that are designed to augment health care provider recruitment and retention efforts in underserved areas of Colorado.

THOMAS WEISNER is professor of anthropology in the Departments of Psychiatry and Anthropology at UCLA. He has written about culture and human development in East Africa, about nonconventional families in California, and about families with children with developmental delays. He coedited *African Families and the Crisis of Social Change* (1997, Greenwood Press) with Candice Bradley and Philip Kilbride.

Subject Index

279

Author Index